WITHDRAWN
St. Scholastica Library
Duluth, Minnesota 55811

Catering
to Every Whim

Catering to Every Whim

A Complete Guide to Catering Sales, Administration, and Operations

G. EUGENE WIGGER

PRENTICE HALL, Englewood Cliffs, New Jersey 07632

Library of Congress Cataloging-in-Publication Data

Wigger, G. Eugene.
    Catering to every whim : a complete guide to catering sales,
    administration, and operations / by G. Eugene Wigger.
        p.   cm.
    ISBN 0-13-120502-1.
    1. Caterers and catering—Management.   I. Title.
TX911.3.M27W54   1991
642′.4′068—dc20
                                                89-38774
                                                     CIP

Editorial/production supervision and
    interior design: Lynda Griffiths
Cover design: Lundgren Graphics, Ltd.
Manufacturing buyer: Mary McCartney / Ed O'Dougherty

 © 1991 by Prentice-Hall, Inc.
A Division of Simon & Schuster
Englewood Cliffs, New Jersey 07632

All rights reserved. No part of this book may be
reproduced, in any form or by any means,
without permission in writing from the publisher.

TX
911.3
.M27
W54
1991

Printed in the United States of America

10 9 8 7 6 5 4 3 2 1

ISBN   0-13-120502-1

Prentice-Hall International (UK) Limited, *London*
Prentice-Hall of Australia Pty. Limited, *Sydney*
Prentice-Hall Canada Inc., *Toronto*
Prentice-Hall Hispanoamericana, S.A., *Mexico*
Prentice-Hall of India Private Limited, *New Delhi*
Prentice-Hall of Japan, Inc., *Tokyo*
Prentice-Hall of Southeast Asia Pte. Ltd., *Singapore*
Editora Prentice-Hall do Brasil, Ltda., *Rio de Janeiro*

Contents

Preface

"A profession is a personal thing that man acquires. It cannot be inherited. It cannot be bequeathed." R. E. Onstad goes on to say, "Only he who, having made the acquisition, puts to use that knowledge and skill with all his ability and complete dedication of purpose can be truly called a professional."

It is because of my desire to share my most valued acquisition that this book has been written. The groundwork for compiling these pages started more than 16 years ago when I began to assemble my experiences for the benefit of other catering staff members. Now, a decade and a half later, after eight hotel openings, this wealth of catering knowledge can be of enormous benefit to the novice as well as the seasoned catering professional.

If you are just beginning your career journey, remember that if at first you don't succeed, you'll get a lot of advice. Grow with each day's experience as you open your mind to change. Experience, after all, is merely knowing a lot of things you should not do. Catering is not a craft that can be mastered in a short time. It can require many years, even decades, of tutorage and self-scrutiny.

What does it take to be a highly successful catering executive? It requires dedication, vast experience, culinary and wine knowledge, leadership, steadfastness, sales ability, diligence, service orientation, theatrics, as well as proven skills in negotiations, humanity, management, motivation, and creativity. Creativity is the only way to make tomorrow better than today. It takes genius and courage to originate.

It is my hope that you will learn from *Catering to Every Whim*. Use my experiences to elevate your own professional career. In doing so, you will have nurtured your most treasured acquisition.

ACKNOWLEDGMENTS ────────────────────────────────

I owe a great deal of gratitude to my beautiful and loving wife, Diane, who is a very talented writer and award-winning magazine editor in her own right. Without her complete understanding and encouragement, this book would never have been completed. Diane also did the early editing in the preparation of this book.

Over the past fifteen years I have enjoyed the work of Joseph Saget Photographer, Philadelphia. His photographs are prominently displayed in this book. Other photographic talents are displayed by Shelia & Rob Hurth of Tiffany Photographic, Fort Lauderdale, and Harvey Bilt Photography, Miami. Thank you to all of these talented individuals.

A special appreciation goes to all the many staff members over the years whose tireless efforts have made me look so good.

This book is dedicated to the memory of William F. Foley, one of the past grand masters of catering, whose several years of guidance early in my career provided the foundation for any contributions I have been able to make.

Catering
to Every Whim

The Professional Catering Executive

Not so many years ago, the number one procurer of catering business for a hotel was called the *function manager*. This individual answered the phone, took the orders, and then serviced the group at the hotel. Competition was almost nil back then.

Then came the hotel-building boom with the Hiltons, Sheratons, Holiday Inns, Howard Johnsons, Western Internationals, and later, the Marriotts, Hyatts, and others. The title quickly changed from *function manager* to *catering manager*.

When many of the hotel groups began moving out of their plush catering kingdoms, the backslapping catering manager was not quite sophisticated enough to provide the leadership needed to get the job done. Thus we saw the advent of the director of catering, who started directing sales efforts with some sophistication, usually supervising one or more catering managers and/or catering sales representatives. It was then that the symbolic cummerbund of the function manager was replaced by the attaché case of today's catering executive. We have become professional special-event planners, although titles may vary from hotel to hotel and chain to chain.

What has all this change meant to us? It has meant higher salaries, more respect for our profession from within our hotels and from the outside world, and, above all else, it has meant that more is expected of us—not only from our managers and corporate officers, but from our clients, our families and friends, and our communities.

As incredible as it may sound, the hotel industry controls the livelihood of many cities and communities. In Washington, D.C., for example, the hotel industry ranks in size just below the federal government and professional associations.

Professionalism has arrived for the hotel catering sales industry—not for everyone, but for the majority. Unfortunately, it is the minority that worries me most and, for that reason, it is that segment I wish to discuss first. It is this group that usually gives us, the professionals, the bad name we sometimes have. Therefore it is this minority that we must train, educate, and coddle into the professional ranks.

When I speak of this minority, I am not necessarily referring to the unethical catering salesperson who lies, intentionally "double books," and cheats the clients, the company and, ultimately, himself or herself. That individual will be weeded out automatically sooner or later. I am referring to those catering persons who have never been trained in the right way nor motivated in the right direction. These are the persons who, for example, represent a property with a ballroom capacity of 800 and approach a client whose only function is an annual dinner for 2,800 guests, yet ignore several telephone inquiries for functions well within their capacities. I'm also referring to the salespeople who have such low regard for themselves and their clients that they don't make appointments. A salesperson should respect his or her own time as well as that of clients or potential clients. If it is worth a personal call, be a professional and make an appointment.

In addition, a professional does not call for the sake of calling or write letters for the sake of writing. The professional does research. It pays off and it is available for the taking. A dictaphone salesperson, for example, does not always know when he or she makes a sales call if the potential client needs dictating equipment. We're more fortunate, in most cases, because we do have avenues of research and we usually know if an organization uses our facilities or may have need of them.

Nonprofessionals sell a client and then forget him or her until it is time for the client's function. That is about as sensible as an appendix transplant. A professional salesperson keeps in touch with constant data, briefing the customer on special events that are happening in the city and that might be of interest to his or her food function or meeting. Informing a client of another group meeting at the same time may also be helpful. It might be a way to serve the client by producing more traffic or by enabling him or her to share the costs of speakers.

As a salesperson (and catering executives should think of themselves as salespersons) you have to be in constant contact with your industry. Professionals are not afraid of long hours or hard work. A person who is in some type of hotel sales and works consistent hours 9:00 A.M. to 5:00 P.M. is a nonprofessional and will ultimately fail. Professionals are hungry—hungry for praise, hungry for hard work, hungry for bookings, hungry for knowledge, and hungry to be involved in their hotel operation, from food and beverage to housekeeping.

Professionals today are asking management for a say in forming the budget and making policy decisions. Professionals are market planners who create a plan of action that details every move that they and their associates make and every dollar they plan to spend. Professionals live by the proven axiom that 80 percent of your business comes from 20 percent of your clients. Today professional hotel salespeople realize that in many instances women are equal to, if not better than, men in sales.

Selling is not just the responsibility of the sales and catering departments; selling must be done by every single employee in the hotel. The extraordinary service, general attitude, and friendliness of employees have become the reasons for repeat customers.

As employees, we must help to build a better mousetrap to snag new clients, more profit, and greater job security. Contrary to what some people may believe, we professionals do not have so much business at our properties that we employ one or more persons just to insult customers. Throughout the entire hotel we must continue to put forth that extra effort that makes one team win over another. If you are ever tempted to relax or slack off, be reminded of the traveling salesman who was seeking advertisements for a local paper. He called on the village grocer and was surprised when, on presenting his card, the proprietor said, "Nothing doing. Been established eighty years and never advertised."

"Excuse me, sir, but what is that building on the hill?"

"The village church," replied the grocer.

"Been there long?" asked the quick-witted salesman.

"About three hundred years."

"Well, are they still ringing the bell?"

Total involvement in the sales program by each member of the hotel staff is vital to effectively develop and maintain maximum results from the sales efforts. To be involved, each employee must understand the workings of the fundamentals of the hotel. A man or woman who is too big to study his or her career is as big as he or she will ever be.

With this in mind, let us detail the basic concepts and procedures in catering management based on actual experience. Many of these topics are so closely related that it is difficult to determine the transition from one to another. So, for the sake of clarity, the responsibilities are divided into three areas: administration (Chapter 3), sales (Chapter 4), and operations (Chapter 5).

CHAPTER 2

The Challenges of Being a Professional

RESPONDING TO CHANGE

The first challenge we must meet in our game plan to become more professional is to acquire the ability to respond favorably to change. Sometimes we change slowly and sometimes we *must* change in a hurry—often when we didn't think we could at all.

In his book entitled *Working,* Studs Turkel writes, "Work is about a search for daily meaning, as well as daily bread. For recognition, as well as cash. For astonishment, rather than boredom. In short, for a sort of life, rather than a Monday through Friday sort of dying." What those few words are talking about is *responding to change.*

What do you change first, your attitude or your behavior? If you wait until your attitude changes before you change your behavior, you will have to wait a long time! *Psych-cibernetics,* a book by Dr. Maxwell Malts, states that if you want to change your attitude, you simply change your behavior. If you deliberately change a habit for 21 to 28 days—just three to four weeks—the new behavior will become the new habit. You can be different in your business; you can be different in your life.

Discipline

Remember that when you point your finger at someone, there are three times as many fingers pointing back at you. The toughest kind of discipline is self-discipline.

As a real pro, you must spend hours and hours behind the scene, preparing, just as a professional athlete does.

The four Fs of good management are:

Firm

Fast

Friendly

Fair

You know what the rules are. You apply them in the same way to everyone in a rapid yet friendly manner.

Recognizable and Attainable Goals

Simply put, if you do not know where you are going, you may end up somewhere else.

It is not enough to reach your goal. You have to get there with the right materials to do the job. You need to establish short-term, midterm, and long-term goals.

1. Are they attainable?
2. Are they challenging?
3. Are they measurable?
4. Are they shared with someone?
5. Are they written down?

In fact, your goals may be a series of small goals just as life itself is a series of small hurdles waiting to be overcome.

Being a Problem Solver

Problem finders abound; what we need are problem solvers. Learn to become part of the solution, not part of the problem. Nobody ever said that life was going to be easy. So we have to use our creative ability to solve problems. When you are a creative professional, you learn to take risks.

Teamwork

Teamwork requires a respect for individual differences. As members of a team we must always be looking for that weak link if we are to remain strong and united in our efforts. Recognition of others and of a job well done is vital, but it also demands that people live up to their potential in serving others. We lead mostly by example.

We sell by our actions, our appearance, our sound, as well as by the words we select. We also have another great ability—to laugh and smile. There must be a reason why we are the only animal that can smile. The greatest sales tool you have is right under your nose!

CREATIVE THINKING

Be awake to every opportunity! The trend today is looking for something different, away from meat and potatoes and toward a more innovative approach to menu planning for meetings and social events. We need to try different ways of preparing and presenting food that will spice up the function and take the "blahs" out of menu planning. That does not mean inventing new foods, but it does mean trying new combinations and new serving ideas. Food is food—the difference is the show, how you serve it, what you call it, and how it looks. This change in attitude toward food can be linked to a new awareness among people about health. Everyone is becoming more weight and health conscious, and the changes are showing up in lighter meals, smaller portions, and more sensible eating habits.

As well as nutritional value, your clients have become very concerned about receiving their value in dollars and cents. This does not necessarily mean they will spend less, but it does mean they want value. You need to excite them, yet make them feel they have gotten a bargain. Bargain does not mean cheaper—it means greater value!

Part of becoming more creative means learning to steal. Steal ideas by becoming a human sponge and absorbing ideas from all around you. People make a great fuss about creativity and the ability to think up new ideas. Yes, creativity is important, but to be a real value, it must be accompanied by two other talents: (1) the judgment to distinguish between a good idea and a bad one and (2) the practical ability to make a good idea actually work.

Lots of people have ideas. The difficulty is to decide which ideas are really worthwhile and find someone who can put them into practice. There are very few "new" things being done in our industry. The most that many of us can hope for is to develop a few new wrinkles. Revive old ideas with a new look. Look around you for ideas that you can adapt to our industry. This is called *transference,* the art of transferring one idea and adapting it, in this case, to a food and beverage activity.

Pointers to Remember When Thinking Creatively

Ideas for making meal functions a creative and imaginative part of your food and beverage operation are endless. The only restrictions are the limits of the meeting program, the audience, the budget, and the location. The following are pointers to make it all a little easier.

Always Know Your Audience
How sophisticated are their tastes? Do they prefer meat or poultry? Will they eat fish? Do the individuals know one another, or are they meeting together for the

first time? Know the group you are planning for, but don't stereotype them. Just because they are sophisticated professionals does not necessarily mean they would not enjoy a country hoedown.

Work with Your Hotel Staff

Since your hotel staff includes many specialists in their fields, it is important for the food and beverage staff to fully recognize and develop their talents and make the most of them. Don't be reluctant to try something out of the ordinary. If you provide some ideas and moral support, most of your staff will come through for your clients.

By all means, do not overlook using the chef in order to win over clients. Include the chef in your initial brainstorming session; ask for his or her suggestions and specialties. Challenge the chef and cooking staff to use their creativity in the planning and preparation. The results will mean the difference between a mediocre function and a sensational one.

Realize the Limits of the Hotel and Staff

Just because an idea worked at one hotel does not mean that the same idea will work at all of them. For instance, if the hotel staff does not feel they do ice carvings well, do not push the selling of them until you have someone on staff who has learned that skill. Also, if the chef has prepared an item new to the menu, you better not offer it to a client until you have done a test meal.

Don't Overfeed Your Guests

Meeting planners and hotel executives have a tendency to go overboard. Because people are much more weight conscious today, both the hotel and customer should avoid rich sauces and heavy starches. Select lighter desserts and consider reducing meat portions by a few ounces.

Make the Most of Your Location

If you are in the South, take advantage of the southern cooking; if you are working in San Francisco, don't forget the seafood and sourdough bread. If you are located in the nation's capital, consider a "Welcome to Washington" opening reception, complete with replicas of Washington monuments: the U.S. Capitol, the White House, the Jefferson and Lincoln Memorials, and the Washington Monument made of sugar, tallow, or pastry; or plan an embassy party where you make use of the location for your decorations, atmosphere, and music. Your menu should be developed to reflect the foods that are indigenous to the selected region or country.

Don't Be Afraid to Try Something New, but Be Prepared with an Alternative

For many guests, fish is still taboo; always have an alternative ready. Also offer an alternative if you are serving pork or lamb. Be aware, too, that some people are vegetarians, and·alert your kitchen staff in advance, if possible.

Remember That People Eat with Their Eyes

Make your functions visually appealing. Think of the colors on the plate, the arrangements, and the shapes and sizes. Equally important is the atmosphere created by the food itself. Try offering new foods, but don't disguise them. Call them by their name, but add to the name to create an atmosphere of interest.

Variety Is the Spice of Life, Especially When It Comes to Food

Take advantage of buffets or receptions to test new foods that you may not offer as an entree. Let others try them. Add variety to your reception buffet by including Swedish meatballs, international cheeses, frog legs sauteed in garlic butter, sauteed pepper steak, a pâté maison display, steak tartare, a display of fresh fruits accompanied by brown sugar, chocolate fondue and whipped cream, anchovies on toast points, medallion of crisp duck with pepper sauce, and sprinkles of scallions, Chinese parsley, and escargot Chablis.

Draw from Ideas Around You

Look at great American family traditions such as the Fourth of July. Notice how these occasions are celebrated and borrow from some of these ideas.

If You Want to Offer Something Different, Convince Your Client to Budget for Something Different

So many clients come to us saying they want something different, but their budgets have no flexibility. Advise your customers to discuss their plans with the hotel staff *before* they draw up their budgets. For a little bit more, they can host a very different and special function that will be remembered with fond memories. *Never* underestimate a client's ability to pay if he or she is excited with the right ideas.

Try to Use the Old Favorites in New Ways

Beef can be served as Beef Wellington or Tournedoes, not just pepper steak and prime rib. Veal is another meat that many function planners are using successfully; Veal Marsala and Veal Marengo are two favorites.

If You Are Uneasy about a Dish, Don't Be Afraid to Have Your Client Sample It as a Test Meal

Provide your clients with a tasting session when new menus have been created. This will give you a chance to sample place setting touches and floral centerpieces. If you really want to impress a committee, hold the test meal right in the kitchen where they can watch the actual presentation. Or suggest that your client drop in, unannounced, at one of the hotel's restaurants. If the restaurant food is good, generally the banquet food will be.

Don't Get into a Rut

Just because you served prime rib to a group last year, that is no reason to serve it again this year. Add interest to the function by updating the event. For example, instead of an Awards Luncheon, make the theme a Parade of Champions Luncheon. Be a little daring in your suggestions and then live up to them.

Brainstorm Creative Ideas and Presentations

Get in the habit of assembling your more creative employees for brainstorming, problem-solving, or new ideas sessions. Open the session to all ideas; do not hold any back. When you come up with an idea and the first thought is "No, we can't do that" or "That's impossible," then discuss why that idea will not work or what would have to be changed to get it to work. Sometimes when you are the most tired and the session is getting a little crazy, some of your best innovative ideas will be produced.

Take one subject and let your minds take that topic as far as possible. Ponder all possibilities and you will see what creative menu planning can do.

Don't Take Orders Off the Printed Menu if You Want Something Different
Each of us should attempt to develop at least one new menu and/or idea everyday. Printed banquet menus are a necessary tool, but they should not become a crutch. Challenge your development of ideas and the ideas of your staff daily. Each hotel has its own personality, but you can direct the behavior of its personality to be unique.

What Is Creative Thinking?

Let's clear up a common fallacy about the meaning of creative thinking. For some illogical reason, science, engineering, art, and writing get tabbed as about the only truly creative pursuits. Most people associate creative thinking with things like the discovery of electricity or polio vaccine, or the writing of a novel, or the development of color television.

Certainly, accomplishments like these are evidence of creative thinking. Each forward step made in the conquest of space is the result of creative thinking. But creative thinking is not reserved for certain occupations nor is it restricted to super-intelligent people.

Well, then, what is creative thinking?

A low-income family devises a plan to send their son to a leading university. That's creative thinking.

A neighborhood turns the street's most undesirable lot into the neighborhood park and play area. That's creative thinking.

A minister develops a plan that doubles his Sunday evening attendance. That's creative thinking.

A catering executive develops a new type of banquet service and theme idea that is new to the hospitality industry. That is indeed creative thinking.

Figuring out ways to simplify record keeping, selling the "impossible" customer, keeping the children occupied constructively, making employees really enjoy their work, or preventing a quarrel—all of these are examples of practical, everyday creative thinking.

Creative thinking is simply finding new and better ways to do anything.

TOOLS OF CREATIVITY

1. Believe. When you believe something can be done, your mind will find the ways to accomplish it. Believe in a solution and you have paved the way to one. Eliminate "impossible," "won't work," "can't do," and "no use trying" from your thinking and speaking vocabularies.

2. Don't let tradition paralyze your mind. Be receptive to new ideas. Be experimental. Try new approaches. Be progressive in everything you do.

3. Ask yourself daily, "How can I do better?" There is no limit to self-improvement. When you ask yourself how you can do better, sound answers will surface. Try it and see.

4. Ask yourself, "How can I do more?" Capacity is a state of mind. Asking yourself this question puts your mind to work to find intelligent shortcuts. The success combination in business is: Do what you do better (improve the quality of your output) and do more of what you do (increase the quantity of your output).

5. Practice asking and listening. By doing this you will obtain raw material for reaching sound decisions. Remember: Big people monopolize the *listening*; small people monopolize the *talking*.

6. Stretch your mind. Get stimulated. Associate with people who can help you to think of new ideas and new ways of doing things. Mix with people of different occupational and social interests.

A study shows us that there are four things that successful people have in common:

Imagination
Enthusiasm
Optimism
Creativity

Act as if you are going to live forever; live as if you are going to die tomorrow.
One of the most creative geniuses of our time was Walt Disney. He affected the lives of almost every human during and since his lifetime. Disney had what he called his *Four Words to Success:*

1. *Think:* Think about where you want to go and set your goals!
2. *Believe:* Believe in your abilities and the abilities of those closest around you. Have a strong faith in your beliefs and make them your life's convictions!
3. *Dream:* Dreaming is vital to planning with a futuristic vision!
4. *Dare:* Dare to be the best at what you do. Dare to be greater than all of your life's competitors!

Also remember the words of Ralph Waldo Emerson: "Whatever you do, you need courage. Whatever course you decide upon, there is always someone to tell you—'you are wrong'. There are always difficulties arising which tempt you to believe that your critics are right. To map out a course of action and follow it to an end requires some of the same courage which a soldier needs. Peace has its victories, but it takes brave men to win them."

CHAPTER 3

Administration

In developing a catering department, the initial phase and the foundation of the entire operation is the administration phase. The mechanical procedures and systems that best suit the individual property are created in this phase. This is also the place where planning, organization, and groundwork for the actual sale begin. Throughout this chapter references will be made to various forms, charts, and letters. Samples of these many organizational tools may be found at the end of the chapter.

Catering is very similar to conducting an orchestra. It takes creativity, planning, timing, and the combined talents of many departments to achieve a satisfying, harmonious event.

POSITION DESCRIPTIONS

Owing to the individual qualities that each hotel possesses, the specific organization and staff size of the department will vary with those qualities and hotel needs. Two factors to consider when determining the size of the staff are the anticipated number of actual functions to be handled and the anticipated total annual dollar volume. However, any relationship between these two factors is not necessary since in most operations, the catering department is responsible for three phases of operation. The foundation of the entire operation is the administration phase. This is also the phase that is primarily concerned with the administration of the planning, organization, and dissemination of the necessary information to the various departments, and the groundwork for the sale that is about to take place.

Sales, the second phase in developing a catering department, is a service that often represents a large percentage of revenue for a hotel or resort. This phase is primarily concerned with the administration of the sales efforts.

Operations is the final phase of any catering department. It is this actuating phase that brings all the vital elements together to produce customer satisfaction and departmental profit. This is the supervision of the execution of all the function arrangements requested by the client. The catering director, with assistance from all members of the catering sales office, provides support to the banquet manager and staff to see that all client promises are fulfilled and then exceeded. At this point, coordination of the sales and administration efforts must blend with the banquet operation as well as the kitchen, the sales department, convention services, beverage, and other related departments. This area of operation is ultimately the responsibility of the catering director.

The position descriptions shown in Figures 3.1 and 3.2 are representative of the general duties and responsibilities most often associated with each position. Specific duties and titles for a particular position will vary in each hotel, depending on the needs and the personnel.

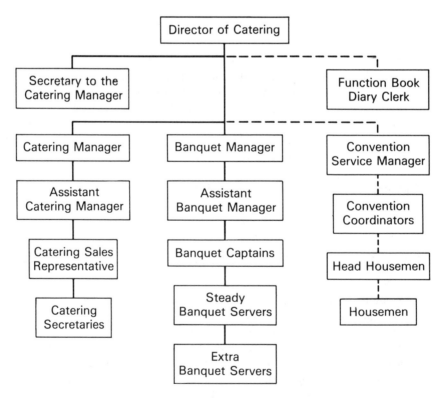

Figure 3.1 SAMPLE CATERING ORGANIZATIONAL CHART

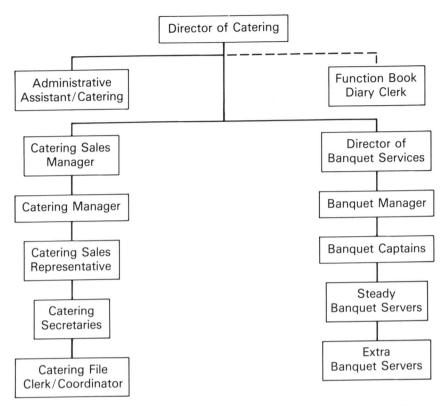

Figure 3.2 SAMPLE CATERING ORGANIZATIONAL CHART

Catering Director

The director of catering must be a highly qualified member of the management team. He or she must be well versed in food and beverage profit and loss, have superb sales ability, as well as be totally organized and a master of details. In addition, the catering director must possess a total knowledge of food, beverage, and all types of service. The success of this particular department hinges on this person's ability to plan for the unexpected. The success of the catering department depends on the rapport that the director of catering establishes with the influential businesspeople of the community as well as the social and society segments.

The director of catering maintains complete supervision of the operation of the catering office and the banquet operation. He or she must oversee the administration of the catering sales program to include merchandising, catering menus, filing, tracing, solicitation procedures, and the evaluation of that catering sales program. He or she gives personal attention to and controls the solicitation and servicing of those conventions, banquets, and important local accounts. In the same vein, he or she controls the assignment of all other conventions, banquets, and local activities to the staff. The catering director prepares or delegates the preparation of reports and gives personal approval of the final product. These reports would include the payroll and the monthly and annual forecasts concerning catering both food and beverage. The catering director also supervises, trains, and assists the sales staff in all phases of catering, both selling and servicing.

The following list includes *some* of the many responsibilities assigned to the director of catering. However, these are not the only duties for which he or she is accountable.

1. Exercises general supervision of food service in all private dining and banquet rooms; assumes responsibility for the profitable operation of all food service and preparation for catering functions

2. Consults with involved personnel regarding the preparation of special dishes and services required

3. Assists in the proper maintenance of food costs control records on coordinating activities with responsible accounting department personnel; works with supervisory staff of kitchen, dining, and banquet rooms in determining work schedules for employees in order to meet requirements for any occasion

4. Analyzes food costs and catering service records to plan and determine necessary adjustments of prices, policies, and services

5. Arranges for necessary details in carrying out transactions for large dinners and other large or special parties; sets and negotiates terms pertinent to the sale of the hotel's catering services

6. Supervises the banquet manager's operation in its entirety

7. Assists management in other matters as required

Catering Manager

The catering manager is directly responsible to and is the immediate assistant of the director of catering. The person in this capacity should be of a caliber to eventually accept promotion to the director of catering position when the opportunity is presented.

The duties of the catering manager are to assist in supervising the operation of the catering office and banquet operation. This individual also assists in the administration of the catering sales programs and in the solicitation and servicing of those conventions, banquets, and local catering functions booked by himself or herself as well as the ones assigned by the director of catering. The catering manager assists, too, in the preparation of reports and forecasts for the department as assigned by the director of catering.

Depending on the size of the catering operation, the hotel may have one catering manager or as many as five. Many hotels avoid the use of the word *assistant* in the title in favor of *catering manager,* since most clients feel slighted if their activity only deserves the attention of an "assistant."

The catering manager's responsibilities include:

1. Assisting in the supervision of food service in all private and dining rooms
2. Assisting in arranging necessary details in executing functions or as assigned by the director of catering
3. Performing any additional tasks as assigned by the director of catering

In addition, some of the large operations retain the services of a catering sales representative who concentrates on developing new business. This person's only responsibility is solicitation; the servicing of the booked accounts is left to his or her colleagues.

Secretary to the Director of Catering

The secretary to the director of catering should have the abilities of an office manager and an administrative assistant, and should be of a caliber to eventually accept promotion to the position of catering sales representative or catering manager when the opportunity is presented.

The secretary is responsible for all of the catering director's correspondence, including catering event orders or changes, letters, and so on. The secretary assists in the preparation of the daily list of activities, including all planned meetings and food functions as well as the weekly list of those activities. In addition, the secretary assists in the preparation of the guarantee sheet on a daily basis for all planned food functions and aids in the preparation of all reports and forecasts for the department.

Some responsibilities of the secretary to the director of catering include:

1. Maintaining and controlling all files and tracing systems
2. Keeping adequate office and catering supplies and reordering when necessary
3. Becoming familiar with the catering operation and its procedures
4. Assisting in maintaining the office reception area so that it is neat and presentable to guests at all times
5. Assisting in directing and channeling office visitors to the proper person and/or office as expeditiously as possible
6. Performing any additional tasks as assigned by the director of catering

Depending on the size of the catering operation, the hotel may have one catering secretary or as many as five. Their qualifications and responsibilities should be the same as those of the secretary to the director of catering.

Banquet Manager or Banquet Maitre d'

The banquet manager derives authority from and is directly responsible to the director of catering. He or she should be totally familiar with all phases of food and beverage service as well as possess a knowledge of food preparation to a certain degree. He or she should be tactful and possess a sales ability as well as a management planning ability and organizational skills.

The banquet manager is in complete charge of the execution of all food and beverage functions. He or she maintains or surpasses the first-class standards set by the hotel and corporation. This person's jurisdiction includes the grand ballroom as well as all private banquet rooms. The banquet manager should be of the caliber to eventually accept promotion to the director of catering or catering manager should the opportunity be presented.

Some of the banquet manager's responsibilities include:

1. Overseeing hotel facilities used for banquet food and beverage functions
2. Supervising the banquet captains, waiters, and waitresses.
3. Scheduling of service personnel for food and beverage functions booked by the catering department and sales department
4. Carrying out instructions as listed on an event order from the catering office
5. Supervising the payroll of waiters and captains
6. Assisting in supervision of set-up and breakdown of all meeting rooms, registration set-ups, and displays as well as all food functions
7. Housekeeping and repairs of all banquet equipment and rooms
8. Performing any additional tasks as assigned by the director of catering

Assistant Banquet Manager and/or Banquet Captains

The assistant banquet manager and/or banquet captains derive their authority from the banquet manager. They should possess skills of service of food and beverage as well as planning and salesmanship.

The assistants help the banquet manager to maintain and surpass first-class standards set by the hotel or corporation. In most union hotels, the only difference between the assistant banquet manager and the captains is the assistant banquet manager does not belong to the union and captains do.

Some responsibilities of the assistant banquet manager and/or banquet captains include:

1. Assisting in the hotel facilities used for banquet food and beverage functions
2. Assisting in taking charge of the waiters and banquet housemen
3. Assisting in scheduling of service personnel for food and beverage functions booked by the catering department as assigned by the banquet manager
4. Assisting in carrying out instructions as listed on event orders from the catering office

5. Aiding in the supervision and set-up and breakdown of all meeting rooms, banquet function rooms, registration set-ups, and displays

6. Assisting in the supervision of housekeeping repairs of all banquet equipment

7. Performing any additional tasks as assigned by the banquet manager

Banquet Service Personnel

The banquet waiters and waitresses are scheduled as functions necessitate and are directly responsible to the banquet manager and the assistant manager and/or banquet captains. They must be well versed in the service of all types of food and beverage.

Some responsibilities of banquet service personnel include:

1. Overseeing the grand ballroom as well as the other private banquet rooms as assigned by the banquet manager

2. Reporting to the banquet manager any need for housekeeping and/or repairs of any banquet equipment and rooms

3. Assisting in the maintenance and organization of all banquet storage space and all banquet equipment and rooms

4. Performing any other tasks as assigned by the banquet manager or assistant banquet manager or banquet captains

THE FUNCTION BOOK

The function book or control diary is used jointly by convention sales and catering sales. To assure that the space available for sale is clearly apparent, and in order to maintain proper control of function space assignment, the function book must be maintained in a neat and orderly manner.

In some smaller operations, each salesperson is responsible for making his or her own entries into the function book. But in the case of abuse or volume, it may become necessary for one and only one individual to be authorized to make entries in the diary.

A tentative booking is one in which the customer has indicated a strong interest in reserving function space, but a letter of confirmation has not been received. The salesperson or diary clerk will proceed by entering the reservation in the function book and the preprinted word *tentative* should be circled in pencil. In some hotels the letter *T* is written. The entire entry is made in pencil and a tentative letter of confirmation to the customer should follow.

A definite booking is one in which a written confirmation accepting the proposal of the hotel has been received from the customer. When the returned confirmation letter has been received, the salesperson or diary clerk must go to the function book and circle in ink the preprinted word *definite* in the status box. This indicates that the reservation has now been confirmed. If the word has not been preprinted then the entering person will simply erase the pencilled tentative indication and place an ink *D*. The returned confirmation letter is then placed in the customer's file as a permanent part of that file.

A cancellation is handled by the salesperson or diary clerk by completely erasing the entry in the function book. In the case of a definite entry, the inked *D* will also be whited out. The salesperson will then acknowledge that cancellation with a letter to the customer. To properly document the file, a Lost Business Report should be prepared.

A change of room, date, or time should be handled by the salesperson or diary clerk by making the proper change in the function book and then acknowledging that change with a letter to the customer requesting a signed and returned copy.

Approximately 10 months before any scheduled function, the function books should be controlled by the catering department. Prior to that time, the books should be the responsibility of the sales department.

Convention programs should be established at the time of booking and the type of function, space, time, and number of guests clearly designated. This information should be confirmed to the guest as well as recorded in the diary on a definite basis.

Whenever an exact program cannot be established at the time of booking, an "All Space Hold" may be established, *but with the approval* of the director of sales. However, this "All Space Hold" should have a 14-month cut-off which will insure a program one year prior to the scheduled meeting. If, at that time, the meeting program is still not established, the "hold" may be extended, again with the director of sales' approval, but since by this time the evening activities will be known, this "hold" is only from 9 A.M. to 5 P.M. It is unusual for there to be planned activities each night of a several-day meeting. This will allow catering evening functions to be booked without delay.

Twelve months prior to the scheduled meeting, "All Space Holds" would be released and replaced with an exact program. If changes occur in the program there-after, they will be accommodated only on a space available basis. After that date, it will be the catering department's responsibility to release "All Space Holds" as an important contribution towards making unused space available for sale.

On the other hand, catering bookings should not be confirmed by the hotel prior to 12 months before the date requested for all major ballrooms and 6 months in advance for all remaining space. This is done in order to give convention sales maximum opportunity to book convention business that might require function space. Exceptions to this rule are annual prestigious social functions since these affairs must be booked prior to one year in advance. This should only be done with the advance approval of the directors of sales and catering.

When the catering salesperson is attempting to book a function but cannot do so due to an "All Space Hold" in the function book, the catering salesperson should prepare a "Request for Clearance of Space" form to bring about that release of space. The form, which requests the clearance of the appropriate space, is submitted to the salesperson who is holding the space. If more than one group is holding space, then a photocopy of the release form is also sent to each appropriate salesperson. Because policies vary with hotel size, forms are sometimes also copied to the food and beverage

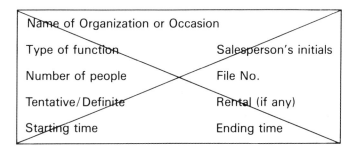

Figure 3.3 SAMPLE FUNCTION BOOK ENTRY

director and/or the general manager. The response for the clearance of space should come within 48 hours. The request should include the appropriate information necessary to make a decision, such as date of request; name of organization requesting space; desired day, date, and year; room or rooms desired; alternate room (if possible); type of function or functions; desired times of functions; attendance; value of this business; desired space now being held; and space for additional comments. There should also be room to note if the space has been cleared and a space for the salesperson's signature.

If the number of "All Space Holds" or "Tentative Holds" is excessive it may be necessary to hold a monthly meeting between the sales, catering, and convention services departments. In some serious situations of abuse, the attendance of top management should be encouraged. This will insure that abuse will at least be minimized.

Tentative bookings should be reviewed regularly at the weekly catering meetings to make certain that there is diligent follow-through on the part of catering salespeople who should either change the tentative bookings to definite bookings, or explain by completing a Lost Business Report.

In some hotels, it may be necessary to note in the function book, along with the entry, if a dance floor prop or piano is required. The same goes for other limited equipment. These entries should stand out for quick notice and can be done with a small red-ink stamp. When making the entry, a large X should be placed to form a block on starting and closing time. This allows the space requirements to be quickly ascertained by the salesperson at a glance. A sample of the function book entry is shown in Figure 3.3.

In some hotels, a line is placed from the upper left-hand corner to the lower right-hand corner if it is tentative. If it is a definite booking, the X is completed with another line from the upper right-hand corner to the lower left-hand corner.

FILE CATEGORIES

The catering file system should be divided into three categories: banquet, convention, and general or miscellaneous sales. This type of file system offers two advantages: fast reference and simple tracing procedures.

Banquet Files

Banquet files contain historical data of local business with active and continuous food and beverage functions. Solicitation and follow-up of these files is the responsibility of the catering office.

On occasion, and at least once annually, random banquet files should be inspected to see that sufficient information is enclosed concerning the prospect—previous functions, records of correspondence, and solicitations for future functions.

New banquet files are obtained from several sources:

1. Catering functions held in the hotel on a regular or repeat basis
2. All other catering functions held in the metropolitan area on a regular or repeat basis
3. Newspaper leads on new catering functions being held or being considered
4. Inquiries coming into the hotel regarding a possible future catering booking

The files for functions booked by the catering department are identified as *B files*. In order to set up a B file the salesperson must complete a "Request to Set Up a B File" form, complete with function history and the approval of the director of catering. This form will then become a permanent part of the B file. A catering secretary will open the file by typing a color-coordinated label showing the name of the organization and a *B* before the file number to be assigned. A master list is kept on banquet files headed: "Numerical Master List—Banquet Files" with the number of the file and the name of the file. For example:

FILE NO.	NAME OF ORGANIZATION
B–1	Touchdown Club
B–2	Symphony Ball
B–3	Lions International, 22-C

Whenever a new B file is set up, it should be added to this list, using the next open number. When a B file is eliminated, it should be removed from this list and that number becomes available for use on a new file. The master list should be kept in a loose-leaf notebook and maintained by the secretary to the director of catering or the file clerk.

At the same time that a file folder has been typed and a number assigned, a 5″ × 8″ card (blue) for the card cabinet and a 1½″ × 8″ card file stuffer (blue) will be prepared with the following information: name of organization, contact name, contact title, address, phone number, file number, salesperson's initials or assignment letter or number, permanent trace date, and function history. In preparing the file folder, the salesperson's assignment letter is placed in the upper right-hand corner of the outside jacket cover as well as the trace date. In some hotels, a stamp is used on the outside cover with blocks for the trace date and salesperson's initials or letter tracing the file. When this stamp is used, only a glance is needed to ascertain the date for which a file has been traced. A sample of the stamp is shown here.

Trace Date	Initials

Convention Files

Catering convention files are set up in the same manner as the banquet files but they do not require the prior approval of the director of catering. This is because the booking generally originates in the convention sales department and usually includes a block of sleeping rooms of at least 25 room nights. The C files contain the bookings of local, state, regional, national, and international conventions. Solicitation and follow-up of these files for future bookings is the responsibility of the convention sales office.

Convention files are identified as *C files* and bear that letter before the assigned file number. In order to open a C file, a copy of the convention salesperson's letter of confirmation or a copy of the convention room assignment program (function booking form) is required. A copy of the sleeping room block form that has been committed by the hotel is also helpful information.

Generally, when a convention is definite and all function space has been assigned, a copy of the program is sent by the convention salesperson to the director of catering for assignment to a particular catering salesperson. These assignments are made according to the size of the group, size of the function, group importance, and other convention assigments already made. Special attention must be given to the latter to avoid overloading any one salesperson which could result in hurried or limited convention coverage. When the assignment has been made, the appropriate catering executive will trace the convention program and function room assignments until approximately three or four months prior to the convention dates. This will depend on the size and complexity of the convention program.

The catering secretary in turn will open the file by typing a color-coordinated label (green) that shows a C before the file number to be assigned. A master list is made on convention files headed: "Numerical Master List—Convention Files," showing the number of the file and the name of the convention. They are logged and maintained in the same manner as the B files. When a file folder is typed and a number assigned, a 5″ × 8″ card (green) for the card cabinet and a 1½″ × 8″ card file stuffer (green) should be prepared with the following information: name of organization, contact name, contact title, address, phone numbers, file numbers, salesperson's initials or letter, and city history if known. In preparing the file folder, the secretary can stamp on the cover the trace date or salesperson's initials or letter. If the stamp is not used, the information should be written on the file cover.

Miscellaneous or General Files

In the catering department, general or miscellaneous files are set up in the same manner as banquet and convention files and, again, no prior approval of the director of catering is required. These files contain the bookings by the catering department that are nonrepeated one-time functions that cannot be resolicited for future business, such as weddings, "Sweet 16" parties, Bar or Bat Mitzvahs, political functions (such as election-time functions), anniversaries, and testimonial functions. Since this category contains only one-time functions, no solicitation or follow-up for future bookings is required. On a few occasions there may be repeat business, such as the marriage of a second daughter, but this hardly warrants methodical solicitation.

Miscellaneous files are identified with an *M* placed before the letter of the alphabet under which they are classified. (If a general file category is used instead of miscellaneous, the letter *G* would be used.) Functions are classified under the name of the client. For example, the Diane Bisciotti wedding would be a *Misc. B* file (first letter of the last name). On the label it would appear as follows: "IHO (in honor of) Diane Bisciotti Wedding Misc. B." Unlike the B and C files, which are filed numerically, the M (or G) files are kept in alphabetical order.

The catering secretary will open the file by typing a color coordinated label (yellow) that shows the name of the occasion or function and a *Misc.* before the letter of the alphabet under which the file is to be classified. A master list is made on miscellaneous files, as it is for B and C files, and headed: "Alphabetical Master List— Miscellaneous Files" showing the alphabetical listing of the affair and the name of the occasion or function. They are logged and maintained in the same manner as the B and C files.

A 5″ × 8″ card and a 1½″ × 8″ file stuffer are not prepared on miscellaneous files since they are one-time functions. These files are maintained on the master list and are kept for approximately one year. The trace stamp is used on the outside cover as with the other files.

Tracing

File tracing is an important follow-up to the file system. It is the responsibility of the director of catering to plan a periodical trace of the banquet files in order to insure that the files are being actively worked. Tracing of B files should be scheduled annually, usually 12 months or more prior to the date of a major function. This allows for ample time and effort to be expended on this important follow-up. Some files need to be traced more than once a year depending on the frequency of their function. Smaller annual functions that are not major in size should be traced approximately six months prior to their scheduled time.

The need for a methodical tracing and solicitation follow-up program cannot be overemphasized. An advanced plan of solicitation must be established well in advance of the client's hotel selection. Rather than wait for inquiries, initiative should be taken to secure every piece of business that is being held and is potentially available. Because of this, files must be traced for follow-up at the appropriate time. This is the very reason a good tracing system is valuable in the day-to-day catering operation.

The ultimate test of an efficient and productive catering operation is repeat business. Once the necessary promises have been made to book the business, those promises must be fulfilled to insure a rebooking. If, for some reason, another hotel has been chosen, no solicitation stone should remain unturned in an attempt to relocate that function at your hotel once again.

During solicitation or following the successful completion of a banquet function, it is necessary to have the ability to retrace the file. This can be accomplished by using a 5″ × 8″ index card where the trace date and salesperson's letter or initials are recorded. In turn, this index card is placed into the tracing system for methodical return to the salesperson.

The tracing system should consist of four tracing accordion files: a daily (1–31) file for the current month's traces, a daily (1–31) file for the next month's traces, a yearly (Jan.–Dec.) file for the current year's traces, and a yearly (Jan.–Dec.) file for the next year's traces. This can be supplemented with additional yearly files if needed.

Each morning, one of the catering secretaries should be assigned the task of pulling all the traces and subject files. The trace card should be attached to the outside of the file and given to the proper salesperson as indicated on the trace. If no name is indicated, the file is given to the director of catering for assignment. Before any file is returned to the filing cabinets, it should be given to the director of catering for review of solicitation efforts.

On the last day of the month, the now empty "current month" file is leapfrogged to become the "next month" file. At the same time, all traces for the next month should be pulled out of the yearly file (Jan.–Dec.) and placed into the daily file (1–31).

Booking Traces

A function book reservation form or booking sheet should be completed whenever banquet space is being held either on a tentative or a definite basis. If it is worth holding banquet space for, then it is worth doing the proper paperwork to insure that the space will be there when you need it, and under the proper space control. Generally, the pink copy of the booking sheet is used by the catering department to trace the booking reservation until it has been removed from the function book (if it is a tentative reservation), or until the successful conclusion of the function (in the case of a definite booking).

The pink copy of the booking reservation form is used whenever it is necessary for the catering office to trace a particular banquet file. With proper tracing, a function space hold will not be entered in the function book to be forgotten.

Some properties prefer to preprint the basic steps to be taken in servicing the booking. Each step taken should be recorded and an appropriate trace date for the next step established and written on the pink booking form. This trace date can be used to follow-up a tentative booking for confirmation, to submit a contract, or to insure proper instructions to the back of the house. All required trace dates should be recorded on the pink sheet. These traces are maintained in the catering office in the date file and pulled daily along with the file, according to the trace date. The preprinted steps on the bottom of the reservation form should include: definite, confirmed, proposed menus, and catering event order. A checkmark beside each completed step will insure an up-to-date and error-free system.

On the day following a function, a thank-you letter should be sent to the client. At the same time, a determination should be made as to the status of the client's next function. The old copy of the pink sheet is destroyed and the 5" × 8" trace card is used for further solicitation of the group until space is held once again. At that time a new pink sheet will be used.

EVALUATING SOLICITATION EFFORTS ──────────────────────────

In the hotel catering office there should be several methods used to measure the success of solicitation efforts and the contributions of each individual. Although the organization of the mechanical procedures are rather basic, they are very important. In addition, in the actual solicitation of catering business, the proper procedures are equally important. The information obtained from catering accounts must be maintained in an organized fashion in order to sell and service each account and to realize maximum income and profit. Methods of selling the best possible product at the best possible price require a systematic or planned approach.

The following reports relate only to local catering business and not to functions generated by convention or group business.

Call Reports

The Call Report is used in conjunction with a solicitation effort and is completed by a catering salesperson after a personal or telephone contact with an account. It is the file record of the solicitation development. All vital data concerning the solicitation and the chronological list of all details should be documented so the report can be placed in the client's file. This can be used as a guide for the proper handling of further traces or for general evaluation of the prospect of future business.

It is the responsibility of the director of catering to be certain that all banquet files are being properly solicited and that the proper solicitation procedures are being followed. Before the subject file is returned to the filing cabinet, the file with the complete Call Report should be reviewed with the director of catering so that he or she is aware of the business in prospect and can *review the progress of all salespersons concerned.* Follow-up letters should be written to acknowledge all solicitation calls. This is done out of courtesy as well as good business sense.

All Call Reports should contain these essential elements: group account name, labor union or association that the call was made on, B file number, date of solicitation call, group address, contact name and title, notation of type of contact call (personal outside call, personal inside call, or a call made by telephone) or by letter only. Other useful information is new or repeat business, the type of function, first and second date choices, frequency of the function, date and place of last function, and office and home telephone numbers of the contact person. The Call Report should be accurate, complete, concise, and properly analyzed. Include either a new or a change in status, but avoid superfluous comments of no consequence to the solicitation effort. The last item to appear on the Call Report is the trace date. This is the date by which the file should be returned to your desk to further your solicitation efforts. You may need it next week following a board meeting or next year just before their annual meeting so that you can solicit for the following year.

The distribution of the Call Report will vary from hotel to hotel. However, a copy should be included for discussion in the weekly catering meeting and subsequently included in the weekly catering meeting minutes.

Monthly Booking Reports

In order to evaluate the success of our solicitation efforts, a Monthly Booking Report should be made by each salesperson. This report should list the number of new bookings, repeat bookings, dates of bookings, covers (the number of people served), and estimated value of business that has been booked during the month. This report should be signed by the salesperson and approved by the director of catering with copies sent to the general manager, the director of food and beverage operations, and the director of marketing and/or sales.

To obtain maximum efforts, goals should be set for the amount of business to be booked by each catering salesperson during a given period.

A summary of all business booked during the month by the catering department is shown on a cover sheet. Also, an analysis should show the comparison of local and convention business as well as the year-to-date figures for each salesperson in dollars and cover counts.

Other useful information that should be included on the monthly bookiing report is the number of outside calls, the number of new B files that were eliminated, and the number of newspaper leads followed during the month.

Lost Business Reports

It is universally recognized that if a salesperson is not losing business, business is not being booked to the fullest capacity. Consequently, it is vital that we know more about any business we have lost than the business we have been able to book. In the preparation of a Lost Business Report, we need to emphasize the reasons for losing business as well as trends that could affect future pricing and booking procedures. These reports will provide a permanent source of information that could affect the future solicitation efforts. Twice annually a study and report should be made and analyzed to evaluate the reasons for lost business during the year. Some of these reasons include parking, prices, location, bad prior experience, date unavailable, and preference for other facilities. You cannot possibly hope to book a business in the future if you do not know the precise reason it was lost in the past. The Lost Business Report should briefly yet concisely outline the steps in solicitation and the reasons for losing a particular piece of business. When preparing the report remember to include the five Ws: *who* the business's decision maker is, *why* the piece of business was lost, *where* the affair will be held, *when* the affair is being held, and *what* might help book the business the next time around.

After the report is approved by the director of catering, copies should go to the subject banquet file, the general manager, the director of food and beverage operations, and the director of marketing and/or sales.

Reader File

The Reader File is a collection of copies of the letters and memos that emanate daily from the catering sales office. This file is distributed weekly to the director of food and beverage and, upon request, to the general manager. A check of the Reader File allows for an immediate evaluation of the style of the letter originating from the catering sales office. It permits an evaluation of the expertise with which business is solicited, confirmed, or gratefully acknowledged by your representatives.

CATERING MEETINGS

Catering meetings should be held on a weekly basis. All members of the catering sales staff should be in attendance as well as the director of food and beverage operations, the banquet chef, the banquet manager, and, whenever possible, the general manager, the beverage director, the sales director, and the executive steward. This meeting is a forum to evaluate the progress and clear up any conflict pertaining to space requirements ("tentative hold" space). In addition, the catering functions for the next 10 days should be discussed in detail.

Management's involvement in these matters is vital in order to underline the importance placed on the results of the solicitation efforts and performance by the catering department.

The scope of the meeting's agenda should include no more than seven to eight items each week. The following subjects are submitted as a basis for a weekly agenda:

- Weekly review of files covered by each catering salesperson
- Call Reports for past week of solicitation efforts
- Lost Business Reports for past week
- Review of high food-cost menus
- Review of high labor costs

- Referrals
- Guarantees
- Condition of big four expenses: glassware, silverware, linen, and china
- Condition of public space
- Progress report of the catering market plan
- Late distribution of menus
- Sales goals for each catering salesperson during certain periods
- Engineering charges
- Evaluation of appearance of meeting room set-ups
- Review of progress report of business booked for each month
- Evaluation of quality of food and service
- Evaluation of effectiveness of ballroom minimums and requirements guidelines
- Review of catering profit and loss reports

Periodically it is advisable to hold meetings jointly between the catering and sales departments.

Catering Office Forms

Samples of various forms used in the administration process may be found at the end of this chapter on pages 40 to 69.

MERCHANDISING CATERING SERVICES ⎯⎯⎯⎯⎯⎯⎯⎯⎯⎯⎯⎯⎯

Each property should design and develop a captivating and enticing preset menu presentation. This presentation can range from the most basic to the most elaborate, depending on property capabilities and budgets. Some of the larger operations have their advertising agencies design these presentations.

When designing menus, keep in mind that items should not read like a telephone book. Rather, they should appear to be selected choices geared to a particular group's budget and desires, and yet provide some upgraded choices.

By the same token, do not place all luncheon or dinner items on one page starting with the lowest-priced item. Instead, try limiting each page to no more than three to five entree items grouped in different price levels. In this way, the catering salesperson can select the highest-priced category that a client's budget can tolerate.

An extensive and varied choice of menus should be offered to include selected international daily choices; cold luncheon items; buffets for breakfast, lunch, and dinner; special reception choices; ladies luncheon choices; and theme parties. A printed list of extra items and arrangements should be included in the menu presentations.

In order to allow an adjustment of catering menu prices without extensive costs and printing delays, prices should not be included on the menus. This exclusion will also allow for obtaining the highest menu prices that the market will bear. For those occasions when printed menu prices must be submitted, a cover sheet with all catering menu prices should be printed. The menu prices can also be handwritten or typed directly on the menu should it be necessary to agree to catering menu prices prior to 60 days before the scheduled function.

Custom-written menus should always be developed for food and beverage functions, other than conventions and groups, whenever possible. Since in almost every case contact with the catering client is in person, the menu should reflect the personal interest of the catering department to create a singular event for this "special" customer. One of the best award-winning menu and brochure design firms in the country is European Graphics, 3740 Park Central Blvd., North, Pampano Beach, FL; 305/971-6004.

Catering Contract Terms

The following list contains suggested conditions that should be included in the finalized agreement, as well as printed on the reverse side of each suggested printed menu.

Any and all proposals, reservations, agreements, and contracts respecting the use of services and facilities of the XYZ hotel are made subject to all hotel rules and regulations and shall include, but not be limited, to the following express terms and conditions:

1. The person or party making arrangements for private functions on behalf of the patron must notify the hotel of the exact number scheduled to attend all private functions Wednesday through Sunday, no later than two days prior to the scheduled function by 12 noon. For functions scheduled on Monday and Tuesday, notice must be given no later than 12 noon of the preceding Friday. Such number shall constitute a guarantee, not subject to reduction, and charges will be made accordingly. The hotel cannot be responsible for service to more than 3 percent over and above the guarantee, up to 50 guests maximum. If said patron or representative fails to notify the hotel by the required time, the hotel will assume the indicated anticipated attendance number previously discussed to be the correct number in attendance; charges will be made accordingly and the patron agrees to pay said charges.

2. All prices are subject to increase in order to meet possible rising costs of food and beverage and other operational expenses existing at the time the hotel is to perform in accordance with its obligations hereunder. Such increases may result from food and beverage costs, labor costs, taxes, and/or currency valuations. The hotel is granted the right to increase the applicable prices when necessary, or to make reasonable substitutions in the menu. The patron agrees to pay such increased prices and accept reasonable substitutions made by the hotel.

3. The patron agrees to pay, in addition to the prices agreed upon and separate from them, all federal, state, and city taxes that are applicable.

4. A gratuity equal to ___ percent of the total food and beverage bill will be added by the hotel unless the patron requests that the banquet waiters and waitresses be permitted to request gratuities from those attending the function.

5. Full payment in advance shall be required, unless the patron has made satisfactory credit arrangements with the hotel. In the event credit has been established, terms of payment shall be worked out at the time thereof. There will be a service charge in the amount of 1½ percent per month on the unpaid balance on all accounts and to be paid within thirty (30) days. If an event is cancelled, the patron shall be held liable for all losses sustained by the hotel, and all deposit monies may be held to cover said losses.

6. Neither the patron nor guests nor invitees shall be permitted to bring food and/or beverages of any kind into the hotel or onto its premises without the express written permission of the hotel. In the event such permission is granted, the hotel is authorized to charge for the service of said food and beverage.

7. The agreement is expressly conditional upon the hotel's ability to perform its obligations hereunder, and the hotel shall not be liable for any damages to the patron or the patron's guests and invitees, in the event that causes beyond the hotel's control interfere with such performance. Causes which may interfere with or prevent performance by the hotel include, but are not limited to: labor disputes or strikes, government controls or restrictions upon food, beverages, or other supplies travel or transportation.

8. The patron agrees to be responsible for any damages done to the premises or any other part of the hotel during the period of time the patron, his guests, invitees, employees, independent contractors or other agents under the patron's control or the control of any independent contractor hired by the patron are on the premises.

9. The XYZ hotel will not assume any responsibility for damages or loss of any merchandise or articles left in the hotel prior to, during or following the patron's function and/or functions.

10. A set-up charge on all seated meal functions will be added. If 25 or fewer guests are guaranteed, an additional set-up charge will be added to the account.

Customer Form Letters

Customer form letters are designed to expedite the mechanical process of written correspondence in catering. An acknowledgment of the reservation in writing is required in *all* cases. The sample letters on pages 70 to 107 will demonstrate how they can be varied to include additional information. The sample letters included are those most frequently used in catering.

1. Confirmation
    A. Reservation Block
    B. Reservation Block—Tentative until 12 months before date
    C. Annual Reservation
    D. Kosher
    E. Specials—Weddings, Bar Mitzvahs, Testimonials
    F. Reservation Block with final menu arrangements
    G. Cover letter with final menu and arrangements
    H. Convention Reservation Block
    I. Failure to return signed letter or proposal

2. Congratulations
   A. Promotion

3. Letter of Condolence

4. School/University

5. Conventions
   A. Request for Convention History
   B. Hospitality Suite
   C. Introductory for catering

6. Inquiry
   A. First follow-up
   B. Second follow-up
   C. Follow-up after visit

7. Option Paragraphs
   A. Six-Month clause
   B. Deposit clause
   C. Two-Week clause
   D. Second-Option clause
   E. Menus Enclosed clause
   F. Hold for Two Weeks clause
   G. Location Change clause
   H. Guarantee clause

8. Solicitation
   A. From another property
   B. Personal referral
   C. Cost-conscious client
   D. No business
   E. Christmas party
   F. Response following inquiry
   G. Convention hospitality
   H. Annual function

9. Thank You
   A. General
   B. General (Committee)
   C. Annual business or possible annual
   D. Wedding or Bar Mitzvah
   E. Regular client
   F. Thank you for the "thank you"
   G. Deposit and/or contract received

10. Floor Plan Requested

11. Cancellation
    A. Second option
    B. Annual (and nonannual) banquets

12. Letter of Refusal for Ads in Programs or Journals

Catering Event Order (CEO)

Often referred to as the *prospectus,* the catering event order is used to convey information about each particular function to responsible departments in the hotel. Copies of the CEO are also sent to the customer for verification of all outlined arrangements and charges. The CEO should be prepared on an 8 ½″ × 14″ proposal sheet and then the required number of copies can be made on a photostat or offset printing machine. The information included should be clear and should be printed in terms that are understandable to the respective departments. More often than not, the CEO is the last communication between the catering salesperson and the responsible departments.

The catering event order should be presented on attractive stationery. The importance of a customized look rather than a preprinted form cannot be overemphasized. A quality hotel operation should have a menu confirmation that will reflect their degree of excellence. Two copies of each menu confirmation should be sent to the guest, one of which he or she is to sign and return for confirmation and acceptance, along with any changes or additions. Notice of terms of contract should always be included with the guest's signature of acceptance.

When submitting a catering event order, as many extra items and arrangements should be included as possible. If appropriate for the function, the following items should not be overlooked:

- General reception room location
- General reception starting and closing times
- Guest of honor or head table reception room location
- Guest of honor or head table reception starting and closing times
- Open doors time
- Dinner service time (starting and closing)
- National Anthem time
- Invocation time
- Speeches (starting and closing times)
- Entertainment and/or dancing (starting and closing times)
- Guests' departure time
- Expected attendance
- Tickets, collected or uncollected
- Beverages (a la carte or added to master account)
- Wines (a la carte or added to master account)
- Gratuities or service charge
- Tax
- Room rental
- Cigars and cigarettes
- Room arrangements and set-ups

- Control tables at entrance
- Music arrangements
- Decorations (floral arrangements, linen selections, placement of candles)
- Mechanical requirements (audio and lighting)
- Additional labor charges
- Fashion show or entertainment special requirements
- Dressing rooms
- Projection equipment
- Meals for musicians, color guard, committee, or models
- Security requirements
- Checkrooms (tipping or no-tipping arrangements)
- Restroom attendants
- Printed materials
- Seating lists and room diagrams
- Easels required
- Photographs
- Flags
- Banners or signs to be hung
- Special decorations
- Prize or gift tables
- Size of dance floor
- Size of bandstand or stage
- Additional service charges
- Special parking arrangements
- Raffle drum
- Deposit received
- Billing or payment arrangements

Once a catering event order has been returned as a customer confirmation, all changes are typed on the original copy and appropriate copies should be distributed to the responsible departments as soon as possible. This should be no later than 10 days and no earlier than 30 days prior to any planned function. CEOs should be distributed once daily, in the late afternoon. Of course, if a rush order is placed, the CEO should be distributed as soon as possible and hand carried. It is important to remember that the few extra seconds it takes to distribute to each department may mean the difference between the success and failure of a function.

Guarantee Sheet

The purpose of the Guarantee Sheet is to notify all responsible departments of the final attendance for which the customer is responsible. It is distributed everyday of the year whether functions are taking place or not. When there are no planned meal functions, the Guarantee Sheet will simply state that fact.

At times the guarantee is adjusted after the Guarantee Sheet has been distributed. If so, the change must be made verbally and the responsible departments notified by telephone and then *followed up in writing.*

No guarantee should be lowered without first obtaining the approval of the director of catering.

In addition to the guarantee, the Guarantee Sheet should contain the name of the function, the room assigned, the file number, the CEO number, and the sales-person's initials or name. Since the Guarantee Sheet contains the minimum number of guests that the customer has agreed to pay for, it is important that the sheet be distributed according to a schedule. The schedule of distribution is as follows:

Monday for Wednesday functions
Tuesday for Thursday functions
Wednesday for Friday functions
Thursday for Saturday and Sunday functions
Friday for Monday and Tuesday functions

Weekly Event List

On Tuesday of each week, a list of all planned meetings and food functions should be drawn up (by date and by group or organization) for the next eight days. For example, on Tuesday, April 10, the Weekly Event List will start with Saturday, April 14 through and including Saturday, April 21.

The day of preparation will vary from hotel to hotel, depending on the day the hotel staff meeting is held. The Weekly Event List should be prepared one day prior to the meeting.

The director of catering or the director of convention services should approve the "Weekly" before the copies are run off and distributed.

The rules of distribution are the same for the Weekly Event List as they are for the Guarantee Sheet.

Daily Event List

The Daily Event List is prepared in a way similar to the Weekly Event List except that the functions are listed as they take place during the day and by group or organization. For example, breakfast is listed first and is followed by meetings, luncheons, recep-tions, and dinners. Each group will have a designated heading in order to quickly locate an activity in the hotel. The "Daily" contains only one (1) day of meetings and food functions. It is prepared each day for the next day. On Friday, the "Daily" must be prepared for Saturday, Sunday, and Monday.

The rules of distribution are the same as those for the Weekly Event List. In addition, a copy of the "Daily" will also be posted in the hotel lobby as well as other possible locations to assist guests in locating these activities.

Function Summary Report (Banquet Manager's Report)

The purpose of this report is to summarize, as concisely as possible, the actual function. The report is filled out by the banquet manager, banquet maitre d', banquet head-waiter, and/or the banquet captain and should be given to the director of catering for his or her review as the first order of business on the following morning. After its critique, the function summary report becomes a permanent part of the organization's file. This report will often settle many disputes, since it provides a cross-reference against the customer's statement of charges. It will also assist in planning the next function for the same group.

Recap of Banquet Sales Report

This report itemizes the charges incurred by each function and provides accounting with the information necessary for posting the daily banquet revenue. This form can be completed by either the accounting department or the banquet manager's office.

Development of Patron's History

Each file should contain as much pertinent information about a function as possible, including any news media coverage. If the salesperson happens to know the chairman drinks Dubonnet, this should be documented in the file. When as much information as possible is collected, it can prove valuable leverage when attempting to rebook the function.

Each function's file should contain (but not be limited to) the following basic information:

- Letter of confirmation (unless booked by convention sales)
- Signed copies of the proposed menus and arrangements
- Signed copy of the Catering Event Order (prospectus)
- Any changes and/or additions
- Guarantee discussed and agreed upon
- Floor plan (if required)
- Copy of the Function Book Booking Form (showing date it was entered in the function book)
- Copy of the Function Summary Report (Banquet Manager's Report)
- Application for credit (if applicable)
- Copy of Request for Clearance Space (if applicable)
- Thank-you letter.

Utilization of Function Space

It is the responsibility of management to establish guidelines with regard to availability of space by the catering department. Once the guides have been established, it is the responsibility of convention sales to determine the convention programs at the time of booking. When an exact program cannot be established at the time of booking, an "All Space Hold," with the approval of the director of sales, is placed on the function space, *but only until 5 P.M.* Evening activities should be programmed at the time of booking, since most groups will require an opening reception and closing banquet. This will allow catering to book evening activities without delay. Also, at this point, judgment must be exercised by convention sales in an attempt to establish the convention program as soon as possible. When a great number of programs can be established in advance, there is a better opportunity for catering to fill distressed periods.

The director of catering and the director of sales *must* establish a strong rapport between their respective departments in order to ensure the maximum occupancy of function space.

Condition of Banquet Rooms

The condition of the banquet facilities can readily help close a sale or kill it. Keeping chairs in good condition, maintaining walls and carpets, and keeping the room arrangement in a neat and orderly manner when it is not in use are important factors when guests are inspecting the facilities.

The general manager, the director of food and beverage operations, the convention service manager, the director of catering, and the banquet manager should inspect the function space regularly to evaluate the condition of the premises. Continual inspection, by these individuals as well as each staff member, to maintain a positive appearance of the banquet facilities not only influences customers' decisions, but it will also affect the morale of the hotel staff.

ACCOUNTING

One of the most difficult problems in catering is in deciding whose credit should be checked. With today's credit risks, a wise policy is to check into each group's credit situation and past history if available. Never assume credit, but do investigate and ask the credit manager to follow through with additional information. In today's economy, no reputable organization will object to proper credit procedures. It should be underscored that to conduct business successfully for any length of time, every proper step must be taken to insure a good accounts receivable program. Whenever there is the slightest doubt, ask for money in advance of the function. The trend, to a large degree, is toward a delay in payment even with a good credit history and a reputable name. In many cases the delay is simply a matter of cash flow, but this is also a reason for concern.

The policy should be to ask for prepayment of all functions booked by individuals as consumers unless the general manager or the credit manager decides an exception is in order. As a general guideline, payment in advance should be obtained for dances, Bar Mitzvahs, weddings, and high-school proms and college functions not arranged directly with the school or university. With respect to *all* political functions, payment in advance should be a standard policy.

All payments should be made *at least* two weeks in advance and preferably by certified check. It is also advisable to collect extra funds to cover any last-minute changes or additions. Such accounts, when delinquent, cannot be written off since such action could be construed as a political contribution. Whenever there is doubt about payment, all information should immediately be turned over to the credit manager's office at the time of booking. Although the responsibility of checking lies with the credit manager, the responsibility of making the credit office aware of all pertinent information rests with the salesperson.

Billing

All charges incurred during a function must be signed by the guest at the conclusion of the function in order to reduce the possibility of disputes. The charges should then be sent to accounting for prompt follow-up. If an account becomes past due, accounting should receive assistance from the salesperson in an attempt to expedite collection.

Forecasting

The process of estimating future revenues is called *forecasting.* The monthly forecast can act as a barometer in staffing and in predicting approximate revenues for the month. Some hotel operations conduct a 30–60–90-day or even a six-month forecast to establish even greater forecast sophistication and accuracy to reaching and surpassing an annual forecast.

In most cases the monthly forecast should be completed by the end of the second week of the month prior to the one being forecasted, and distributed no later than the 15th of that month. In order to compensate for short-lead business booked within that period, a percentage should be built into both the covers (the number of people served) and the food revenue. The percentage to be built in can only be obtained from past history and experience.

The steps for this type of forecasting are as follows: The forecaster goes through the function book day by day for the forecasted month. The number of covers booked for each breakfast, lunch, dinner, and reception on each day are noted. After placing them in their respective columns, the forecaster must then total them and add in the pickup (anticipated last-minute bookings). This figure is then placed under total covers. The total cover-to-date column is a cumulative of several covers. Actual to-date represents the actual covers served. The food revenue is calculated by multiplying the price per person times the number of covers for each function on each day and then adding in the pickup. The beverage revenue is calculated by dividing the forecasted total number of covers for the month one year ago. This figure is then multiplied by the forecasted total covers on a day-to-day basis.

The validity of using covers as an effective statistic is often questioned. Contrary to the belief that covers bear little relationship to the dollar figures, it should be emphasized that they indeed have a direct impact. For example, when the monthly income is compared against the number of covers served in that month, it is possible to determine the average check. In turn, the average check is a barometer for the minimum rate structure in determining if costs are in line.

DEVELOPMENT OF SUPPLEMENTARY RESOURCES

Within each catering department there is often a need, on behalf of the customer, for ancillary services such as music, decorations, flowers, photography, and projection and audio equipment. This can often develop into a large source of revenue for your hotel. Generally, a hotel will receive a percentage commission for making the contract.

The catering department should exercise caution in this area, however, since a recommendation can turn out to be a failure. The customer should engage these services based on their own approval and not the approval of the catering department. For purposes of billing and commission, it is possible for the hotel to act as a liaison between the customer and the agent.

MENU COMPOSITION

There are two types of catering menus: preset and custom written. Regardless of which kind is used, four basic factors enter into the composition: planning, costing, design, and selling.

In the planning stage, the catering director should work closely with the executive chef to determine what can be produced most effectively. To achieve the most productive relationship, the catering director should:

1. Determine the strengths and weaknesses of the executive chef and the chef's key personnel.

2. Challenge his or her knowledge of creative and attractive menu composition. Always consider if items can be produced in volume.

3. Learn which regional foods are preferred and keep abreast of the consumer market.

4. Understand which advantages can be developed by using locally grown items. Certain items may be exclusive to your area and a delicacy elsewhere.

5. Try new items and sources, but be cautious as to the size and habits of the group. When selecting a menu for a group, most customers tend to be conservative, and with good reason. They may have experimented and met with failure in the past.

Once the menus are planned, they must be costed to determine profitability to the hotel and salability in the particular economic climate. It is extremely important to determine what comprises cost in banquet menu planning. The sale price of the menu depends entirely on the profit that the particular property must achieve from catering.

Some hotels attempt to prevent the food costs from exceeding 25 percent, whereas others may allow 33 percent as the ceiling. Once the price has been established, however, it is important to keep the costs continually in line. In this way, the price structure can be adjusted to meet future costs. This method is the most accurate since it reflects actual costs. A simple guide to determine if the price structure is in line prior to the sale is to request a portion cost sheet from the food and beverage controller such as the example shown below. The figures can be adjusted weekly or monthly. Theoretical guidelines can be especially helpful when creating custom-written menus. All the catering salesperson needs to do is to calculate the total cost and multiply that figure by the desired markup. The following example represents a proposed dinner menu:

Lobster Bisque...$ .78

    *   *   *

Princess Salad ....$ .46
  Romaine lettuce—$ .08
  Fresh sliced mushrooms—$ .07
  Hearts of palm—$ .12
  Cherry tomatoes—$ .05
  Gourmet cheese dressing—$ .14

    *   *   *

Filet Mignon au Champignon/Accoutrements $6.62
  8-oz. filet—$5.54
  Champignons—$ .10
  Sauce Périgourdine—$ .33
  Pommes Duchesse—$ .22
  Artichoke bottom—$ .25
  Florentine tomato Provencale—$ .18

    *   *   *

Rolls and Butter..$ .44
  Fresh rolls—$ .32
  Butter—$ .12

    *   *   *

Frozen Raspberry Souffle....................................$ .47
Fresh Raspberry Sauce.....................................$ .41
Petits Fours/After-Dinner Mints ....$ .38
      *   *   *

Coffee ....$ .15
COST $9.71

     Charge: 4 × $9.71 = $38.84 or 25 percent

Once you have the marketed items, plan the menu layout in such a way as to create interest on behalf of the customer. Offer traditional items along with new ideas, and design the menus so that eye appeal will flow logically from one item to another.

It is very important to understand *how* to sell a menu. Knowing the composition of a menu will aid in cost-effective selling. For example, a fresh fruit cocktail could be substituted for shrimp cocktail when the entree is a type of fish. In this way, cost can be kept down while maintaining an attractive and salable menu.

REQUEST FOR CLEARANCE OF SPACE

To: _____ Date of Request: _____

CC: Mr. or Ms.: _____

From: _____

Name of Organization Requesting Space: _____

By: _____ Date: _____

Room Desired: _____

Alternate Room (if any): _____

Type of Function: _____

Attendance: _____ Value of Business: _____

Space Now Being Held for: _____

(group name)

Additional Comments:

Space Cleared: _____ Not Cleared: _____

Reason:

_____

Person Releasing Space (Signature)

40

REQUEST TO SET UP "B" FILE

Date: _____

Organization: _____   File No.: _____

Name of Executive: _____   Office Phone No.: _____

Title: _____   Home Phone No.: _____

Address: _____

City and State: _____   Zip: _____

Annual Events	Attendance	Approx. Date

Annual Trace: _____   Requested by (Salesperson): _____

Approved by: _____
(Director of Catering)

41

INQUIRY CALL SHEET

Name of Group: _____   File No.: _____

Posting Instructions: _____

Person in Charge: _____

Address: _____

_____   Phone: _____

Booked by: _____   Tentative _____   Definite _____   Inquiry _____

(BOOKING INFORMATION)

Date	Hours	Function	Room	Number of Persons	Rate

CALL REPORT

By: _____   Telephone _____

Date: _____   Letter _____

File #: _____   Personal Call _____

New Business _____   Inside Hotel _____

Repeat Business _____   Outside Hotel _____

Name of Organization: _____

Type of Function: _____

Dates: 1st _____   2nd _____

Frequency of Function: _____

Last Function: Hotel _____   Date _____

Person Contacted:

Name: _____

Address: _____

_____

Telephone: Office _____   Home _____

Remarks: _____

Approved: _____   Trace Date: _____
                Director of Catering

MONTHLY BOOKING REPORT

BANQUET SOLICITATION PROGRAM

DEFINITE BOOKINGS—MONTH OF _____ YEAR _____ SALESPERSON _____

Name of Organization	Local/ Conv.	File No.	New Bus.	Rep. Bus.	Date	Type of Function	Size	Estimated Value
TOTALS								

Number of outside calls: _____

Number of new B Files this month: _____

Number of B Files killed this month: _____

Number of newspaper leads followed this month: _____

Salesperson _____

Approved by _____

Director of Catering

REPORT OF LOST BUSINESS

Date: _____

Name of Group: _____ File No.: _____

Contact: _____ Title: _____

Date of Function: _____ Type of Function: _____

Size: _____ Estimated Value: _____ Hotel Selected: _____

Source of Lead and Date Received:

Report of Solicitation:

Reasons for Losing Business:

_____   _____
Approved by Director of Catering   Catering Contact

Copies:

PROPOSED SAMPLE MENU

Hotel Logo

American Ocean Organization
Attendance: 750 guests
In Charge: Ms. Kathryn Miller

Catering Department
Proposed Menu (SAMPLE)
Saturday, May 4, 1991
6:30–7:30 P.M. Reception—Foyer
7:45 P.M. Head Table Introductions
8:00–9:15 P.M. Dinner
9:15–Midnight—Dancing—Presidential Ballroom

RECEPTION

From an attractively decorated buffet table,
we will serve the following selection
of hot & cold hors d'oeuvres
(approximately 9 pieces per person):

Hot & Cold

Baby Lamb Chops
Beef Fondue with Sauces
Oysters Rockefeller
Brochette of Duckling with Kumquat
Croustade St. Jacques
Baby Shrimp Canapés
Crab Claws Supreme
Prosciutto & Melon
Celery with Roquefort

$ Price

DINNER

Gulf Shrimp Cocktail
Sauce Remoulade
*   *   *
Tender Bib Lettuce
with Red Pimento
Marinated Mushrooms
Esquire Dressing
*   *   *

Filet Mignon Grillé

Sauce Choron

Fondante Potato

Green Beans Sauté

Tomato Duxelle

*   *   *

Strawberries Romanoff

*   *   *

Coffee or Tea

$ Price

Extra Items and Arrangements:

Beverages:

From 6:30–7:30 P.M.—Foyer   We will provide 10 hosted bars and 10 bartenders to serve a complete selection of highballs & cocktails at a flat rate charge of $____ per person, using Premium brands. Bartender charges are included in the per person price. We will also have domestic beer and appropriate mixes available, also included in the per person price. Full bar set-up.

With the Entree   We will be pleased to serve Cabernet Sauvignon, California at $____ per bottle (approximately 4 bottles per table) to be charged as consumed and added to the account.

From 9:15 P.M.–Midnight—Presidential Ballroom   We will provide 4 cash bars and 4 bartenders at $____ each and 4 cashiers at $____ each to serve a complete selection of highballs and cocktails at $____ per drink, using House brands. We will also have available imported beer at $____ per bottle, domestic beer at $____ per bottle, and soft drinks at $____ each. We will provide appropriate mixes and full-bar set-up. All above cash bar beverages are inclusive of gratuity and tax.

Gratuities:

____% on all food and beverages (except cash bar beverages) added to the account.

Tax:

____% state sales tax on all food and beverages (except cash bar beverages) added to the account.

Linen:

We will provide sandalwood linen and walnut napkins.

Candles:

We will provide silver candelabras on the head table, complimentary.

Flowers:	Creative Flowers to provide 2 long and low floral centerpieces for the head table at $_____ each. We will also provide individual floral centerpieces for the banquet round tables. Each centerpiece will have (2) 18″ tapered candles incorporated in a bouquet of spring flowers, at $_____ each.
Checkroom:	By each guest.
Arrangements:	*Reception Foyer* A serpentine-shaped buffet table will be placed on the east wall. Intimate groupings of cocktail tables and chairs will be placed where space permits. Bars to be placed in the appropriate locations. Two 6′ rectangular tables to be placed at the entrance to the foyer area for Committee control.
	Dinner—Presidential Ballroom Head table of 30 guests with table podium on the east wall. Round tables of 10 guests each, seating according to diagram. Bandstand on the south wall with a large highly polished dance floor in the center of the room. Cash bars to be placed in strategic locations around the room.
Music:	Own arrangements have been made with Big Band Productions, Inc., for 14 musicians.
Mechanical:	One microphone attached to the podium at head table, complimentary, and 3 additional microphones at the bandstand at $_____ each.
Rental:	Complimentary
In Charge of Service:	Mr. William Vaccaro, Banquet Maitre D′
Billing:	American Ocean Organization Attn: Ms. Kathryn Miller 12 Sailfish Way Ocean City, Florida 13002
Arrangements by:	G. Eugene Wigger, Director of Catering (Signature) Hotel Name

PROPOSED SAMPLE MENU

Hotel Logo

Catering Department
Proposed Menu (SAMPLE)
Saturday, Dec. 7, 1991
7:00 P.M.–1:00 A.M.—Coatcheck—
Outside Presidential Foyer
7:30 P.M.–8:45 P.M.—Reception—
Presidential Foyer
8:45 P.M.–11 P.M.—Buffet Dinner

In Honor of the Bryan Weiner Bar Mitzvah
Reception/Dinner/Entertainment/Dance
Attendance: 350 Adults, 45 Children
In Charge: Mr. and Mrs. Saul Weiner

11:00 P.M.–11:30 P.M.—
Entertainment
11:30 P.M.–1:00 A.M.—Dancing—
Presidential Ballroom

THE MOST SPECIAL ATTENTION
WHITE GLOVE SERVICE

THE MOST SPECIAL ATTENTION
WHITE GLOVE SERVICE

RECEPTION

A stark white cubic construction
designed to present the following:

A Mélange of Fresh Seafood

Captured in giant iced seashells,
a selection of:
Giant Jumbo Shrimp
Clams and Oysters on the Half Shell
Langostinos
Whole Pieces of Crabmeat and Lobster
Served in Coconut Shells
Garnished with Lemon Stars,
Cocktail Sauce, and Horseradish
*   *   *

A Presentation of Fresh Vegetables

To include:
Zucchini, String Beans, Cauliflower, Broccoli,
Carrots, Mushroom Caps, and Cherry Tomatoes
Served with a Mustard Curry Dip and a Fresh Dill Dip
*   *   *

Whole Nova Scotia Smoked Salmon
Sliced by a Chef at the Table
Served with Pumpernickel Bread
and the Appropriate Garniture
*   *   *

A Display of International and Domestic Cheeses
To include:
Bel Paese, Danish Bleu, Camembert, Wisconsin Sharp Cheddar,
Boursin, Edam, Brie, and Muenster
Garnished with Whole and Sliced Fresh Fruits
*   *   *

BUFFET DINNER
WHOLE RACK OF LAMB, NICOISE
Sauce Diable,
Sliced at the Table
WHOLE LARDED BEEF TENDERLOIN
Sauce Bearnaise and Sauce Périgourdine,
Sliced at the Table
WHOLE SADDLE OF VEAL
Sauce Morille,
Sliced at the Table
ROTISSERIE DUCK
a l'orange,
Carved at the Table
FILET OF FRENCH TOURBOT
Meuniere
*   *   *

SNOW PEAS WITH WATER CHESTNUTS
WILD RICE
TOMATO BOUQUETIERE
A Whole Tomato Stuffed with a
Fleurette of Broccoli and Cauliflower
Sauce Hollandaise

ZUCCHINI BOAT
Stuffed with Mushrooms
SPECIALTY BREAD DISPLAY
A Collection of a Variety of Breads
To include:
Rolls and Other Bread Items

*   *   *

A SWEET TABLE
To include:
Chocolate Chip Cheesecake, Marzipan Torte, English Trifle,
Black Forest Cake, Lemon Bavarian Tart, Zugger Kirsch Torte,
and a Variety of Other Specialties of the Chef's selection
and
A SPECIALLY PREPARED BAR MITZVAH CAKE

*   *   *

Coffee or Tea

*   *   *

CHILDREN'S BUFFET

A Super Six-Foot Submarine Sandwich
will be used as an edible centerpiece,
placed in the center of this separate buffet.
In addition,
we will present:
Golden Brown Fried Chicken
McBryan Hamburgers
Foot-Long Hot Dogs
Deep-Dish Pizza
French Fries
Cole Slaw
A Complete Assortment of Relishes
and Appropriate Condiments

*   *   *

A Special Presentation of our
SUNDAE EXTRAVAGANZA
A Custom-Made Sundae with 100 Scoops of Ice Cream
To include:
Chocolate, Vanilla, Strawberry,
Chocolate Chip, Assorted Sherbets;
Served with a Selection of Hot Fudge, Fresh Strawberries,
Mixed Nuts, Brandied Peach Sauce, Rum Raisin Sauce,
AND
A
CHERRY
*   *   *
Milk and Assorted Soft Drinks

$_____ per person, ADULT
$_____ per person, CHILDREN

Extra Items and Arrangements:

Beverages: *From 7:30 P.M. to 8:45 P.M.*   We will provide 5 hosted bars and 5 bartenders to serve a complete selection of highballs using Premium brands at $_____ per bottle, *to include the following liquors:* Chivas Regal Scotch, Dewars White Label Scotch, Tanqueray Gin, Smirnoff Vodka, Canadian Club, Bacardi Rum, Johnnie Walker Black Label Scotch, Jack Daniels Black Label Bourbon, Beefeater Gin, Stolichnaya Vodka, Crown Royal, and Jose Cuervo Gold Tequila. We will have Dry Sack Sherry at $_____ per bottle, Michelob Beer at $_____ per bottle, and Heineken and Lowenbrau Beers at $_____ per bottle. *In addition,* we will have a variety of red, white, and rosé wines available at $_____ per glass. Bartenders will be charged at $_____ each for the first three hours and $_____ for each hour thereafter. Appropriate mixes and full bar set-up included.

From 8:45 P.M.–1:00 A.M.   We will provide 3 hosted bars and 3 bartenders located in the *Presidential Ballroom, serving the same liquors as outlined above.* The prices of the bartenders will be as quoted in the overtime charges stated above. *With the salad,* and continuing on through the meal, we will serve a *Pouilly Fuissé, Louis Jadot, 1976* at $_____ per bottle and a *Cote de Beaune Villages, Louis Jadot, 1974* at $_____ per bottle. These wines will be made available to the guests during the entire meal. Each waiter will offer a choice accordingly. *With the coffee,* we will serve *from multiple Cordial Carts,* a presentation of the following liqueurs: Courvoisier, Remy Martin, Hennessey, Drambuie, B & B, Grand Marnier, Kahlua, Galliano, Harvey's Bristol Creme, and Creme de Menthe Green, at a charge of $_____ per drink.

Gratuities: _____% on all food and beverages, to be added to the account.

Tax: _____% state sales tax to be added to the account.

Decorations: *Linen:* Special table arrangements and linen provided by Omnibus, and special napkins provided by Mrs. Weiner.

Flowers: Table arrangements, floral decor, and all other decor throughout the Reception and Ballroom has been separately handled between Mr. and Mrs. Weiner and Omnibus Decorators. The charges incurred for this service are not a part of this arrangement.

Candles: Incorporated in the decor of the evening.

Checkroom: The Concierge's desk will operate a coatcheck to be placed outside the Presidential Ballroom foyer, in the mirrored alcove across from the elevator. This will be done compliments of the host at a charge of $_____.

Arrangements: *Guests' Arrival* Valet parking will be available from the front door of the hotel. Full service will be rendered for arrival and departure of guests, at a charge of $_____.

Reception—Presidential Ballroom Foyer We will have five bars, cocktail tables, cubic arrangements to support the buffet, with a full floor plan to follow.

Dinner—Presidential Ballroom Buffet design incorporated with Omnibus Decorators. Full details to follow. The guests will be seated at six-foot round tables of 10 guests each.

For the Children A separate buffet will be created for the children's buffet. The SWEET TABLE will be introduced at approximately 10:30 P.M. There will be two separate buffets apart from the main buffet and the children's buffet for this particular service.

Hotel Staff Attire: All members of the hotel staff servicing the evening's affair, including all levels of management and service personnel, will be dressed in formal white tie and tails, at a cost of $_____.

China and Glassware: China and glassware will be a specially purchased crystal water goblet and glass showplate to be used as well as a rented Gold China pattern for the service of the evening, at a cost of $_____. *Specially constructed cubic design at a cost of $_____.*

Bandstand, Dance Floor, Buffet Arrangements, and Table Placement will be fully detailed in a floor plan.

Music: The entertainment and music for the evening will *set-up* at approximately 2:00 P.M. on Saturday, December 1st. All arrangements are under the separate control of Mr. and Mrs. Saul Weiner. *Piano required for the reception.*

Mechanical: *For the entertainment,* positioned at the bandstand, the Engineering Department will provide a power source having single phase, 60 amp., 120 volts, at a charge of $_____.

Rental: Complimentary.

In Charge of Service: Mr. William Vaccaro, Banquet Maitre D'

Billing: As mentioned in the cover letter and if agreeable to Mr. and Mrs. Saul Weiner, the following arrangements will be in effect: A check to be returned with the signed arrangements in the following amount: $_____, which covers full payment.

Price Breakdown:
350 Adults at $_____ per person...............................$
45 Children at $_____ per person ....$
350 Adults at an approximated
    beverage cost per person of $_____ ....$
Gratuity at _____% on food and beverage ....$
Tax at _____% on food and beverage....................$
Extra Items...$
Grand Total..$
Less Deposit ....$
Balance Due...$
For record purposes, note the following address:
Mr. and Mrs. Saul Weiner, 4364 NW 67th Way, Coral Springs, FL 33067

Arrangements by: Respectfully Submitted:
(Signature) G. Eugene Wigger, Director of Catering

DISTRIBUTION LIST FOR CATERING EVENT ORDERS

(PROSPECTUS)

Customer (original for sign & return + 1 copy) ....1 copy
Executive Assistant Manager, F&B..1 copy
Director of Catering ....1 copy
Catering Manager ....1 copy
Catering Secretaries ....2 copies
Banquet Manager ....2 copies
Customer File..1 copy
Director of Convention Services ....3 copies
Executive Chef ....5 copies
Executive Steward...2 copies
Purchasing Agent ....2 copies
Beverage Manager ....2 copies
Comptroller ....1 copy
Head Cashier...1 copy
F&B Control...1 copy

A total of 26 copies are to be run off and distributed. After the original is signed and returned, it is kept in the customer's file. (Distribution will vary according to size of operation and hotel policy.)

BANQUET CHANGE

American Ocean Organization
Annual Reception & Neptune Awards Banquet
Attendance: 750 Guests
In Charge: Ms. Kathryn Miller

Saturday, May 4, 1991
6:30–7:30 P.M.—Reception—
Foyer
7:45 P.M. Head Table
Introductions
8:00–9:15 P.M. Dinner
9:15–Midnight—Dance,
Presidential Ballroom

In connection with the above function, please note the following changes:

Menu: Instead of the Gulf Shrimp Cocktail, we will now serve the ALASKA KING CRABMEAT—SAUCE REMOULADE.

Price: The per person dinner price will now be $____ per person.

Beverages: Reduce number of bars to 9 bars and 9 bartenders @ $____ each during the Reception. Four cash bars to remain during the dance.

Attendance: 650 guests are now expected.

Arrangements: Reduce head table to 24 guests.

All other arrangements remain the same.

SAMPLE MENU WORK SHEET

Group Name: Date:

Type of Function: Times:

Attendance: Guests:

In Charge: Room:

Extra Items and Arrangements
    Linen:
    Candles:
    Flowers:

    Checkroom:
    Arrangements:

Menu Price:

Extra Items and Arrangements:
    Beverages:

    Music:
    Mechanical:
    Rental:
    In Charge of Service:
    Billing:
    Arranged by:
    Gratuities: Date:
    Tax: File:

BANQUET GUARANTEE

G—Stands for Guarantee   S—Stands for Set

TO: Messrs: Executive Chef, Food and Beverage Director, Banquet Manager, Purchasing Director, Executive Steward, Beverage Director, Comptroller

            Mesdames: Secretary to Director of Catering, Catering Secretary

FROM: G. Eugene Wigger, Director of Catering

SUBJECT: SAMPLE GUARANTEE SHEET—MONDAY, MARCH 25, 1991

NATIONAL ASSOCIATION OF
CLOCK WINDERS   WIG-C-8

G778/S800	Reception	Grand Foyer	
G778/S800	Banquet	Grand Ballroom	

CORAL SPRINGS TEACHERS UNION   WIG-B-14

G25/S27	Luncheon	Salon III

EXECUTIVE SECRETARIES, INC.   MD-B-22

G125/S130	Luncheon	Salon IV

BISCIOTTI CORPORATION   WIG-B-20

G57/S60	Breakfast	Board Room

DISTRIBUTION LIST FOR GUARANTEE SHEET

Executive Assistant Manager, F&B...1 copy
Director of Catering...1 copy
Catering Manager..1 copy
Catering Secretaries..2 copies
Banquet Manager..2 copies
Director of Convention Services ....3 copies
Executive Chef (original + 3 copies)...3 copies
Executive Steward...2 copies
Purchasing Agent ....1 copy
Beverage Manager ....1 copy
Comptroller ....1 copy
Room Service Manager ....1 copy

A total of 19 copies are to be run off and distributed. The Executive Chef receives the original + 3 copies. (Distribution will vary according to size of operation and hotel policy.)

SAMPLE WEEKLY EVENT SHEET

SATURDAY, MARCH 23, 1991

National Association of Clock Winders

General Session	Grand Ballroom	9:00 A.M.–4:30 P.M.	800 PP
Breakout Meeting	Junior Ballroom B	4:30 P.M.–5:30 P.M.	250 PP
Breakout Meeting	Junior Ballroom C	4:30 P.M.–5:30 P.M.	375 PP
Breakout Meeting	Junior Ballroom D	4:30 P.M.–5:30 P.M.	150 PP
Breakout Meeting	Salon I–II	4:30 P.M.–5:30 P.M.	50 PP
Breakout Meeting	Salon III–IV	4:30 P.M.–5:30 P.M.	50 PP
Breakout Meeting	Salon V–VI	4:30 P.M.–5:30 P.M.	50 PP
Breakout Meeting	Conference Room	4:30 P.M.–5:30 P.M.	50 PP
Reception	Grand Foyer	7:00 P.M.–8:00 P.M.	1,000 PP
Banquet/Show/Dance	Grand Ballroom	8:15 P.M.–1:00 A.M.	1,000 PP

Coral Springs Teachers Union

Meeting	Conference Parlor I	10:00 A.M.–12:00 Noon	12 PP
Luncheon	Conference Parlor II	12:00 Noon–1:30 P.M.	12 PP

Executive Secretaries, Inc.

Luncheon	Conference Room	11:30 A.M.–2:00 P.M.	100 PP

Bisciotti Corporation

Breakfast/Meeting	Meeting Room A	7:30 A.M.–10:30 A.M.	60 PP

SUNDAY, MARCH 24, 1991

IHO Beth Zaharako & Jim Patton Wedding

Reception	Junior Foyer	12:30 P.M.–1:30 P.M.	225 PP
Luncheon/Dance	Junior Ballroom	1:30 P.M.–5:00 P.M.	225 PP

St. Mary's Church

Reception	Conference Room	1:00 P.M.–1:30 P.M.	200 PP
Annual Luncheon	Grand Ballroom B	1:30 P.M.–3:00 P.M.	200 PP

Perry Corporation

Exhibit Set-Up	Meeting Room I	3:00 P.M.–Eve	—

DISTRIBUTION LIST FOR WEEKLY EVENT SHEET

General Manager...1 copy
Executive Assistant Manager, F&B...1 copy
Executive Assistant Manager, Rooms..1 copy
Director of Catering..1 copy
Catering Manager..1 copy
Banquet Manager..1 copy
Director of Convention Services..1 copy
Executive Chef...1 copy
Executive Steward...1 copy
Purchasing Agent..1 copy
Beverage Manager..1 copy
Comptroller...1 copy
Head Cashier...1 copy
Outlet Manager...1 copy
Outlet Manager...1 copy
Outlet Manager...1 copy
Outlet Manager...1 copy
Outlet Manager...1 copy
Room Service Manager...1 copy
Director of Security...1 copy
Hotel Hostess Director..1 copy
Assistant Managers...1 copy
Director of Sales...1 copy
Director of Engineering...1 copy
Front Office Manager..1 copy
Chief PBX Operator..1 copy
Public Relations Director...1 copy
Bell Captain..1 copy
Garage Supervisor..1 copy
Function Book Diary Clerk..1 copy

A total of 30 copies are to be run off and distributed. The original copy will be retained by the Diary Clerk. (Distribution will vary according to size of operation and hotel policy.)

SAMPLE DAILY EVENT SHEET

SATURDAY, MARCH 23, 1991

National Association of Clock Winders

General Session	Grand Ballroom	9:00 A.M.–4:30 P.M.	800 PP
Breakout Meeting	Junior Ballroom B	4:30 P.M.–5:30 P.M.	250 PP
Breakout Meeting	Junior Ballroom C	4:30 P.M.–5:30 P.M.	375 PP
Breakout Meeting	Junior Ballroom D	4:30 P.M.–5:30 P.M.	150 PP
Breakout Meeting	Salon I–II	4:30 P.M.–5:30 P.M.	50 PP
Breakout Meeting	Salon III–IV	4:30 P.M.–5:30 P.M.	50 PP
Breakout Meeting	Salon V–VI	4:30 P.M.–5:30 P.M.	50 PP
Breakout Meeting	Conference Room	4:30 P.M.–5:30 P.M.	50 PP
Reception	Grand Foyer	7:00 P.M.–8:00 P.M.	1,000 PP
Banquet/Show/Dance	Grand Ballroom	8:15 P.M.–1:00 A.M.	1,000 PP

Coral Springs Teachers Union

Meeting	Conference Parlor I	10:00 A.M.–12:00 Noon	12 PP
Luncheon	Conference Parlor II	12:00 Noon–1:30 P.M.	12 PP

Executive Secretaries, Inc.

Luncheon	Conference Room	11:30 A.M.–2:00 P.M.	100 PP

Bisciotti Corporation

Breakfast/Meeting	Meeting Room A	7:30 A.M.–10:30 A.M.	60 PP

DISTRIBUTION LIST FOR DAILY EVENT SHEET

General Manager ....1 copy
Executive Assistant Manager, F&B...1 copy
Executive Assistant Manager, Rooms ....1 copy
Director of Catering ....1 copy
Catering Manager ....1 copy
Banquet Manager ....2 copies
Director of Convention Services ....6 copies
Executive Chef ....1 copy
Executive Steward ....1 copy
Purchasing Agent ....1 copy
Beverage Manager ....1 copy
Comptroller ....1 copy
Head Cashier ....1 copy
Outlet Manager ....1 copy
Outlet Manager ....1 copy
Outlet Manager ....1 copy
Outlet Manager ....1 copy
Outlet Manager ....1 copy
Room Service Manager ....1 copy
Director of Security ....2 copies
Hotel Hostess Director ....1 copy
Assistant Managers..1 copy
Director of Sales ....1 copy
Director of Engineering...2 copies
Front Office Manager ....1 copy
Chief PBX Operator ....1 copy
Public Relations Director...1 copy
Bell Captain ....1 copy
Garage Supervisor..1 copy
Function Book Diary Clerk ....1 copy
Catering Secretaries ....2 copies

A total of 40 copies are to be run off and distributed. The original copy will be retained by the Diary Clerk. (Distribution will vary according to size of operation and hotel policy.)

BANQUET MANAGER'S FUNCTION SUMMARY REPORT

Name of Organization: _____

Type of Function: _____

Date: _____ File No.: _____

Function Room: _____ Salesperson: _____

Did function start and end on time? _____

_____

Room cleaned following function? _____

_____

Air conditioning and lights turned off? _____

_____

Remarks: _____

_____

_____

_____

Guests' Comments: _____

_____

_____

Articles left in room: _____

INCOME

Hors d'oeuvre food: _____

Other food: _____

Beverage: _____

Wine: _____

Gratuity: _____

Tax: _____

Other: _____

Total: _____

COVER COUNT

#Guaranteed _____

#Set _____

#Plated _____

#Served _____

#Charged _____

_____
In Charge of Service

RECAP OF BANQUET SALES

Date _____

| Check # | Name | Sales | | | Other Items | | Sales Tax | Function Tips | | Totals | Charge To | | | Number Served | Typ. Fun. |
		Public Rooms	Food	Beverage	Explanation	Amount		Food	Beverage		City Ledger	Guest Ledger	Cash		
Food															
Total Food															
Beverage															
Total Beverage															
TOTAL BANQUET SALES															

66

APPLICATION FOR CREDIT

_____ Organization   _____ Profit Organization

_____ Individual   _____ Nonprofit Organization

Name of Company (or Group): _____
                            Responsible for payment

Address: _____

_____ Telephone: _____

Credit References:

  1. Bank: _____
         name   branch

     Address: _____

     Account #: _____ Telephone: _____

  2. Previous Function: _____ Date: _____

     History with Hotel: _____ Date: _____

  3. Previous Other: _____ Date: _____

     Bookings: _____ Date: _____

It is my/our understanding that if granted credit, my/our account will be settled in full within thirty (30) days.

_____
signature of company or group official

_____

To Be Completed by Sales Office:

  Date of Function: _____

67

Sales Value of Event:　Rooms: _____

Food: _____

_____　Beverage: _____
salesperson

Total: _____

_____

Credit Decision:　Dun & Bradstreet _____ (rating)

Approved: ____　Disapproved: ____　Remarks: _____

_____

_____

_____　_____
credit manager　　　　　　　　　　　　date

68

BANQUET EXTRA WAITER PAYROLL REPORT

No. _____

Date _____

Food Ck. No. _____ Amt. _____ Grat. _____
Food Ck. No. _____ Amt. _____ Grat. _____
Bev. Ck. No. _____ Amt. _____ Grat. _____
Bev. Ck. No. _____ Amt. _____ Grat. _____

Function _____

Group _____

Total _____
Less 19% _____

Room _____ Set _____ Served _____ Net Grat. Ch _____

Captain's

Meal Price _____ Signature _____

Employee Name	Station	Basepay	Overtime	Extra Covers	Setup	Clear	Total Wages	Grat.	TOTAL

Comments:

White copy: Payroll   Yellow copy: Banquet Manager   Pink copy: Union

1. CONFIRMATION

A. Reservation Block

(Date)
(Name)
(Position or Title)
(Company)
(Address)
(City, State, Zip Code)

Dear _____:

Following our (recent telephone conversation or conversation during your recent visit to the Hotel), I am delighted to acknowledge the following tentative reservation:

(NAME OF ORGANIZATION AS POSTED—ALL CAPS)
(Starting and Closing Times)—Reception
(Location—if different from Dinner)
(Starting and Closing Times)—Dinner
(Starting and Closing Times)—Program/Dancing (when applicable)
(Location—Name of Ballroom Assigned)
Rental: ($____ when applicable)
Attendance: Approximately (number) Guests
(DAY AND DATE—ALL CAPS)

If you wish to make this a definite reservation, will you please sign one copy of this letter and return it to us (along with $ amount as an initial nonrefundable deposit—when applicable) within (number) days. This signed and returned letter will serve as your confirmation of the above reservation.

At your convenience (and as we get closer to the date), I will be pleased to get together with you to finalize the menu and all other arrangements for your forthcoming (type of function).

Please be assured (name of addressee) of our continued interest and cooperation at all times in making this event the outstanding success you wish it to be.

Sincerely,

(Catering Executive)
(Title)
(Hotel)

1. CONFIRMATION

B. *Reservation Block—Tentative until 12 months before date*

(Date)
(Name)
(Position or Title)
(Company)
(Address)
(City, State, Zip Code)

Dear _____:

Following our (recent telephone conversation or conversation during your recent visit to the Hotel), I am pleased to acknowledge your tentative reservation:

(NAME OF ORGANIZATION AS POSTED—ALL CAPS)
(Starting and Closing Times)—Reception
(Location—if different from Dinner)
(Starting and Closing Times)—Dinner
(Starting and Closing Times)—Program/Dancing (when applicable)
(Location—Name of Ballroom Assigned)
Rental: ($____ when applicable)
Attendance: Approximately (number) Guests
(DAY AND DATE—ALL CAPS)

As we discussed, we will be delighted to hold the above space on a tentative second-option basis until approximately twelve months prior to the requested date. At that time, if the space is still available it will be reconfirmed to you on a definite basis (and an initial nonrefundable deposit will be requested).

In the meantime, may I assure you that we look forward to being of service to you. If you have any questions, please feel free to contact me.

Sincerely,

(Catering Executive)
(Title)
(Hotel)

1. CONFIRMATION

C. Annual Reservation

(Date)
(Name)
(Position or Title)
(Company)
(Address)
(City, State, Zip Code)

Dear ——————:

Indeed, it was a pleasure for us to host the annual (name of organization function) here at the XYZ Hotel on (date). We hope this will mark the beginning of a long and friendly relationship. In order to protect the date for your annual (event), I am most happy to confirm the following reservation on a tentative basis:

(NAME OF ORGANIZATION AS POSTED—ALL CAPS)
(Starting and Closing Times)—Reception
(Location—if different from Dinner)
(Starting and Closing Times)—Dinner
(Starting and Closing Times)—Program/Dancing (when applicable)
(Location—Name of Ballroom Assigned)
Rental: ($—— when applicable)
Attendance: Approximately (number) Guests
(DAY AND DATE—ALL CAPS)

If you wish to make this a definite reservation, will you please sign one copy of this letter and return it to us within (number) days. (Insert deposit clause when applicable.) This signed and returned letter will serve as your confirmation of the above reservation. If additional time is needed in order to place this reservation in our books on a definite basis, we would appreciate hearing from you.

Many thanks for your valued patronage. We look forward to the privilege of again welcoming your guests to the XYZ Hotel.

Sincerely,

(Catering Executive)
(Title)
(Hotel)

1. CONFIRMATION

D. Kosher

(Date)
(Name)
(Position or Title)
(Company)
(Address)
(City, State, Zip Code)

Dear _____ :

Following our (recent telephone conversation or conversation during your recent visit to the Hotel), I am delighted to acknowledge the following tentative reservation:

> (NAME OF ORGANIZATION AS POSTED—ALL CAPS)
> (Starting and Closing Times)—Reception
> (Location—if different from Dinner)
> (Starting and Closing Times)—Dinner
> (Starting and Closing Times)—Program/Dancing (when applicable)
> (Location—Name of Ballroom Assigned)
> Rental: ($____ when applicable)
> Attendance: Approximately (number) Guests
> (DAY AND DATE—ALL CAPS)

If you wish to make this a definite reservation, will you please sign one copy of this letter and return it to us (along with $ amount as an initial nonrefundable deposit—when applicable) within (number) days. This signed and returned letter will serve as your confirmation of the above reservation.

We will be pleased to place our fine accommodations at your disposal and arrange to serve your guests an excellent menu prepared in strict accordance with Hebrew Dietary Laws and under the supervision of Rabbi (name) (Chairman of the Beth Din of Greater (city) and Vice-President of the Union of Orthodox Rabbis of the United States and Canada).

At your convenience (and as we get closer to the date), I will be happy to get together with you to finalize the menu and all other arrangements for your forthcoming (type of function).

Looking forward to the opportunity of serving you and assuring you of our best efforts on your behalf at all times, I am

Cordially yours,

(Catering Executive)
(Title)
(Hotel)

1. CONFIRMATION

E. Specials—Weddings, Bar Mitzvahs, Testimonials

(Date)
(Name)
(Position or Title)
(Company)
(Address)
(City, State, Zip Code)

Dear (Mr. & Mrs.) —————— :

I am pleased to acknowledge the following tentative reservation:

> IN HONOR OF (NAME OF BRIDE & GROOM, BAR MITZVAH YOUTH,
> OR TESTIMONIAL HONOREE—ALL CAPS)
> (Starting and Closing Times)—Reception
> (Location—if different from Dinner)
> (Starting and Closing Times)—Dinner
> (Starting and Closing Times)—Program/Dancing (when applicable)
> (Location—Name of Ballroom Assigned)
> Rental: ($____ when applicable)
> Attendance: Approximately (number) Guests
> (DAY AND DATE—ALL CAPS)

If you wish to make this a definite reservation, will you please sign one copy of this letter and return it to us (along with $amount as an initial nonrefundable deposit) within (number) days. This signed and returned letter will serve as your confirmation of the above reservation.

As we discussed, our adopted Hotel policy dictates that the full estimated amount of the function be paid to the Hotel no later than two weeks prior to the planned affair.

It will be my personal pleasure to finalize the many arrangements for (Name of Bride, Bar Mitzvah Youth, or Testimonial Honoree). Please be assured of our continued interest and cooperation at all times in making this event in your lives the lasting memory you wish it to be.

Most sincerely,

(Catering Executive)
(Title)
(Hotel)

1. CONFIRMATION

F. Reservation Block with final menu arrangements

(Date)
(Name)
(Position or Title)
(Company)
(Address)
(City, State, Zip Code)

Dear _____ :

Following our (recent telephone conversation or conversation during your recent visit to the Hotel), I am delighted to acknowledge the following tentative reservation:

    (NAME OF ORGANIZATION AS POSTED—ALL CAPS)
    (Starting and Closing Times)—Reception
    (Location—if different from Dinner)
    (Starting and Closing Times)—Dinner
    (Starting and Closing Times)—Program/Dancing (when applicable)
    (Location—Name of Ballroom Assigned)
    Rental: ($___ when applicable)
    Attendance: Approximately (number) Guests
    (DAY AND DATE—ALL CAPS)

If you wish to make this a definite reservation, will you please sign one copy of this letter and the enclosed Banquet Event Order and return them to us within (number) days along with any changes and additions. This signed and returned letter and Banquet Event Order will serve as your confirmation of the above reservation.

Please be assured (name of addressee) of our continued interest and cooperation at all times in making this event the outstanding success you wish it to be.

Sincerely,

(Catering Executive)
(Title)
(Hotel)

1. CONFIRMATION

G. Cover letter with final menu and arrangements

(Date)
(Name)
(Position or Title)
(Company)
(Address)
(City, State, Zip Code)

Dear _____:

Following our (recent telephone conversation or conversation during your recent visit to the Hotel), I am pleased to enclose the final menu and arrangements for your perusal.

In order to complete our records and if all meets with your approval, would you please sign the appropriate copies and return within (number) days, along with any changes and additions.

Please be assured of our continued interest and cooperation through the successful completion of this (event).

Sincerely,

(Catering Executive)
(Title)
(Hotel)

1. CONFIRMATION

H. Convention Reservation Block

(Date)
(Name)
(Position or Title)
(Company)
(Address)
(City, State, Zip Code)

Dear _____ :

Following our (recent telephone conversation or conversation during your recent visit to the Hotel), I am delighted to acknowledge the following tentative reservation:

(NAME OF ORGANIZATION—ALL CAPS)

Day and Date			
Hospitality	Room Assigned	Start and Close Time	Attendance
Meeting	Room Assigned	Start and Close Time	Attendance
Luncheon	Room Assigned	Start and Close Time	Attendance
Day and Date			
Hospitality	Room Assigned	Start and Close Time	Attendance
Meeting	Room Assigned	Start and Close Time	Attendance
Luncheon	Room Assigned	Start and Close Time	Attendance

As we discussed, the total rental for the above space, for both days, will be a special price of $(amount). If you wish to make this a definite reservation, will you please sign one copy of this letter and return it within (number) days. This signed and returned letter will serve as your confirmation of the above reservation.

At your convenience (and as we get closer to the date), I will be happy to get together with you to finalize the menu and all other arrangements for your forthcoming (type of function(s)).

Please be assured (name of addressee) of our continued interest and cooperation at all times in making this event the outstanding success you wish it to be.

Sincerely,

(Catering Executive)
(Title)
(Hotel)

1. CONFIRMATION

I. Failure to return signed letter or proposal

(Date)
(Name)
(Position or Title)
(Company)
(Address)
(City, State, Zip Code)

Dear _____ :

In reviewing our files, we find you have not as yet signed and returned the copy of the (confirmation letter or proposal) which we sent to you on (date).

Would you please sign the designated copy and return it to us, for the completion of our records, as soon as possible.

If I may be of any further assistance to you at this time, please do not hesitate to call upon me.

Sincerely,

(Catering Executive)
(Title)
(Hotel)

2. CONGRATULATIONS

A. Promotion

(Date)
(Name)
(Position or Title)
(Company)
(Address)
(City, State, Zip Code)

Dear _____ :

News of your recent (appointment or election) to the position of (_____) of (name of company or organization) was read with much interest.

Please accept this letter as an expression of our most sincere congratulations.

I am certain the (name of company or organization) and the XYZ Hotel will be business associates for many years to come. Any time we can be of service, we stand ready to comply with your wishes. Our beautifully appointed Banquet Rooms and Ballrooms are especially attractive.

Again, congratulations and our best wishes for a very happy and successful tenure.

Cordially yours,

(Catering Executive)
(Title)
(Hotel)

3. LETTER OF CONDOLENCE

(Date)
(Name)
(Position or Title)
(Company)
(Address)
(City, State, Zip Code)

Dear _____:

Allow me to offer my sincere condolences upon the loss of your (wife, mother, son, etc.).

Having enjoyed the privilege of knowing (him, her), I can understand your grief during this time.

Please accept my heart-felt sympathy in your bereavement.

Sincerely yours,

(Catering Executive)
(Title)
(Hotel)

4. SCHOOL/UNIVERSITY

(Date)
(Name)
(Position or Title)
(Company)
(Address)
(City, State, Zip Code)

Dear _____ :

With the closing of the school year, we trust this letter will find you soon on your way to a well-deserved vacation, and you have our very best wishes for fine weather.

We are very interested in establishing a closer relationship between the XYZ Hotel and your school, as we believe that such an association would be mutually beneficial.

We can offer your faculty, student, and alumni activities a wide choice of very attractive accommodations and a cuisine selection second to none.

Against the background of our (hotel, resort), these events will have an even greater prestige and importance. Furthermore, you will be surprised to learn how little it costs to have the very best at the XYZ Hotel.

Looking ahead to next season, we would like very much to contact, in September or October, the student advisors and the students who will be in charge of the various social affairs that will be planned for this winter and next spring.

Accordingly, we will contact your office in September or early October in order to ascertain the names of those individuals. We would also welcome, at any time, a visit from your representatives so that we may show them the accommodations available here at the hotel. If you wish, at that time, we can discuss arrangements which, I am confident, will be made to their satisfaction and within their budget.

Thank you for your kindness, and I look forward to welcoming (school) to XYZ Hotel in the future.

Cordially,

(Catering Executive)
(Title)
(Hotel)

5. CONVENTIONS

A. Request for Convention History

(Date)
(Name)
(Position or Title)
(Company)
(Address)
(City, State, Zip Code)

Dear _____ :

We have the pleasure of hosting the (name of convention) during (month, days, and year). It is our understanding that your hotel hosted this same convention during the dates of (month, days, and year).

In order to better serve them, we would very much appreciate it if you could supply us with their Convention History, including the number of sleeping rooms picked up, a list of their various Banquet Functions, as well as the number of covers and the per person meal costs. Certainly, this would enable us to do a better planning job.

Indeed your cooperation is greatly appreciated. Many thanks, in advance, for your help.

Sincerely,

(Catering Executive)
(Title)
(Hotel)

5. CONVENTIONS

B. Hospitality Suite

(Date)
(Name)
(Position or Title)
(Company)
(Address)
(City, State, Zip Code)

Dear _____ :

This is to acknowledge (our recent telephone conversation or your letter of) (date). (*or* We have been advised by (name) of our (department) that you plan to host a hospitality suite here at the XYZ Hotel during the (name of organization, as posted), convention.) We are delighted to confirm the following accommodation:

(NAME—ALL CAPS)
(Firm Name)
(Accommodation)
Arrival: (Date)
Departure: (Date)
Rate: ____plus usual taxes
Attendance: (number) MAXIMUM

Please be advised that all food and beverage used for entertainment purposes must be purchased from the Hotel. Enclosed are appropriate food and beverage selections for your perusal. In order to best serve you, we request that you forward us the necessary requirements at your earliest convenience.

If the above meets with your approval, kindly sign and return the enclosed copy of this letter within (number) days. We look forward to serving you.

Sincerely,

(Catering Executive)
(Title)
(Hotel)

5. CONVENTIONS

C. Introductory for catering

(Date)
(Name)
(Position or Title)
(Company)
(Address)
(City, State, Zip Code)

Dear _____ :

I was delighted to learn from (salesperson) that the XYZ Hotel will have the pleasure of hosting the (organization).

As (Director of Catering or appropriate title), I will be more than happy to handle all food and beverage arrangements for your meeting, and I am most anxious to assist you in any way possible.

Enclosed are several menu suggestions for your perusal. Please note that the enclosed menus are our current prices which are subject to review six months prior to your meeting.

I am certainly looking forward to the pleasure of working closely with you as your plans progress. Please feel free to call me if there are any other questions that I can answer at this time.

Cordially,

(Catering Executive)
(Title)
(Hotel)

6. INQUIRY

A. First Follow-up

(Date)
(Name)
(Position or Title)
(Company)
(Address)
(City, State, Zip Code)

Dear _____ :

Thank you for the courtesy extended to me during our recent telephone conversation. I am delighted to know that you will give favorable consideration to the XYZ Hotel in planning your next event.

We are anxious to have the privilege of serving your group and we would be happy to place our facilities at your disposal and arrange to serve you an excellent menu within the limits of your budget, and to your complete satisfaction.

The XYZ Hotel offers the finest in comfort, convenience, and luxury. If you could visit our hotel, it would be my personal pleasure to show you our distinctive and luxurious facilities.

We look forward to the pleasure of serving you.

Cordially,

(Catering Executive)
(Title)
(Hotel)

6. INQUIRY

B. Second Follow-up

(Date)
(Name)
(Position or Title)
(Company)
(Address)
(City, State, Zip Code)

Dear _____ :

On (date), you expressed interest in the XYZ Hotel's facilities. Since we have not received a response to our letter of (date), we are most anxious to learn how plans are progressing for your organization's function(s).

Since space is already at a premium in (month), we would like to hear from you concerning the dates that are under consideration so that we might set aside tentative reservations to assure you of necessary accommodations.

Needless to say, we would be most privileged to host your fine organization.

We hope to hear from you soon.

Sincerely,

(Catering Executive)
(Title)
(Hotel)

6. INQUIRY

C. Follow-up after visit

(Date)
(Name)
(Position or Title)
(Company)
(Address)
(City, State, Zip Code)

Dear _____:

It was a pleasure to have had the opportunity of meeting with you and discussing the banquet facilities that are available at the XYZ Hotel.

More and more of the top leaders in business, industry, and on the social scene are discovering that the XYZ Hotel is the choice locale for meetings, private parties, or banquets of distinction.

We certainly hope that you, too, will allow the XYZ Hotel to be the site of your next function. Your consideration is very much appreciated and, if given the opportunity, we will do our utmost to make your occasion a memorable one.

Cordially yours,

(Catering Executive)
(Title)
(Hotel)

7. OPTION PARAGRAPHS

The clauses below can be inserted into any one of the sample letters.

A. *Six-Month Clause:* Please note that the enclosed menus are our current prices which are subject to review six months prior to your function.

B. *Deposit Clause:* If you wish to make this a definite reservation, will you please sign one copy of this letter and return it to us, along with $(amount) as an initial nonrefundable deposit, within (number) days. This signed and returned letter will serve as your confirmation of the above reservation.

C. *Two-Week Clause:* A company policy has been adopted whereby the estimated balance will be due the Hotel two weeks prior to the affair.

D. *Second-Option Clause:* Please note that we are holding the (name) Ballroom on a second-option basis. As soon as we receive a release from the organization now holding the space, on a tentative basis, we will contact you at once.

E. *Menus Enclosed Clause:* Enclosed are several menu suggestions for your perusal.

F. *Hold for Two Weeks Clause:* If you wish to make this a definite reservation, will you please sign one copy of this letter and return it to us prior to (two weeks from the date of letter) in order that we may complete our records.

G. *Location Change Clause:* Any substantial increase or decrease in expected attendance may necessitate the change in location of the function!

H. *Guarantee Clause:* The Catering Office must be notified no later than 12 Noon, two days prior to the scheduled function, of exact attendance expected. For functions scheduled on Monday or Tuesday, the exact expected attendance must be given to the Catering Office no later than 12 Noon of the preceding Friday, due to the weekend. This number shall constitute a guarantee, not subject to reduction, and charges will be made accordingly. The Hotel cannot be responsible for service to more than 3% over and above the guarantee, up to fifty guests maximum. If no guarantee is given at the appropriate time, the Hotel will assume the indicated anticipated attendance discussed heretofore to be correct, and charges will be made accordingly, and the organization agrees to pay said charges.

(Note: Some hotels require guarantees 72 hours ahead of each function, excluding the weekends.)

8. SOLICITATION

A. From another property

(Date)
(Name)
(Position or Title)
(Company)
(Address)
(City, State, Zip Code)

Dear _____ :

We read with much interest that the (organization) recently held a banquet at another facility here in the (locale) area.

May we take this opportunity to extend to you a most cordial invitation to hold your next function at the XYZ Hotel where we offer you an unusually attractive choice of private function rooms, plus cuisine and service that is second to none.

Your decision to make the XYZ Hotel the site of your next (activity, meeting, breakfast, luncheon, dinner, benefit) will, I am certain, meet with your members' and guests' enthusiastic support and approval. You may be certain that if favored by your valued patronage, we will spare no effort to please you in every way and make your activities outstanding and successful.

Indeed, I will be privileged to have you as our guest for lunch, at your convenience, to give you a sample of our well-known cuisine and service. I look forward to hearing from you.

Sincerely,

(Catering Executive)
(Title)
(Hotel)

8. SOLICITATION

B. Personal referral

(Date)
(Name)
(Position or Title)
(Company)
(Address)
(City, State, Zip Code)

Dear ——————:

Following my conversation with (name), I would like to take this opportunity to extend a most cordial invitation to you to allow us to host your next affair at the XYZ Hotel.

International experts in culinary foods and service have come together here at the XYZ Hotel to offer you a new dimension in catering.

I will be contacting you in the immediate future in order that I may have the opportunity to further discuss our renowned Hotel. In the meantime, if I can be of any assistance, please do not hesitate to contact me.

Sincerely,

(Catering Executive)
(Title)
(Hotel)

8. SOLICITATION

C. Cost-conscious client

(Date)
(Name)
(Position or Title)
(Company)
(Address)
(City, State, Zip Code)

Dear _____ :

Thank you for the courtesy extended to me during our recent telephone conversation. It was indeed a pleasure to learn that you will give favorable consideration to the XYZ Hotel in planning your next affair.

As you indicated, price is certainly a consideration, as I am sure quality is. We are certainly comparable with the major operations in the (locale) area and would be happy to work with you to the best of our ability in trying to keep these ever-rising costs in line.

In the meantime, I am enclosing a brochure for your perusal. Please do not hesitate to contact us in the future, as the need arises.

We look forward to being of service to you.

Sincerely,

(Catering Executive)
(Title)
(Hotel)

8. SOLICITATION

D. No business

(Date)
(Name)
(Position or Title)
(Company)
(Address)
(City, State, Zip Code)

Dear _____ :

We have noted that it has been some time since we have been host to the (name of organization).

Our expanded service can now offer you, more than ever, that special touch in catering. Let us help you plan your next dinner, lunch, or private party.

I am looking forward to welcoming you back to the XYZ Hotel and catering to your every whim.

Sincerely,

(Catering Executive)
(Title)
(Hotel)

8. SOLICITATION

E. Christmas party

(Date)
(Name)
(Position or Title)
(Company)
(Address)
(City, State, Zip Code)

Dear _____ :

We have already begun! In only a few short (months, weeks) the Holiday season will be upon us. We are extremely excited about our plans for making the XYZ Hotel the perfect location for a Holiday party. We even offer a special plan that we believe will provide your guests a truly memorable experience, while staying within the limits of your budget.

We hope you will honor us soon with a visit so that we may personally conduct you on a tour of our fabulous facilities.

The staff at the XYZ Hotel promise to do our part to make your Holiday celebration the most memorable and enjoyable ever.

Cordially yours,

(Catering Executive)
(Title)
(Hotel)

8. SOLICITATION

F. Response following inquiry

(Date)
(Name)
(Position or Title)
(Company)
(Address)
(City, State, Zip Code)

Dear _____:

We are delighted to learn of your interest in the XYZ Hotel. Enclosed for your consideration is a brochure describing our Banquet facilities.

Since we are now booking many annual functions as well as first-time activities, may we suggest that you contact us in order that we may immediately enter a reservation for you and the accommodations of your choice. This reservation is, of course, subject to your confirmation.

We look forward to the pleasure of hearing from you in this regard and assure you that the XYZ Hotel will provide you with its traditional excellence in cuisine and service.

Cordially yours,

(Catering Executive)
(Title)
(Hotel)

8. SOLICITATION

G. Convention hospitality

(Date)
(Name)
(Position or Title)
(Company)
(Address)
(City, State, Zip Code)

Dear _____ :

We understand that you will soon be arriving at the XYZ Hotel in connection with the (name of convention) beginning (date) through (date).

Since we are constantly striving to better serve our guests, we are pleased to offer you a comprehensive hospitality plan. All details are enclosed. May we remind you that no food or beverages of any kind will be permitted to be brought into the Hotel.

Our advance order plan has been designed in order that you may truly be our "guest" at your own affair. We look forward with much pleasure to having you with us.

Sincerely,

(Catering Executive)
(Title)
(Hotel)

8. SOLICITATION

H. Annual function

(Date)
(Name)
(Position or Title)
(Company)
(Address)
(City, State, Zip Code)

Dear ——————:

Having been unable to reach you by telephone, I am writing in order to extend to you a most cordial invitation to hold your (function) here at the XYZ Hotel as you did last year.

Since we are now booking many parties and other future activities in (month and year), may we suggest that you contact us in order that we may immediately enter a reservation for you and the accommodations of your choice. This reservation is, of course, subject to your confirmation.

We look forward to the pleasure of hearing from you in this regard, and assure you that the XYZ Hotel will provide you with its traditional excellence in cuisine and service.

Cordially yours,

(Catering Executive)
(Title)
(Hotel)

9. THANK YOU

A. General

(Date)
(Name)
(Position or Title)
(Company)
(Address)
(City, State, Zip Code)

Dear _____:

Please accept my sincere thanks for the privilege of serving the (name of organization) on the occasion of your (function or functions) on (day or days, month, and date).

I sincerely hope that the preparations for all of your functions (or your affair) met with your approval, but as we are constantly striving to improve our services, we would appreciate any comments or suggestions you may have regarding your recent (function or functions).

If I can ever be of assistance to you in any way, please do not hesitate to call upon me. We look forward to the privilege and pleasure of serving your organization in the not too distant future.

Sincerely,

(Catering Executive)
(Title)
(Hotel)

9. THANK YOU

B. General (Committee)

(Date)
(Name)
(Position or Title)
(Company)
(Address)
(City, State, Zip Code)

Dear _____ :

It was indeed a pleasure having you and your guests utilize our facilities for your (type of function) held at our Hotel on (day or days, month, and date).

Needless to say, the excellent cooperation we received from you and (name of client's colleagues) made our job much easier, and I only hope that our food and service measured up to your expectations in every way.

May I take this opportunity to express our sincere appreciation for your valued patronage, and we look forward to your return visit.

Sincerely,

(Catering Executive)
(Title)
(Hotel)

9. THANK YOU

C. Annual business or possible annual

(Date)
(Name)
(Position or Title)
(Company)
(Address)
(City, State, Zip Code)

Dear _____ :

It was indeed a pleasure working with you on the details and arrangements for the successful completion of your (function) which was held here at the XYZ Hotel on (date).

Considering that this (function) is an annual affair, we would be most happy to reserve a tentative date for your (organization) for 19__, to assure you of the necessary accommodations. Do not hesitate to contact me if I can assist you in planning the arrangements for your next function.

We will strive to serve you in a manner meriting your good will and continued patronage.

Sincerely,

(Catering Executive)
(Title)
(Hotel)

9. THANK YOU

D. Wedding or Bar Mitzvah

(Date)
(Name)
(Address)
(City, State, Zip Code)

Dear —————— :

Please accept my sincere thanks for the privilege of serving your family on the occasion of your (son's or daughter's) wedding (*or* (youth's name) Bar Mitzvah).

I sincerely hope that all the preparations for the celebration met with your approval.

If I can ever be of assistance to you in any way, please do not hesitate to call on me.

Kindest personal regards.

Most sincerely,

(Catering Executive)
(Title)
(Hotel)

9. THANK YOU

E. Regular client

Each time a regular client (one who uses the facilities on a regular basis) has a function, a short, personal note should be sent. For fear of repetition, a form for this particular letter is not enclosed.

9. THANK YOU

F. Thank you for the "thank you"

(Date)
(Name)
(Position or Title)
(Company)
(Address)
(City, State, Zip Code)

Dear —————:

I was delighted to receive your cordial letter of (date of letter or "recent date") and appreciate your many gracious comments on the food, service, and arrangements for the (organization) (function) on (date of function) in our (ballroom).

It is always most gratifying, both to the members of our staff and to me, to know that our efforts have succeeded in making a function such as yours a memorable event, and we look forward with much pleasure to having you with us on many, many more occasions.

Please accept my heartfelt appreciation once again for your thoughtfulness in writing, and I assure you of my personal interest and utmost cooperation at all times.

Sincerely,

(Catering Executive)
(Title)
(Hotel)

9. THANK YOU

G. Deposit and/or contract received

(Date)
(Name)
(Position or Title)
(Company)
(Address)
(City, State, Zip Code)

Dear _____ :

Just a short note to acknowledge receipt of your check for $(amount) as a nonre-fundable deposit for (name of function—if wedding, use daughter's name; if Bar Mitzvah, use youth's name; e.g., Elizabeth's wedding) to be held here at the XYZ Hotel on (date).

(If contract is also enclosed):
Just a short note to acknowledge receipt of your check for $(amount) as a nonre-fundable deposit for (name of function, see example above) and the signed copy of our (letter or contract) dated (date prepared).

As we approach the date of (name of function), I will be contacting you in order to finalize all arrangements. If you have any questions in the meantime, please do not hesitate to call on me.

Sincerely,

(Catering Executive)
(Title)
(Hotel)

10. FLOOR PLAN REQUESTED

(Date)
(Name)
(Position or Title)
(Company)
(Address)
(City, State, Zip Code)

Dear _____:

Enclosed you will find a floor plan for our Banquet facilities, as you requested. We hope that this will supply you with all the necessary information you may need.

I am looking forward to seeing you in the near future, and if I may be of any further assistance to you, do not hesitate to call on me.

Sincerely,

(Catering Executive)
(Title)
(Hotel)

11. CANCELLATION

A. Second Option

(Date)
(Name)
(Position or Title)
(Company)
(Address)
(City, State, Zip Code)

Dear _____:

We have recently learned that the organization holding the first option reservation for our (name) Ballroom on (date) will indeed be using our facilities on that date.

Consequently, we must release your second-option reservation on the same facility. However, as an alternative, may we offer the following reservation:

    (NAME OF ORGANIZATION AS POSTED—ALL CAPS)
    (Starting and Closing Times)—Reception
    (Location—if different from Dinner)
    (Starting and Closing Times)—Dinner
    (Starting and Closing Times)—Program/Dancing (when applicable)
    (Location—Name of Ballroom Assigned)
    Rental: ($___ when applicable)
    Attendance: Approximately (number) Guests
    (DAY AND DATE—ALL CAPS)

If you wish to make this a definite reservation, will you please sign one copy of this letter and return it to us (along with $amount as an initial nonrefundable deposit) (when applicable) within (number) days. This signed and returned letter will serve as your confirmation of the above revised reservation.

At your convenience (and as we get closer to the above date), I will be delighted to get together with you to finalize the menu and all other arrangements for your forthcoming (type of function).

Please be assured (name of addressee) of our continued interest and cooperation at all times in making this event the outstanding success you wish it to be.

Sincerely,

(Catering Executive)
(Title)
(Hotel)

11. CANCELLATION

B. Annual (and nonannual) banquets

(Date)
(Name)
(Position or Title)
(Company)
(Address)
(City, State, Zip Code)

Dear _____ :

We have recently learned with deep regret that the (name of party, reception, luncheon, dinner, etc.) scheduled for (date) will not be held at the XYZ Hotel due to reasons you have indicated.

Accordingly, we have cancelled the reservation for our (name of ballroom, room, etc.) and sincerely hope that we will hear from you should plans be reconsidered.

Assuring you that we look forward to the opportunity and pleasure of serving you in the not too distant future, I am,

Cordially yours,

(Catering Executive)
(Title)
(Hotel)

12. LETTER OF REFUSAL FOR ADS IN PROGRAMS OR JOURNALS

(Date)
(Name)
(Position or Title)
(Company)
(Address)
(City, State, Zip Code)

Dear _____ :

I am in receipt of your letter of (date) with a request that we advertise in the (name of program or journal).

You can realize, I am certain, the innumerable number of requests we constantly receive for such advertisements, and it is utterly impossible for us to accede to all of them.

Therefore, rather than risk displeasing any of our friends through a seeming display of favoritism, our policy is, of necessity, to refuse them all.

Though this course may appear arbitrary, I am certain you will understand the reasons that motivate it, and anticipating your indulgence in this instance, I remain, with every good wish,

Sincerely yours,

(Catering Executive)
(Title)
(Hotel)

CHAPTER 4

Sales

Sales, the second phase in developing the catering department, is a service that often represents a large percentage of revenue for a hotel. The objective of sales is to maximize the occupancy of function space, keeping within management's guidelines, and to sell those products that are most profitable.

DEVELOPING PRODUCT KNOWLEDGE

One of the first facts to recognize about catering sales is that the salesperson need not be a chef, gourmet cook, or connoisseur of fine wines. As in any occupation, any knowledge gained from past experiences is helpful, but most important is knowing the quality of your product and how it compares to your competition's product. One of the best ways to learn catering sales is by a reverse procedure or first training in the operation phase. In this way, the product can be observed firsthand.

Each salesperson should be thoroughly acquainted with the layout of the property and know the capacities of the function rooms for various set-ups, what the engineering capacities are (e.g., electrical demands, etc.), which combination of rooms is most compatible, and, if given a choice, which rooms would be reserved first because of advantageous location (nearness to the kitchen or elevators). Knowing the limitations of your product is as important as knowing the capabilities. This knowledge is not to discourage the potential customer, but to give the salesperson the opportunity to seek and create new alternatives.

DEVELOPING SOURCES OF BUSINESS ───────────────────────

Catering sales can originate from a number of sources. Included below are some of the most popular.

Convention sales.   Convention sales refer to any business that has been booked into the hotel with sleeping rooms and requires food and/or beverage activities in catering. The convention sales department will send a copy of the booking sheet to the director of catering. Unless there is a special request, such as sending menus, the director of catering will file the copy in date order until 12 months prior to the convention dates. At that time the catering director will assign the account, noting that convention assignment in a control central book. This control book should be broken down by months and years. Each catering salesperson should have a page for his or her assignments under each month. In this way, it is easy to ascertain the monthly assignments for each salesperson and prevent overloading or neglecting any one salesperson.

Walk-in inquiries.   Walk-in inquiries include those potential customers who have made no specific appointment with a salesperson. Although some salespersons feel that this type of customer is just shopping for competitive prices, do not be surprised if this customer becomes one of your valued accounts.

Written inquiries.   Written inquiries are those that show an interest in reserving space via a letter. All correspondence should be responded to as quickly as possible and should include the suggestion of an appointment so that the potential customer may tour the facilities. Sending printed menus will rarely guarantee a booking from this type of inquiry. It will take sales personality and personal attention to close the sale.

Telephone inquiries.   Telephone inquiries are by far the largest source of repeat business in catering. Most customers, including many who have scheduled a successful function, will reserve future space over the telephone.

Referrals from sister hotels.   Referrals from sister hotels take place when there are two or more sister hotels within the same city or state. Since this is a source of keeping potential revenues in the same corporation, it is important to refer a customer to a sister hotel when your hotel is booked for a particular date. This brings up the importance of knowing the names of key personnel at your sister hotels and having a general idea of their function room capacities. However, *never* quote rate structures for another hotel.

Trace of internal past accounts.   As mentioned previously in the section covering Call Reports (Chapter 3), it is up to the discretion of the director of catering to establish a procedure for pulling and evaluating past accounts. The salesperson should attempt to learn if the business still exists and, if so, where, who is in charge, and what reasons prompted the client to move the company's business elsewhere. Following this conversation, the salesperson should then fill in the Call Report.

Competing hotel accounts.   Accounts from competing hotels act as a good source of business. Some hotels send personnel out to the competing hotels each day to report what is taking place. News clippings are also a good source of information when looking for what is taking place locally.

Sales considerations.   Sales considerations are those factors that are taken into account with regard to minimum rate discount.

When is a discount allowed and why? Any discount or menus should be the decision of the director of catering. Once the minimum rate structure has been established, it is not to be lowered without the consent of the director of catering and, in some cases, the director of food and beverage operations and/or the general manager. Concessions on price are made only after all other avenues of approach have been exhausted and it is still desirous to have the function at the hotel.

Some functions that may fall into this category are conventions during slow months, short-term bookings, charitable organizations, or multifunction organizations.

If the business climate is such that there are several multifunction organizations offering business, the catering department may want to propose a special campaign price subject to approval of the director of catering. With regard to conventions, the catering director and possibly upper management should first look at the overall financial return on the convention before discussing a price concession.

Charitable functions often realize the greatest return in press coverage for a hotel. Usually, the chairperson is aware of this and it becomes a factor in price negotiations. Before appearing overly grateful for any publicity that the organization may be bringing to you, it should be recognized that the group may be coming to your particular hotel because the hotel itself receives good coverage. Every effort should be made to hold a firm line on minimum rates. If a price concession is considered, it is the responsibility of catering to have a preliminary profit and loss statement made on the function.

PSYCHOLOGY OF CATERING SALES ————————————————

Selling a catering function is similar to other kinds of sales. The salesperson must plan what approach will be used for each prospect while asking himself or herself: What is the customer like? What are her needs and desires? What is the best way to appeal to him? The salesperson should think about any objections that are likely to be made in each case and determine in advance the best way to overcome them. Notes about the last discussion should be reviewed to be sure there is nothing about the prospect's situation of which the salesperson is not aware. If necessary, introduce the client to various department heads such as the chef, the banquet manager, and, if possible, the general manager.

In short, the salesperson should settle for nothing less than total customer satisfaction and total hotel satisfaction. This can be accomplished most efficiently by increasing the effort on the basics. All files in the banquet department should be reviewed, via the trace system for the past two-year period, well in advance of the function date. This process should be accelerated in light of current sales trends to include all local food and beverage functions.

Leads from newspapers, trade journals, and other media should be checked daily. At least five promising new leads can be obtained daily from these sources. Even if a form letter is sent by you in response, your exposure to potential business— either in rooms or in food and beverage—will be increased on a local level.

Competitive shopping of function boards, although not particularly aimed at short-term business, can be effective in generating leads for the future. This should be a standard practice in all catering offices. One member of the catering sales team, preferably a catering sales representative, depending on staff size, should be assigned to obtain the function listings from at least the top five hotels at least once a week and preferably daily. If your staff is small, this task can be assigned as a secretarial duty. These lists should be reviewed and the businesses called immediately after the function for booking at your hotel the next time around.

Increase the supply of sales personnel.   With present business conditions, there is a need for more salespeople in our hotels without increasing the payroll. There are measures that will help to increase the sales effort without increasing the staff. An emphasis on the scheduling of time can do a great deal to increase the sales effort from the catering department. The staff has the responsibility of handling details of function business in the hotel, but they can also make a scheduled number of sales calls each day. One-half hour in the morning can mean three well-handled personal calls.

There should be a clear-cut emphasis on sales in the catering department. The program "Everyone Sells" is designed to accomplish this goal. The results of this program are different for each property, but it is evident that if the program is carried out to the letter, sales will be generated. Using employees who are not trained in sales is not an ideal situation, but a short series of training sessions can help to at least direct them on how to use the phone effectively and how to turn leads over to the sales department. The reports from most sales positions have been consistent in that once an employee receives a commission, that individual will increase his or her effort.

Sales effort can be increased in this program in the following ways:

1. Instruct department heads to use the phone effectively. (More information to help employees get accustomed to phone solicitation will follow.)

2. Publicize any cash-incentive awards to all the employees. Give them incentive by making the tangible benefits visible.

3. Set a target for the results of the program in your property and post a chart showing the number of calls, definites and tentatives, against a team goal. Give the staff something to shoot for.

Increase the competitive stand of your product.   Emphasize the need for competitive shopping by your sales and catering staff. It is the director of catering's responsibility to always be apprised of how the price structure of the hotel compares with those of the competition on all major food and beverage items sold at banquets. These prices should be in line, remembering that people buy on comparative value as well as price. If you are serving the same item at the same price as your competitor, it should taste better, look better on the plate, and be served better. This message must be delivered to the customer. Supply pictures of the major food items plated attractively, have the various rooms set up for functions, and present some type of service in action. Sell your advantage even if you have to create one.

In order to remain abreast of competitive hotels' current prices, a spread sheet should be prepared at least once each year, showing a comparison of banquet prices for breakfast, lunch, dinner, and so on. This spread sheet should include your own hotel as well as your competing hotels. One copy of each of these spread sheets should be distributed to the following: general manager, director of sales, director of food and beverage, each catering salesperson, and the area director of food and beverage. If the competition in your area extends to country clubs, catering halls, and resorts, include these in your spread sheet.

Take careful note of this emphatic word of caution: All prices on the comparison sheet must be obtained through general market sources and *not* from direct communication with competitors. (See Figure 4.1 for a sample comparison sheet.)

Increase the effectiveness of your product.   All unique touches to your menu and service that will help a guest make up his or her mind in your favor are ways to increase your product's effectiveness. Some properties offer these unique-type banquets, complete in every detail. This adds a lot of work to your job, but it also adds another dimension to your banquet operation. There is no better way to

Hotel Name: Name of Your Hotel or Resort

Date Conducted: _____

Entree/Item for Comparison	Your Hotel's Present Prices	Your Proposed Revised Prices	Hotel A	Hotel B	Resort C	Hotel D	Hotel E	Resort F	Hotel G	Hotel H
Date of Last Revised Menu Price	6/90	6/91	7/90	6/90	8/90	4/90	2/90	7/90	3/90	6/90
Continental Buffet Breakfast	$ 7.00	$ 7.25	$ 7.50	$ 6.50	$ 7.50	$ 6.75	$ 7.00	$ 6.75	$ 7.25	$ 6.50
Full Breakfast with One Meat	$ 8.95	$ 9.25	$ 9.50	$ 8.50	$ 9.50	$ 8.75	$ 8.75	$ 8.75	$ 8.95	$ 8.50
Chicken Breast Luncheon	$ 15.95	$ 16.75	$ 17.25	$ 14.95	$ 17.00	$ 15.25	$ 15.75	$ 15.25	$ 16.50	$ 15.25
Sliced Beef Luncheon	$ 20.25	$ 21.50	$ 22.25	$ 19.50	$ 21.75	$ 19.25	$ 19.95	$ 19.95	$ 21.25	$ 19.75
Filet Mignon Luncheon	$ 24.95	$ 26.50	$ 27.25	$ 24.25	$ 26.95	$ 24.50	$ 24.75	$ 24.50	$ 25.95	$ 24.50
Minute Steak Luncheon	$ 20.95	$ 22.25	$ 22.75	$ 20.25	$ 22.50	$ 20.50	$ 20.75	$ 20.50	$ 21.95	$ 20.50
Chicken Breast Dinner	$ 22.50	$ 23.75	$ 24.50	$ 21.95	$ 24.25	$ 21.75	$ 21.95	$ 22.25	$ 22.95	$ 21.75
Prime Rib of Beef Dinner	$ 33.50	$ 35.50	$ 36.50	$ 32.75	$ 36.50	$ 32.95	$ 32.95	$ 32.95	$ 36.25	$ 32.50
Filet Mignon Dinner	$ 35.50	$ 37.75	$ 38.75	$ 34.50	$ 38.50	$ 34.25	$ 34.75	$ 34.95	$ 37.95	$ 34.75
Sirloin Steak Dinner	$ 36.50	$ 38.75	$ 40.75	$ 35.50	$ 40.50	$ 35.25	$ 35.95	$ 35.95	$ 37.95	$ 35.50
Drink Rate — Name Brands	$ 3.75	$ 3.95	$ 4.50	$ 3.50	$ 4.25	$ 4.00	$ 3.75	$ 3.50	$ 4.00	$ 3.50
Drink Rate — Premium Brands	$ 4.25	$ 4.50	$ 5.00	$ 4.00	$ 4.75	$ 4.50	$ 4.00	$ 3.95	$ 4.50	$ 4.00
Cash Bar Drink Rate — Name Brands	$ 4.00	$ 4.50	$ 5.00	$ 3.50	$ 4.50	$ 4.00	$ 3.50	$ 3.50	$ 4.00	$ 3.50
Cashiers (3 Hours)	$ 50.00	$ 60.00	$ 50.00	$ 45.00	$ 65.00	$ 35.00	$ 35.00	$ 60.00	$ 45.00	0
Bartenders (3 Hours)	$ 50.00	$ 60.00	$ 50.00	$ 45.00	$ 65.00	$ 35.00	$ 35.00	$ 60.00	$ 45.00	0
Flat Rate Hour — Name Brands	$ 7.75	$ 8.00	$ 9.00	$ 7.00	$ 8.50	$ 6.50	$ 7.25	$ 7.00	$ 6.50	$ 7.00
Additional Hour	$ 6.00	$ 6.50	$ 7.50	$ 5.50	$ 7.00	$ 5.00	$ 6.25	$ 5.50	$ 5.00	$ 5.50
Flat Rate Hour — Premium Brands	$ 9.00	$ 9.50	$ 10.00	$ 8.00	$ 10.00	$ 7.00	$ 9.25	$ 8.00	$ 7.00	$ 8.00
Additional Hour	$ 7.00	$ 7.50	$ 8.00	$ 6.00	$ 8.00	$ 5.00	$ 7.25	$ 6.50	$ 5.00	$ 6.50
Hors d'oeuvres (100 Pieces)	$155.00-$195.00	$160.00-$200.00	$165.00-$200.00	$150.00	$175.00-$200.00	$155.00	$150.00	$145.00	$160.00	$150.00
Jumbo Shrimp (100 Pieces)	$295.00	$325.00	$350.00	$325.00	$350.00	$300.00	$275.00	$250.00	$300.00	$250.00
Steamship Round of Beef	$595.00	$625.00	$650.00	$575.00	$650.00	$475.00	$600.00	$550.00	$500.00	$525.00

Note: All prices listed on this comparison sheet must be obtained through general market sources and *NOT* from direct communication with competitors. When making comparisons in your city, use hotel names in place of hotel letters.

Figure 4.1 COMPARISON OF COMPETITIVE HOTEL CATERING PRICES

113

add revenue dollars. Examples of these events include: A night in Paris (French menu and wine, special dessert, and strolling violinists) or a German Beer Festival (hot or cold German buffet, beer by the pitcher, checkered tablecloths, and a stein to take home). Be imaginative; there are many local customs in your area that will help in tailoring a special party for a special group.

Increase the sales power of your banquet menus.   As an experiment, select the top-selling entrees from your banquet menus and have a small supply of individual menus run off consisting of each item as an individual dinner or luncheon with the price at the bottom. When prospective clients are choosing a menu, show them these individual meals one at a time rather than a complete list of entrees and prices. Use this as a sales tool to get the highest average check that you can without using pressure. Size up the group as to what their approximate budget should be and present an individual menu slightly higher in price so that you can come down if necessary without going to the lowest limit. This will give you more ability to sell the group on a menu rather than having them select a meal solely based on low price. Make up a sales pitch including service points and guest satisfaction to go along with each menu.

Use your past guests to help you sell.   Each catering and sales department should have a book that contains the letters of past groups that have enjoyed your facilities. Testimonials can be a key to establishing your quality in the minds of your present guests. This book should be attractively assembled (leather binding is recommended), with clear plastic pages inserted. On the left page present the letter from the group, and on the right side show a clean typed menu of what was served, including any special arrangements. Select the letters for this book from a wide range of functions such as business meetings, charity functions, political fund raisers, weddings, military groups, and so on. Be proud of your history.

Business can be created.   Business will not always come knocking, especially in the present business cycle. There are ways to create action on your function facilities during slow periods. Choose a group, club, or company organization that meets regularly and make them an offer that will aid them and yourself. Offer them the use of your ballroom or other function rooms at a competitive price. Needless to say, this should only be done on a very short-term basis, and in some properties you may have to charge a nominal labor charge to cover your costs. If the size of the group warrants it, and the projected attendance, beverage revenue, and profit allow, donate a small sum of money to the group for their use in promoting the function. This can often create enough action in the hotel to help your regular outlets before and after the function.

"EVERYONE SELLS" PROGRAM _____

Basic Information for Participants in Solicitation

The following information on telephone solicitation can be used in conjunction with training meetings conducted by the sales and catering departments to help individuals in the correct procedures of telephone sales. It is offered as a good example of the information that should be provided to make this program produce maximum results for your hotel.

In addition, each participant should receive the following:

1. Directory of all other properties (if your hotel is part of a chain)
2. Up-to-date Tariff Sheet of your hotel
3. Function information including function room capacities and contact people for specific information
4. Directory of your hotel's services
5. Short background of your hotel, outlining your services and the strong selling points such as location, transportation, rates, restaurants, and so on
6. Banquet food and beverage menus and prices

Telephone Solicitation

This section is designed to assist you in your telephone solicitation program. Telephone personalities can be developed through practice. You are easily evaluated by a listener through the quality of your voice, sincerity, and ease with which you speak. Your listener can readily determine if you are a person who has something worthwhile to say, expresses yourself clearly, and can get to the point.

A natural flow of conversational exchange has conviction. The tone of your voice should reflect self-confidence. Be careful of your diction. The listener will quickly detect a conned variety of solicitation if your speech is poorly paced and hurried. The exchange of thought must be natural and pleasantly aggressive when information is needed. Be prepared to supply facts as requested by your listener. In the beginning, telephone conversation exchanges can be awkward, but with each call you will improve your telephone personality as you become more certain of your ability.

The "Everyone Sells" Program depends largely on solicitation to market ways to the end that overall occupancy will be improved and food and beverage sales increased.

Each telephone call is to be reported on the Call Report form (see end of Chapter 3). The reports are to be completed in duplicate. The original copy should be retained in your program file for follow-up and the second copy should be referred to the catering director, general manager, or the director of food and beverage operations. If any leads develop, they will be either followed up by you or the sales and catering offices.

A sample telephone solicitation presentation is included. There are various ways of approaching a new client and various ways of getting people to talk. Your own intuition and common sense will help you as you become experienced.

Do not ignore calling small companies. There is always a chance of potential leads or a market for your facilities and services. You may feel a great many calls are a waste of time, but a fair share of them will be productive. Think of the extra business the hotel would not have otherwise obtained without your effort.

Suggested Telephone Presentation

"Good Morning/Good Afternoon. This is _____ at the XYZ Hotel. May I please speak to the member of your firm who makes your in-town hotel reservations?" (Try to get a name.)

If the answer is no, then say, "Does your company ever have occasion to use (your city) hotels for rooms, meetings, or food functions?" If the answer is no, then say, "Well, if we at the XYZ Hotel can ever be of service at any time, please call us." (Give the telephone number of the hotel.)

If you have the name of the person who is handling reservations, ask for him or her and then say, "This is _____ at the XYZ Hotel. For the convenience of you and your company, we are in a position to assist you and your company in making instant out-of-town reservations for your traveling personnel or for visitors coming to _____." If the client's interest is aroused, mention your special reservation number or 800 number. Have a directory at your fingertips, if your hotel is chain connected. "Call us any time. We will be glad to give personal attention to your reservations and banquet and meeting room requirements at the _____."

Then ask, "Are there any other departments in your company that might have need for our hotel services?" (Get name and department.)

Wind up the conversation with, "Thank you very much for your time. We are sending you a folder describing the XYZ Hotel and our individual rates. We have special low rates for groups which we will be glad to discuss with you whenever convenient. Please call on us for assistance at any time."

When a person who handles hotel accommodations or travel arrangements responds with, "We usually send a letter or call long distance," just go on briefly with your presentation and explain your special reservation number or 800 number.

If the person says yes, then explain that you will be happy to send information. Get the correct spelling of the individual's name for your report and for mailing. Remember, if a person is reluctant to listen to you or speak to you, or really does not have time to speak with you, bow out gracefully, giving him or her as little or as much information as the situation will allow.

When you talk to a person who says that the company has very little traffic out of town, make a note that the company is local and may, from time to time, have a luncheon, meeting, or gathering during the year. Make a pitch for your banquet facilities. People who have friends, relatives, or visitors who need local accommodations may find no better place than the XYZ Hotel.

If you cannot get beyond the receptionist or switchboard operator, be certain to explain who you are and what your hotel can do for them. Always try to leave your telephone number—you will be surprised at how many switchboard operators and receptionists are the people in the company who make reservations. Try to get his or her name for follow-up.

These ideas are merely suggestions. You must inject your own personality into your telephone conversation exchanges. When taking down information, be certain to get the full name of the party to whom you are speaking, his or her title (if possible), the full name of the company, and the address.

When reporting your calls, be explicit and do not leave out any details. Follow the form as you progress through your conversation. The form is far more detailed than these suggested presentations indicate. I suggest that *before* the telephone call is made the form be filled out insofar as the name of the organization, the address and phone number, and the name of contact (if known) are concerned. Reports should be turned in as they are completed, on a daily basis.

PERSONAL SELLING

Without a doubt, of all the various sales tools in your arsenal, *personal selling* should be considered your ultimate weapon. The reasons why personal selling is your most potent sales tool are many. Looking a sales prospect "eye to eye" will give you, the seller, advantages that no other type of selling has. The customer can form an opinion of the product or service for sale based on the impression created by the salesperson. It does not necessarily follow that an eye-appealing salesperson means an excellent product, but that favorable first impression surely gets you off to a running start.

The advantages of selling face-to-face are:

Direct contact

Personal impression

Opportunity to present a product or service directly to the right buyer

Chance to overcome objections and correct false impressions

Opportunity to answer questions

Best of all—getting a signed, definite commitment or advance booking (individual reservation, group room or meeting business, banquet or function)

Contrary to general opinion, personal selling does not require any unique charm or technique. There is nothing tricky about it. All it takes is the willpower to get up, go out, see potential clients, and ask them for business.

Let's take a look at the basic technique used in making a sales call on someone in his or her home or office. It is almost as simple as introducing yourself, stating the purpose of your visit, listening, asking for business, getting a commitment, thanking the client, and leaving.

It is almost that simple, but not quite. Prefacing the above must be product knowledge. You must know what you are talking about; you must be informed with all the statistical data about your property; and you must know rates, prices, measurements and capacities of facilities, hours of operation, availability of special equipment, and so on.

Basics of Personal Selling

Plan the call. As stated earlier, the salesperson must plan what approach will be used for each prospect while asking himself or herself: What is the customer like? What are her needs and desires? What is the best way to appeal to him? What offer can be made that will get action?

Have a specific purpose or definite goal that you want to accomplish. A goal is more than a dream; it is a dream being acted upon. It is more than a hazy, "Oh, I wish I could. . . ." A goal is a clear "This is what I'm working toward." Get a clear fix on where you want to go. Set your goals high—and then exceed them!

Have all the information with you, but remember—you do not have to know all of this by memory. It is perfectly acceptable to refer to material while you are talking, but you must either have the information down pat in your head or available at hand so you can come up with accurate information when necessary. Some salespeople think they can impress a prospect by using personal charm. Some of these super salespeople also think they can "free-wheel" it or make a sales presentation without reference material. It cannot be done. You must be knowledgeable.

Introduce yourself clearly and remember to include your affiliation. When you make a call in person or by phone, always jot down the names of the other people (secretaries and receptionists). On follow-up or return calls, the last instant before entering the office or making a phone call, look at your file or call card, check the names, and then call the receptionist or secretary by name. Is there anything more flattering than the sound of one's own name? Will you have any trouble getting back in to see the client? Well, at least it should be easier.

State the purpose of your call. The best possible sales pitch is to state your name, affiliation, and precisely what you want—as briefly as possible. Probably the best sales talk ever is something like: "I'm Jane (John) Doe from the XYZ Hotel. We'd certainly like to get you to send us some business—especially people who come to see you from out of town."

The recipient of such a sales talk will appreciate your brevity and directness.

From an old boat, a mélange of seafood includes jumbo shrimp, langostinos, and golden gulf crab claws, garnished with lemon, mustard, and remoulade and cocktail sauces.

TIFFANY PHOTO

This mosaic display of international cheeses, garnished with fresh fruit, is displayed on a 5½-foot table-size mirror.

TIFFANY PHOTO

Creativity adds the final touch to the cheese display.

TIFFANY PHOTO

TIFFANY PHOTO

An elaborate Tropical Fruit Fantasy display is highlighted by a large crystal ice carving.

TIFFANY PHOTO

The tempura station is attended by tropical-shirted servers manning giant woks. In addition to Vegetable and Shrimp Tempura, the preparation of Beef Chow Yoke and Oriental Stir-Fried Vegetables are cooked tableside to order.

TIFFANY PHOTO

This treasure chest is made from pineapple skins.

The Chocoholic Bar adds a memorable sweet side to the evening.

TIFFANY PHOTO

TIFFANY PHOTO

Open wide—there's always room for chocolate of any kind.

HARVEY BILT PHOTO

The Culinary Christmas Cruise Around The World reception provided four very authentic replicas of different areas of the world at Christmas time. Here is the Far East set, made entirely from styrofoam, which makes the decor very inexpensive.

HARVEY BILT PHOTO

The European backdrop provides an appropriate setting for the service of delicacies from Germany, England, France, Hungary, and Italy.

HARVEY BILT PHOTO

The Latin American setting presents foods from Colombia, Argentina, Mexico, Guatemala, and Venezuela.

HARVEY BILT PHOTO

The North American display includes Santa and his tiny reindeer in route to bringing joy to the hearts of children around the world.

HARVEY BILT PHOTO

The highlight of the North America setting is the New England and Florida Raw Bar with a crystal seahorse ice carving.

HARVEY BILT PHOTO

From separate carving stations, we present Whole Roast Turkeys, Whole Smithfield Hams, and Whole Steamship Rounds of Beef.

HARVEY BILT PHOTO

The international dessert selection is displayed uniquely on giant white kydex and mirrored cubes with burgundy velvet ribbons.

HARVEY BILT PHOTO

Hanging snowflakes and international flags, as well as white branches and floral displays, lure you into the Winter Wonderland of Desserts.

HARVEY BILT PHOTO

Special beverage stations feature wines, beers, and sparkling waters of the world.

HARVEY BILT PHOTO

Various stations offer selections of international teas and coffees.

HARVEY BILT PHOTO

This is the prop used as the entrance to an Art Deco Casino for The Gaming Crowd Casino Party.

HARVEY BILT PHOTO

The pace is quick, the stakes are high, and the air is charged with the titillating excitement Lady Luck brings with her. The sure thing here is the quality of food and drink.

HARVEY BILT PHOTO

The huge fountain provides that grand up-scale feeling.

JOE SAGET PHOTO

What a great day it is going to be!

HARVEY BILT PHOTO

Super sports on the beach.

HARVEY BILT PHOTO

A shipwreck display complements the outdoor atmosphere.

HARVEY BILT PHOTO

An evening in the twilight makes a night to remember.

After dinner in the ballroom, how about crepes prepared to order under the stars?

HARVEY BILT PHOTO

TIFFANY PHOTO

Travel to the Caribbean Islands for Bahamian Conch Fritters, Skewered Fruit, Sweet and Sour Shrimp, and Petite Chicken & Pineapple Kabobs.

TIFFANY PHOTO

Grab a ride on the Orient Express with Far East delicacies.

TIFFANY PHOTO

Costumed staff prepares Tempura, a variety of seafood and vegetables dipped in batter and deep fried.

TIFFANY PHOTO

Pristine elegance reception includes a silver starburst as a backdrop.

TIFFANY PHOTO

The reception includes mirrored tabletops and classical music.

TIFFANY PHOTO

Servers offer canapés from gleaming silver trays as well as champagne, white wine, and mineral water.

JOE SAGET PHOTO

Displays atop, around, and on rectangular cubes with satin multicolored banners draped from the ceiling create a colorful atmosphere.

JOE SAGET PHOTO

Classical food presentations atop stark white cubic construction steal the show from priceless works of art.

JOE SAGET PHOTO

Lose yourself in the luxury and opulence of days gone by and taste the forbidden fruits of Prohibition. "The Way We Were" is the way you'll want to be again!

JOE SAGET PHOTO

Paté Maison display is decorated with plumage on silver mirror, the Marquis Selection of cold canapés on marble, and gleaming silver chafer of Zucchini Boats filled with puree of Gingered Carrot.

JOE SAGET PHOTO

Display shows off Gallantine of Duck, garni, and Saddle of Cold Venison.

JOE SAGET PHOTO

This petite display is of vegetable crudités, garnish of carved fresh vegetables, and silver chafers of hot vegetable selections.

JOE SAGET PHOTO

A simple but elegant table setting. Fresh gardenias floating in water-filled fish bowls add the fragrance desired, as well as the visual impact.

Whole wheels of Brie with toasted almonds and carved apple bird are complemented by whole Stilton cheese with port wine and silver trays of homemade melba toast, biscuits, crackers, and French bread.

JOE SAGET PHOTO

JOE SAGET PHOTO

Here, we show select fresh strawberries with stem on, fresh blueberries, raspberries, cherries, dates, whole poached figs, ripe pears, accompanied by white and dark chocolate fondue, sour cream, whipped Chantilly cream, and brown sugar.

JOE SAGET PHOTO

This re-created 1920s drug store soda fountain features: vanilla, butter pecan, strawberry, and chocolate ice cream, as well as whipped cream, cherries, chopped nuts, chocolate jimmies, strawberry sauce, marshmallow topping, hot fudge, butterscotch sauce, crushed pineapple, bananas, and sugar cones. In addition, a soda-dispensing unit for soft drinks, chocolate syrup, and crushed ice shall be provided.

JOE SAGET PHOTO

At resort properties, food functions are held outdoors at an
increasing rate. Here, a conch shell is filled with cascading
dendrobium orchids on a table mirror.

JOE SAGET PHOTO

This fresh fruit fantasy offers
freshly made fruit yogurt,
glass decanters of fresh-
squeezed juices, and sculp-
tured ice casks that serve
fresh orange juice.

All prospects are busy. They do you a favor by assigning some of their listening time to you. Don't waste that time. Let them know precisely what you want. Naturally, you can enlarge on this approach as you go on, but never waste a prospect's time with unnecessary chit-chat about the weather or other unrelated chatter. If the client directs the conversation into some other field foreign to the subject, fine. Go along with it. But do not try to be off-beat, or clever, or witty. Just state your case and stay with it—this is a business call.

Explain the sales points of your product or service as simply and briefly as possible without leaving out any salient fact. Also think about the objections that are likely to be made in each case and figure out in advance the best way to overcome them. It is also important for the salesperson to review all notes made on previous discussions to be sure that there is nothing new about the prospect's situation. In short, the salesperson should settle for nothing less than total customer satisfaction. This can be done best by increasing the effort on the basics.

Listen to the prospect if and when he or she wants to talk. Remember: People don't care how much you know until they know how much you care. We have to learn to respond to people's needs, not just to their wants. People always get what they want, but professionals recognize what they need and sell it to them.

Ask for the Order

The point is simple: Ask for business. Ask everyone you meet, anywhere, under just about any circumstance. Every time you ask someone for business, that is personal selling. Ask and you'll receive. An important part of personal selling is to keep in mind that prospects will not make a definite commitment or booking of any kind unless you ask them to. Explaining the merits and advantages of your hotel in elegant, sparkling prose with dramatic word pictures means little, no matter how convincing you are, unless you say, "How about it?" or "I will definitely hold the dates for you" or "If you'll just sign this Catering Event Order, everything is confirmed" or "When shall I make the first room reservations for your company's representatives coming in from out of town?"

Along these lines, try to get a definite commitment; if that's not possible, at least get a tentative commitment (for a food function, meeting, convention, wedding, or whatever). How do you get a commitment? If you are on an outside sales call, ask the prospect if you may use the phone, call your office, ask if the dates are open, then reserve the space.

Ask your client for what you want, ask for it again, then ask for it again. "No" is a reaction at a specific moment—not a definite answer. What "no" really indicates is that "yes" may be forthcoming. Or maybe all it means is "give me more information." Remember: To progress to your place in the sun, you must always put up with some blisters.

When a customer indicates that the interview is over—*leave*. When the customer agrees to do whatever it is you have asked for (make a room reservation, send all the company's or association's people to stay at your place, or book a meeting, food function, or convention)—when he or she says yes—*leave*. And do not forget to thank the prospect for giving you time from his or her busy schedule.

The next time you miss a sale, review the following checklist, item by item. You can check each statement with a yes or no response. Too many yes responses may indicate that you should brush up on your sales techniques.

- I was lacking in self-confidence. I was afraid the buyer would say no.
- I needed more information about my own product and competing products in order to be sure of my ground.
- I lost the order to a lower-priced supplier because I didn't have enough facts to demonstrate that our firm was worth the money.
- I neglected my prospect too long. A competing salesperson beat me to the order because he or she was there asking for it.
- I let myself get into an argument with the buyer. Maybe I won, but maybe he or she didn't like the idea of being beaten.
- I waited too long before asking for an order. I talked myself into a sale—then I talked myself out of it.
- I tried to pressure the buyer. I lacked tact and finesse in trying to close the deal.
- I failed to see everybody who may have influenced the sale. On the other hand, I may have seen too many people. Maybe disagreement among themselves lost me the order.
- I let a ticklish credit situation beat me out of the order.
- I aroused the buyer's resentment because I spent so much time knocking competing firms and I did not drive home the advantages of my own.
- I let the buyer scare me. I felt apologetic and I felt as if I were asking a favor.
- I neglected to reinforce my sales talk with visual aids.
- I should have made my presentation more complete. I did not "touch all the bases." Maybe I overlooked something that the prospect considers extra important.
- I talked about too many things. Maybe I ought to boil my presentation down to fewer points and make these points stick better.
- I forgot the prospect's name, or I failed to use it often enough.
- I failed to show enough interest in the prospect's business or profession and/ or problems.
- I counted too much on getting by on "inspiration." I did not plan the interview beforehand.
- I interrupted the prospect too much. I did not give him enough opportunity to talk.
- I don't always use the "tools of the trade."

TWELVE POINTS OF SELLING

1. Understand who you are and enjoy yourself.

2. Plan your time, which will allow you to make the most of it.

3. Keep yourself in the pursuit of customers.

4. Get the customer's full attention before you begin your presentation.

5. Let persistence be the rule. Do not get discouraged when you are first refused the sale.

6. Know your customers.

7. Know your product and present *ideas,* not just a product. Use samples to present ideas.

8. Always be well-groomed.

9. Be honest at all times.

10. Do not be afraid to ask for the order.

11. Take a "moon shot" once a week at the "Big Sale."

12. Let your sales actions and follow-through speak for themselves.

CHAPTER 5

Operations

Operations is the summation and actualization of the administration and sales phases of catering. It is this phase that brings all the vital elements together to produce customer satisfaction and departmental profit.

TRANSITION

The point at which sales ends and operations begins is a finite transition. In reality, the transition is accomplished through the work of the banquet manager, banquet headwaiter, or banquet maitre d'. The realization of all operational effort is done through him or her.

The Banquet Manager, Banquet Headwaiter, or Banquet Maitre d'

This individual is responsible for the hiring of qualified service staff, such as captains, waiters, waitresses, and housemen, and, just as important, training these people in the methods and standards of the department. The banquet manager, banquet headwaiter, or banquet maitre d' must be able to organize, to delegate responsibility to the captains and waiters and waitresses, and remain the undisputed leader of the group. He or she must keep everything in perspective, being able to set priorities, eliminate unnecessary work, and cope with the immediacy of the situation. By doing this, the individual will instill confidence in himself or herself as well as in the subordinates. Furthermore, this person must be able to deal with customers—putting them at ease and letting them know that all arrangements will be handled expertly and professionally. Finally, the banquet manager must be flexible. Many last-minute details may develop on catered functions that were not called for on the Catering Event Order. The banquet manager must be able to enact a customer's desires on a minute's notice and maintain a positive attitude.

The Banquet Manager must be aware of room size, capacity, arrangements, and special requirements such as lighting and sound. He or she should examine the menu to determine if any special requirements are mentioned and if any special services are ordered. Furthermore, he or she must communicate these facts to the staff and familiarize them to the point where they can successfully complete their assignments.

Captains, Waiters, Waitresses, and Housemen

Captains, waiters, waitresses, and housemen form the backbone of the catering operation. They are in the most direct contact with the public and, therefore, create the image not only of the department but often of the hotel as well. The key to any successful operational phase is a well-trained staff, and the key to such a staff is good selection and training methods. The regular house staff should feel confident in their jobs and, like the banquet manager, make customers feel confident in their selection of the hotel. Courtesy, enthusiasm, and capability should be developed in these personnel.

Extra personnel are needed when the function exceeds the capabilities of the regular house staff. Using house personnel to their fullest advantage is of primary concern. Therefore, it is important to determine the optimum size of the regular banquet staff and maintain a well-trained crew at that level. Additional call lists must be prepared when the need arises, or, in the case of a union house, contact the waiter/waitress union for assistance.

FUNCTIONAL PROCESSES OF CATERING OPERATIONS

The operations phase can be divided into five functional processes: planning, organizing, staffing, actuating, and controlling. The operations of a catering department is simply a mix of these functions.

During *planning,* the necessary information such as menus, size of the function, room arrangements, special services, and special arrangements are gathered.

During the *organizing* function, this information is analyzed and an action plan is developed. Special problems are brought to light and solutions are developed.

Staffing is a key function within the catering operation. Since labor makes up a sizable percentage of operations costs, it is necessary to minimize the number of people working on a banquet. In many hotels, the number may be determined by union contract; that is, the union may set a maximum number of customers one waiter or waitress can serve during a function. The union may also set a specific number of captains and busboys. In other cases, there may be no requirements.

In any case, achieving the optimum productivity is the main consideration. An example of effective staffing may be used to establish goals for labor-cost guidelines. Assume that a 10% labor cost as a percentage of gross revenue is desired. By multiplying the guaranteed number of persons times the price per person, a gross revenue estimate is determined. Then, simply take 10% of that figure and schedule as many people as possible. Sometimes there may not be enough personnel and sometimes there may be too much help; consequently, adjust the number as necessary. Since labor is a variable cost in this case, the cost should be kept to a minimum to maximize profit. It must be noted, however, that at no time should scheduling convenience turn into a reason for lowering service. Once service standards are met, they should be maintained. It is difficult to upgrade service once it starts to slip.

Actuating is the service function. This means the actual service of the food and beverage. It is at this point that all the preliminary work done by the administration and sales phases is enacted. If this function goes badly, the entire effort suffers. It is the "moment of truth" for any catering department. If the proper elements are brought together accurately and are clearly understood, the catered affair will be successful for the customer and the hotel. Managerial attention should be focused on this point to assure customer satisfaction and departmental profit.

Finally, *controlling* is a multifaceted function involving summation of all the operational activities. First, the billing of the customer and paying of personnel must be considered. Accuracy of both is vital. Customers become irritated if they receive inaccurate statements. The catering department may feel the effect of errors if the bill is too small. Payroll is just as important since serving personnel expect and should receive their correct salary. If allowed to continue, mistakes can become demoralizing.

Another important facet of control is the Function Summary Report (see end of Chapter 3), which summarizes everything that occurred during the affair and leaves plenty of space for customer comments. These are very important sources of feedback and should be noted by all concerned.

A final review with the director of catering may also be needed to bring out problems encountered and to develop solutions for future bookings. In any case, an open channel of communication between the administration, sales, and operational phases of the catering department must be realized and used continually to create an effective organization.

Catering Market Plan

The need for advanced knowledge and preparation on solicitation efforts is emphasized throughout this book. Solicitation on repeat and regular business and the catering and servicing of convention banquets are the foundation of the catering business. Often a caterer will become so involved in handling the usual that he or she will sometimes neglect the unusual, which is what makes one banquet production superior to that of a competitor.

Special programs and promotions have a way of not materializing if they are not planned in advance. Therefore, the catering department of each hotel should prepare a market plan that covers all programs and promotions for the coming year. This should be developed toward the end of the year for the following year. This plan should cover all market areas concerning the catering office, including regular and repeat business, special solicitation efforts, and catering sales promotions. It should be precise and concise.

WHY A MARKET PLAN IS NECESSARY

The purpose of the Catering Market Plan is to increase food and beverage revenue. Your goal is to take advantage of all possibilities that will increase your revenue. Excellent teamwork, interest, and esprit de corps of all department members is required to surpass anticipated achievements.

Your Market Plan should be a plan of attack and a goal of achievements of your operation. It will be the key to achieving the goals outlined in your annual forecast. The Market Plan will help you concentrate your efforts on developing new business and generating more dollar sales volume from the customers you already have.

Hand-in-hand with the problem of greater business volume is the problem of greater profit. While you continue to sell every service your customer wants, regardless of the price per sale, you should be constantly alert to all opportunities to convert a low-dollar volume sale into a larger, more profitable sale. This is called step-up-selling (SUS).

STEP-UP-SELLING

SUS is used by the most successful firms in the country. If salespeople employed by these firms did not use step-up-selling to increase quality and quantity of goods purchased, our entire national economy would be 20 to 30 percent lower.

With this in mind, your Market Plan should include how your department plans to deal with SUS, which, in our business, serves two ends. It has a marked effect on both volume and profit. Your volume goes up when you step-up a sale, so that your customer has a more completely planned function and a function that will include more of the features that his or her guests will enjoy. Surely, a function that gives the guests the quality of food and service that they really desire will satisfy them most.

Your profits will also benefit from SUS because the average check or total guest bill will increase, which goes a long way in helping keep food costs in line.

Step-up-selling is accomplished most effectively by:

- First, sell the customer completely on whatever he or she had intended to purchase.
- Then, offer helpful ideas and suggestions pertaining to the customer's wishes. The customer will recognize your sincere effort to help him or her carry out those wishes, for his or her maximum satisfaction.
- Next, whet your customer's appetite for other items or additional pleasures and conveniences.

The opportunities for SUS are so vast that it is difficult to list them all. In fact, it is easy to overlook many of these opportunities if you do not remind yourself of them regularly. A few examples of SUS are listed below. They demonstrate how easy it is to increase your business volume by stepping up the sale from the customers you already have.

SUS EXAMPLES

- When a customer returns to the hotel to finalize arrangements covering a banquet function, you should review the menu carefully and suggest adding wine if it has not been included.

- If wine has been included, suggest stepping-up the entree from capon, for example, to roast prime rib of beef.
- Another step-up opportunity for a banquet dinner function is to suggest a rolling cordial cart to add that extra touch to a well-planned function.
- Wedding reception functions offer excellent step-up opportunities.
- In addition to stepping-up the entree and adding the many extra touches, you should offer the services of your orchestra, photographer, florist, and audio-visual firm. These are all SUS examples because your hotel should receive a percentage on the total sales from all of these services.

In these economic times, we must be cognizant of the tight-money market. Even with a well-deserved quality reputation, a certain number of your clients will be very price conscious. More than ever, price is an important factor to this special segment of our business. With this in mind, to offer these customers *all* the services you feel and know they need would only drive the business to your nearest competitor. On the other hand, if you do not make an effort for the extra sale, your volume will experience no additional increase.

YOUR CATERING MARKET PLAN

All catering sales personnel should be involved in the preparation of your Market Plan. Each of these persons should be responsible for at least one of these projects: to organize the plan, to submit suggestions for promotion, to estimate the budget, and to direct the project to its completion and success.

By November 1 of each year the Market Plan should be submitted for management approval, complete with programs, internal and external advertising recommendations, rehabilitation, budget, and salesman assignments. Goals must be established and the director of catering should administrate the entire plan to its culmination. A copy of this report should also be sent to your area or divisional director of food and beverage.

Your plan should be reviewed monthly and may be supplemented by a "Special Market Plan" for a particular soft period. This supplemental plan should include:

Standardized outline and format

Checklist for completeness

Example and information

This suggested outline represents only the minimum information that should be included. It does not take into consideration any special additional factors that should be considered for properties located near resort areas, airports, suburbia, or any special local community. It is intended to refine the format for all hotels so that the Market Plan will become a truly effective means to increase catering food and beverage volume.

Contents of Your Market Plan

I. INTRODUCTION

Your Catering Market Plan should begin with a short introduction to set the tone of
the Market Plan as well as the theme of the marketing strategy.

II. FOUR-YEAR CATERING TRENDS

Using the sample here, compile a four-year overview of trends (two preceding years,
plus the current year and a forecast for next year).

	19XX	19XX	Current Year 19XX	Forecasted Year 19XX
House Occupancy %				
Banquet Food $				
Breakfast				
Lunch				
Dinner				
Other				
Total				
Banquet Beverage $				
Breakfast				
Lunch				
Dinner				
Other				
Total				
Banquet Covers				
Breakfast				
Lunch				
Dinner				
Other				
Total				
Banquet Average Check $				
Breakfast				
Lunch				
Dinner				
Other				
Total				

III. COMPETITION

If you hope to sell successfully against the competition, you must understand who they are, what they can offer, and what their strengths and weaknesses are. Every salesperson should know the present and future competition which is direct and indirect.

A. Direct Competition

1. Present

Name of Establishment	(Name) Largest Ballroom	Total Number of Banquet Seats
1.		
2.		
3.		
4.		
5.		
6.		
7.		
8.		
9.		
10.		

2. Future (to be opened in the next 24 months)

Name of Establishment	(Name) Largest Ballroom	Total Number of Banquet Seats
1.		
2.		
3.		
4.		
5.		

B. Indirect Competition

1. Present

Name of Establishment	(Name) Largest Ballroom	Total Number of Banquet Seats
1.		
2.		
3.		
4.		
5.		
6.		
7.		
8.		
9.		
10.		

2. Future (to be opened in the next 24 months)

Name of Establishment	(Name) Largest Ballroom	Total Number of Banquet Seats
1.		
2.		
3.		
4.		
5.		

IV. OUTSELLING COMPETITION

The purpose of this section is to highlight your primary present direct and indirect competition and to amplify all items *as seen through the eyes of the customer*. This section should be written so as to be useful to the assistants in the catering department when "selling-up" your hotel.

A. Direct Competition

A paragraph should be included for each establishment that is in direct competition and listed under Roman numeral III. Briefly include important points *only as they might be accepted by the customer.* Such items should include type and size of facility, training, view, location, quality of food, equipment, service, price, experience, logistical resources, local image, uniforms, locality, flexibility, parking facilities, parking costs, and so on.

B. Indirect Competition

Explained in paragraph above. Again, list each establishment that was mentioned under Roman numeral III.

V. ACHIEVEMENTS

In this section you should describe the five most important achievements of your catering department *last year.* Include how these achievements relate to increased food and beverage profits.

VI. OBJECTIVES FOR 19XX

This is the most important section of your Market Plan. It should include a detailed action plan for the guidance of your entire department for the next year. After meeting with your general manager and food and beverage director, you should briefly list specific objectives for the coming year in an organized manner. Below are a few suggested topics. Incorporate any others you feel are important. This review of objectives should *not* be confined to one page. *Specific goals should be developed* in each area and a check point should be established that can be checked periodically during the year to be sure that your goals are reached by the end of the year.

A. People—Present Staff

Consider evaluation, training, restructure, alignment of responsibilities, and the like. Coordination with the sales department should also be discussed.

B. Product and Equipment

This section is very important. Reevaluate your present menu presentation, budget, quality, and replacement. Think about new solutions to old problems, theme menus or parties, newly created products, package plans, drinks or hors d'oeuvres by the hour, and so on.

C. Market

Reinforce your *existing markets*. Increase market share, average check, image, and publicity. Explore *new* markets that were previously untapped. (Review the checklist on pages 136 to 139 for reference.)

D. Solicitation Techniques

Consider new and improved solicitation techniques all based on available resources and your business savvy in outsoliciting and outselling the competition.

E. Policy and Price Change

Evaluate if your existing structure of minimums, price levels, and so on, are still appropriate. Consider new approaches, sales commissions on flowers, music, audio-visual, and the like (rebatable to hotel).

F. Cover and Dollar Goals for Year

Establish realistic goals for each salesperson on a monthly basis; to be reviewed at catering meetings, monthly.

Some Other Sample Objectives

Maximize space allotments.   In order to surpass your goal, the objective of the catering department should include an effort to maximize the sale of all public space in order to produce the highest revenue possible. Due to your limited amount of public space, it is necessary to work closely with the sales department in order to use the public space to achieve the maximum profit for your hotel. Also, you may want to consider decreasing the maximum convention block, thereby emphasizing the transient market more and opening more public space for local banquet business. An open line of communication will enable both departments to effectively maximize the sale of your public space through the diligent and proper management of space allotments. And, in doing so, the overall profit picture of your hotel will benefit accordingly.

Additional suggestions for improving space assignments in your sales department for conventions include *holding space until 5:00 P.M. only* and having a convention program as early as possible and no later than *six months in advance.*

Also, if a pattern has developed in your hotel that shows a great deal of private banquet business (both local banquet and sales oriented) with fewer than 50 guests, you should exercise extreme caution in this area due to the high cost of producing a private function that does not create a greater sales volume. It may be a situation of exchanging dollars or possibly even losing money. One consideration may be to introduce a service charge to be added to all small functions, such as: "If 25 or fewer guests are guaranteed, an additional service charge of $50.00 (or higher) will be added to the account."

Annual local catering business.   Another possible goal would be to establish a base of annual catering business from which a higher sales volume will be attained in future years. This can be done by establishing a repertoire of catering files. Through methodical solicitation, you can research, pursue, and develop a local catering business of both existing and new markets.

Convention groups.   Serve all convention groups in such a way as to maximize dollar volume and insure the repeat status of this business. Remember to "sell-up" in order to obtain the highest potential from this market and, at the same time, do intelligent menu planning to maintain the lowest possible food costs. In order to attract the lion's share of the convention market, you and your staff must build a better mousetrap—a new style of service, a new level of creativity, a truly different repertoire of thematic affairs, or anything that your hotel can do better than the competition.

Increase profits.   Increase profits and revenue by obtaining better prices on existing menus and minimizing overproduction through better control.

Direct sales.   With the food and labor costs continuing to rise, you should work toward the following:

1. Increase your average check and obtain maximum profit during prime periods.
2. Stay firm on the guarantee clause, so the set-up figure is only 3 percent above the guarantee figure.
3. Preset menus to reduce production and food costs and increase sales to multiply markets.
4. Stress the strengths of the facilities and your hotel's reputation.
5. Underscore service as a main point by being one of the few hotels that is still emphasizing customer service and complete customer satisfaction.
6. Create new ideas to further enhance annual groups.
7. Increase mail solicitation to overall organizations, groups, and communities.

Operation goals.   Once the piece of business has been secured for your hotel, greater profits can be experienced through the proper controls; for example:

1. Establish the option of changing the assigned function room if—and as soon as—a drop in attendance is detected.

2. Greater emphasis needs to be given to the service segment of your catering operation so that waiters and waitresses may assume their appropriate roles in the total sales picture. This can only be done through constant service training.

3. Incorporate regular meetings between the catering staff and the banquet service personnel, toward establishing a better working relationship.

4. Improve the office appearance and increase office productivity. Steps can be taken to help eliminate office noise, such as installing typewriter sound covers, and so on. Also, better customer impressions can be accomplished by displaying photographs of various catered functions, a prepared slide show in a self-contained unit for presentations, or a wine display or a china, silverware, and napkin folds and color display. This office appearance should be maintained throughout the year.

Special Marketing Programs.   The following are suggested as possible goals to be added to your Market Plan.

1. VIP Client Luncheons and Dinners—These are designed to serve as a maintenance program with regard to annual and other special clients. These functions could take the format of a Chef's Round Table Luncheon, a Theme Dinner, or possibly a Gold or Platinum Service presentation.

2. Local Corporate Party—This is intended to attract and support your local corporate catering business.

3. New Year's Eve—This provides extensive planning with an early execution date (completion date by September 1st) so as to provide greater exposure.

4. Christmas in July—In an attempt to visit and solicit your clients for new business and to demonstrate your appreciation for their past patronage, hand-carry pastry or other goods to them and, most important, in their environment.

5. Good Customer Party—This is an opportunity to say thanks to clients who have remained loyal to the hotel for their past patronage.

6. Gold or Platinum Service—This series of small-meal functions is designed to create an intimate atmosphere for clients, salespersons, and management to spend time in a social atmosphere.

7. Summer Extravaganzas—These are designed to fill the soft areas during the summer season. These functions could take the form of Big Band entertainment or Big Name entertainment and would be open to the public as scheduled.

Miscellaneous.   In addition to the goals already mentioned, consider the following:

1. Advertise your facility in your local market areas to increase volume and exposure. Cultivate the local press and news media for better coverage of existing

events taking place at your hotel. Also, avail the catering staff to local groups that require speakers, demonstrations, or lectures on party planning, themes, and events.

2. Continue to determine soft spots in catering sales and attempt to fill those spots with quality catering business. There should be constant review of forecast figures to identify areas and coordinate sales efforts to fill those specific areas. Some hotels may consider the development of a totally professional tour menu package consisting of menus, inclusive prices, beverage selections, and the like. A package will encourage tour groups to book banquet functions and group meals during their stay at your hotel. Also, there should be a constant review of function space held for conventions to determine available space utilization and maximize your potential sales. You may want to consider the development of a mailer to local business and social clubs suggesting breakfast and weekend luncheon activities to fill natural slow periods in your catering/banquet areas.

3. Continue to upgrade catering menu presentations in order to expand the menu presentations and keep your prices competitive with your city or area competition. Offer an impressive catering menu package created for your convention *and* local clients. If you are trying to attract social business, then include menu presentations geared to the social market, not just convention-oriented menu presentations. You should update prices on a regular schedule to keep pace with inflation and market trends, and send these updates to regular and new customers. Add and delete items to refresh existing menu ideas. Utilize portions of the menu package for specific market solicitation (i.e., convention backup groups, incentive travel groups, special local events, etc.).

4. Increase availability of beverage and beverage revenue over your previous year's activity. One way to increase volume of wine sold per function is to suggest four bottles per table over the traditional three. Suggest a wine or champagne toast to start or conclude an affair to increase sales volume. Your hotel should always be prepared to offer a la carte wine/beverage service for events that order limited amounts or none at all. Also, if a hard-liquor reception is not planned, you may suggest aperitifs.

5. Continue the development of creativity, organization, and selling techniques within your catering staff. There should be continued direction and adminis-tration of the catering office by the catering director with specific, effective administration guidelines. There should be increased exposure to developments in the industry through conventions, publications, seminars, and communication within sister and competitive properties. Your entire department needs to keep working on the improvement of sales techniques through seminars, publications, and continued exposure to experts in the industry. There must be an organized solicitation and revised annual listing of catering events on a regular basis.

6. Improve banquet service for all catered events. Expand and upgrade full-time service staff through training, involvement, and stimulation of interest in their jobs and guests. Your hotel needs to be involved in training and policy input

into your local source for additional service personnel. In some markets, this may be your food service and hospitality local union.

7. Maintain your metropolitan area's "Cream of the Annual" business activity. Each year you need to update the annual events and key contracts. A member of your staff should attend the annual affairs that you wish to accommodate the following year but that are not currently being held at your hotel. Special effort must be made to contact and personalize in-house tours and meetings for key decision makers immediately before or after the current year's events.

VII. IDENTIFYING MARKET AREAS

A. Existing Markets

This is a local catering business that is available to you. If a particular piece of business has been booked at another hotel, you need to know *why* it was booked there and *how* it would be possible for you to obtain this event as future business. Proper sales techniques will help you to get these answers.

1. Annual listing.   These are functions that are held on an annual basis during the same time period each year. A master list should be kept and compared monthly with the previous year's list. It should also be updated with functions not held in previous years that you know took place in either your hotel or at other hotels in your city or area. Special emphasis should be given to the solicitation of the accounts that you know book at other hotels. On a monthly basis, this annual listing should be reviewed and solicited. This solicitation should be handled by the director of catering. It should be his or her responsibility to check each file as to the status of that account to date. This annual listing must be updated continually. Also, at least once a year all "banquet" files and "social" files should be purged and updated.

2. General solicitation of existing files.   Methodical solicitation should be made and recorded by Call Reports. Then, at your weekly catering meetings discuss the potential business that exists in all present catering files. These files should be solicited in the course of your normal program of solicitation outlined above. This should be done through continual solicitation, which will be necessary to insure complete coverage of every file, *at least* once a year.

B. New Markets

Your department must constantly attempt to develop new markets in your hotel from the many available sources.

1. Prestigious social functions.   A list should be compiled of all known prestigious social functions, giving you information as to the size, preferred date, and the type of function. This list should be periodically updated and revised to provide the most accurate information available. Due to the desire to book these functions one year in advance and because most clients are very price conscious and "looking for a deal," it is still doubtful that your hotel can afford to overlook this important segment of available business. However, special care needs to be taken in the solicitation of these prestigious social functions, which should be in a continual solicitation program.

2. Follow-up of newspaper leads. Particular attention should be given to the social columns and business sections and other features in the local publications, which might prove advantageous in developing new leads. Daily solicitation must follow on all newspaper clippings and other hotel functions. Outside solicitation should be used on all accounts, new and old, that have been held elsewhere. Phone solicitation is used to determine a thorough and in-depth manner of where definite and potential business exists. This is followed up by a letter or outside call. If you do not have a catering brochure, you should consider developing one that includes room layouts and pictures, along with the various hotel facilities. The catering staff should coordinate all newspaper leads that involve food functions in your city and report their findings directly to the director of catering.

3. General solicitation.

a. *Developing New Business*—Through memberships in local organizations and through the friendships you have established with individuals in various organizations, it should be your intention to *discover* new leads, new organizations, and other potential sources of income. It is important that you do not discount the value of friendships in procuring new business. Each department member should have the project of inviting *at least* one person from a new organization to lunch or dinner *each week*. This is in keeping with your intention of developing new friendships, thereby producing new leads for new business.

b. *Multi-Events*—These include functions that take place in connection with or as part of the overall program for a group staying in your hotel, having meetings or other functions, for any extended period of time. These groups are normally booked by and the programs are coordinated through the sales department.

c. *Dances*—There are groups that request no planned food service but have a desire for beverage service only as well as a dancing prerequisite. These are treated the same as a banquet, incorporating normal seating by a diagram. This type of business has been found to be extremely profitable and is primarily booked during slow periods or within six to eight weeks prior to the scheduled affair. The profit of this type of function is assured by the establishment by using a package plan that includes a bottle of each House scotch and House bourbon; appropriate mixes (3 quarts); potato chips, pretzels, and peanuts on each table; and appropriate room charge, gratuities, and tax on all items included at an approximate price for a table of ten guests. In addition, on all dances, the hotel should require one security guard for each 100 to 200 guests, scheduled one-half hour before the event and until one-half hour following the affair. These charges, of course, should be passed along to your clientele. Generally, this type of business is done only on a cash-in-advance basis.

  d. *Ethnic Groups*—The hotel needs to solicit all communities within the city, as well as encouraging many community groups outside the city to come into the city or vice versa. The functions being booked fall into all categories (i.e., social, annual, dances, charity, fund raising, etc.).

  e. *Charity*—Charities are solicited frequently, prior to and following the event, whether at your or another hotel. Price structure may deter many from utilizing your hotel even though your hotel may meet or surpass their requirements.

  f. *Business and Corporate*—Close contact must be utilized in business accounts since they are sporadic in their bookings. In addition, a closely coordinated relationship should exist between the sales and catering departments, utilizing any Executive Reservation Program and the commercial and industrial sales department efforts.

  g. *Fund Raising*—This covers many categories (e.g., multi-events, charity, social, annual, etc.). Most have higher budgets than charity events and are held at hotels more frequently. These also include political parties. Because of their prestige, every effort should be made to insure that political parties are held at your hotel. Again, all fund-raising functions should be paid well in advance and by certified check.

  h. *General/Social Files*—Periodically review the general/social files to develop what you initially thought to be a one-time function into a productive file of recurring catering business.

  i. *Competition Function Boards*—This includes the solicitation of competition function boards as well as newspaper leads of events held at other hotels.

  j. *Christmas Parties*—This market is practically limitless and is comprised of most of the aforementioned markets.

  4. Other possible market areas.   The following is a somewhat incomplete list of market areas to be considered for solicitation. In each case, *the particular area should be assigned* to an individual in your department, together with clearly specified objectives. Each city should be reviewed to take advantage of any special markets that may be important to that city.

   Professional Clubs
   Banks and Financial Institutions
   Savings and Loan Associations
   Bar or Bas Mitzvahs
   Weddings
   Kosher Business and Jewish Organizations

Sweet 16 Parties

Hospitals

Industry

Radio and TV Stations

Religious and Church Institutions

Tour and Travel

Garden Clubs

Civic Groups

Automobile Shows

Masonic Groups

Travel Agencies and Showings

Social Clubs

Debutante Balls

Embassies and Embassy National Holidays

Colleges (Faculty, Alumni)

Transportation Industry

College Fraternities and Sororities

Airline Functions

City-Based Labor Unions

Political Functions

Sports-Connected Activities

Interline Airline Clubs

High Schools

VIII. MARKET ADVANTAGES

In this section, you should list all the advantages your hotel has over the other hotels in your market such as prestige, location, food quality and presentations, service, reputation, new facilities, elegance.

IX. MARKET DISADVANTAGES

You also need to list your hotel's disadvantages. Some items that are listed as advantages may also appear as disadvantages; for example, location can appear in both lists.

X. MARKETING CALENDAR

This section will help you accomplish the department objectives you have set and will aid in setting up some accountability of those accomplishments. Under each month, briefly list which marketing objectives will be accomplished, the date of completion, and which member of the department has been assigned that task. This marketing calendar needs to be reviewed during the catering meeting *each and every month*.

XI. INNOVATIONS

The entire department needs to brainstorm this section, but here are some examples to get your creative juices flowing:

A. Meet Competitive Prices

Increase business by meeting competitive prices with better selling. You may find it expedient to sell a 6-ounce filet mignon at a lower price in order to meet your competition rather than to lose a party. You can do this and still keep your food costs in line. In addition, by selling specially selected menus at a lower cost, you can offer your customers a better menu at a lower selling price. Consideration should be given to booking food functions during slow periods or at the last minute, allowing lower prices, if necessary, in order not to lose the business. A set of special and confidential printed menus should be prepared by the chef and the director of catering for this purpose.

B. Work Closely with the Chef

Work closely with your chef for better production in costs and sales. The guarantee spread should be only 3%, which should minimize overproduction. In addition, the banquet manager and all charge captains should give the chef an accurate count on all functions *as soon* as the guests are seated. This count should be given to the chef before the main course (based on the guarantee figure) is dished out. This will eliminate dishing out food and wasting food if attendance figures happen to fall below the guarantee.

C. Review Function Space Reservation Book

Establish a monthly meeting with a member of management, the directors of sales, catering, and convention services, as well as the sales and catering staff to review the function space reservation book in order to eliminate dead options and to make sure proper procedures are being followed in connection with reservations in the function book. You should also attempt to get convention programs as quickly as possible. In addition, you should attempt to institute a new program for all convention bookings whereby the entire space can only be held until 5:00 p.m. Functions after 5:00 p.m. in connection with the convention must be programmed when the convention has been made definite. A convention meeting planner may not be certain of his or her many break-out meetings, but generally the person will know which nights there will be receptions and/or dinners. Before the first of each month, a list should be made of "Hold All Space" conventions for the following six- to nine-month period. This meeting should be instituted and carried out throughout the year for better allocation of space and proper management.

D. Review Banquet Menus

Review all present banquet menus and eliminate, if possible, any high-cost menus. Banquet menu prices need to be revised as the market increase demands. Generally, banquet menu prices should be revised once or twice a year.

E. Apply Additional Charges

Get additional revenue whenever possible by applying service charges and passing labor costs along to your customers. Here are some examples:

> "Buffet breakfasts, luncheons or dinners under the minimum requirement will incur an additional $2.00 charge, for each 20 guests under the minimum, added to the per person buffet price."
>
> "All receptions with a minimum of food service will require a server labor charge of $35.00 per server for three (3) hours and $15.00 each hour thereafter. One (1) server is required for each one hundred (100) guests."
>
> "Extra labor charges for breakfast scheduled prior to 7:00 a.m."
>
> "Waiter/waitress service time is a three-hour maximum period, including required setup time. Overtime charges of $15.00 per hour, per waiter/waitress, will be added to the account."
>
> "On all seated meal functions, if 25 or fewer guests are guaranteed, an additional $50.00 (or higher) service charge will be added to the account."

Other additional charges may be applied for the following:

Shuckers

Carvers

Bartenders

Cashiers

Beertenders

Hostesses

Security Guards

Spotlight Operators

House Light Operators

Sound Technicians
Traffic Directors
Parking Attendants
Chefs to carve
Chefs to prepare
Coat Check Attendants
Washroom Attendants

F. Duplicate Some Items

Before selling a function for a given date, every member of the catering department should check the menu file and attempt to sell the same items that are already being prepared for that day. Granted, the same menu cannot be completely duplicated, but the selection of the same appetizer, vegetables, and/or dessert would help to control production costs. In many cases, this is not possible, but it is up to the catering staff to make every endeavor to see that a menu is duplicated whenever possible.

G. Know Your Food Costs

Be aware of food costs month by month, so that the expensive items can be avoided during certain periods (e.g., serve carrots instead of tomatoes when tomato prices are up, etc.).

H. Promote Wine Sales

To increase your banquet revenue, a new program for wine sales should be established. Your staff should recommend wine with all food functions, mainly dinners, and approach the guest by recommending wine to enhance his or her dinner and to make it more successful. By serving three bottles of wine for a table of 10 guests, the selling price of the wine could be as low as $5.40 per person, plus gratuities and taxes, if the house wine sells for $18.00 per bottle. Based on experience, if a customer is told the cost on a per-person basis, he or she is more receptive.

I. Show Evidence of Success

A letter book of Bouquets (thank-you letters) should be kept in the reception area of the sales and catering offices. These books should be brought up to date frequently since this is an extremely fine sales tool. This should be maintained directly by the director of catering.

J. Break Down Menus

Preprinted menus designed to increase productivity should be utilized to increase sales. These menu breakdowns limit the variety of items offered. Also, they should be designed in such a manner that they do not read like a telephone book. Prices should be printed on a separate price page to allow the catering salesperson to "sell up."

K. Determine Minimum Guarantees

Establish suggested minimum guarantees (attendance and/or dollar volume) for the major function space designed to maximize the use of all facilities and reduce the percentage of overhead expenses. In turn, a greater revenue could be obtained from each facility.

L. Move the Function to a Smaller Room

In all contracts, a paragraph should be devoted to giving the hotel the permission to move any group that falls below the attendance requirements that were established at the time of booking to a smaller room. This allows you to sell the larger facilities to another group. Of course, this move should be done at the *earliest detection* of a decrease in group size.

M. Include the Chef

A close relationship needs to be established between the chef and the catering sales staff, utilizing the chef's experience and knowledge for all social functions or special parties. The chef, on frequent occasions, should sit in on customer meetings to discuss menu and food preparation. This is an extremely helpful tool in selling. It makes the customer feel that the chef is personally involved in his or her function.

N. Improve Communications

The banquet manager's office should incorporate a system for major functions in which the waiter or waitress obtains a roast slip (a slip that indicates a beef entree pickup) from the captain in charge to obtain the entrees from the chefs/stewards staff. In addition, the captain's count is made prior to the entree service and given to the chef. This aids in less overproduction, which lowers the overall food cost. The three-way check system—food and beverage control's count, the chef's count, and banquet manager's count—has proven to be a most successful idea.

O. Decrease Your No-Show Ratio

To eliminate overproduction, the difference between the guarantee figure and set-up figure should be reduced to 3 percent. This should prove to increase covers and also reduce food costs because of the number of no-shows present at any large function.

P. Review Portion Costs

Monthly reports should be done by the food and beverage controller or executive chef, listing the portion cost on items most frequently served. This allows the catering staff to know at all times what the cost of a new menu is prior to the sale.

Q. Sell Wine a la Carte

As an incentive for the customer to purchase wine, you should have cards listing several different wines at a feasible selling price. When desired, you can place these cards on all dinner tables prior to the guests' seating, especially at large functions. You will be selling the wines on an a la carte basis, and, in most cases, you will generate additional beverage dollars.

XII. ADVERTISING

Special attention should be given to this section. Your advertising needs to convey excitement, elegance, and your message to your area's competitive market. Care should be taken to insure that advertising dollars are spent where they will most effectively reach the desired market. Trade-outs and direct mail promotions should also be considered.

XIII. CATERING STAFF MARKET SOLICITATION RESPONSIBILITIES

In this final section, the solicitation responsibilities of each member of the catering staff should be listed.

CHAPTER 7

Convention Food and Beverage Functions

"Know thy property!" These words should hang on the wall of every hotel executive who wants to build a successful convention business. The axiom provides a realistic base from which to assess the size and complexity of the conventions the hotel can serve. It eliminates the wasted time and cost of pursuing convention business that is not compatible with the facility. And it forms the backbone of one of the most valuable services you can give a potential buyer—accurate information.

Even before working with a convention bureau and related sources on developing a prospect list, the immediate knowledge of your property should be used to develop an information package for the buyer. This should include:

1. A detailed summary of the types of accommodations available in all ranges
2. A detailed description of each function room, with accurate scale drawings showing ceiling heights, post locations, dividers, access—a "total" floor plan showing locations of all public rooms, corridors, service areas, etc.
3. A list of the technical equipment available for meeting support
4. An accurate outline of the support the convention services department can give the meeting planner
5. Special features that make the property unique or highly appealing
6. A complete description of the property's restaurants, entertainment, and sports facilities

7. A list of the types of service and shops available on the premises

This is a high-powered arsenal in the drive to develop meeting business.

After talking to and selling the meeting planner on your property, the convention bureau representative should know what tentative dates have been blocked. Naturally, when the definite bookings come through, the convention bureau should be notified immediately.

A BIT OF HISTORY

The hotel executive must be familiar with the past convention history of any organization he or she is dealing with and should double-check early in the game to make sure that adequate rooms, meeting and exhibit space, equipment, and services that the organization will need can be provided.

A full-scale outline should be worked out with the meeting planner so that both people know exactly how many rooms can be made available. Each type of accommodation should be specified, including the number of single rooms, doubles, twins, suites, and hospitality rooms.

Room rates should be clarified and, to the best of your knowledge, the period over which these rates will apply should be stated. If the meeting planner is not tied to a specific time of the week, month, or year, it should be pointed out if there are any rate advantages of off-season or other nonpeak periods.

If the hotel has a specific or negotiable policy about complimentary rooms, it should be spelled out for the meeting planner. The hotel planner may be depending on V.I.P. accommodations that cannot be provided by the hotel. If so, this should be brought out early in the planning stages.

FUNCTION OBJECTIVES

With the matter of accommodations completely clear, function space should be outlined with the meeting planner. This can be done by listings and diagrams of meeting rooms and exhibit areas to define what the meeting planner will need. If the convention set-up will involve special charges, the meeting planner should be informed at this time.

This is also an opportunity to list other charges that will affect the convention. Any special facilities, equipment, or services that will involve a charge should be explained. The meeting planner should also be told what cannot be provided in the hotel, and an outside source should be mutually agreed on for these services that will be required for a smooth-functioning convention.

If the property is bound by any special rules or regulations regarding licenses, taxes, beverage control, or union contract agreements, the meeting planner should be informed.

WHO HANDLES WHAT? _____

As the meeting planner provides the hotel executive with an authorization sheet that lists the names, addresses, phone numbers, and responsibilities of all persons from the organization with whom the planner expects to deal, the hotel executive should do the same. He or she should give the meeting planner the same information for the hotel staff, along with an outline of the methods and procedures that will be used in servicing that convention.

DOWN TO DETAILS _____

Now that all the preliminary groundwork has been covered, a meeting with the meeting planner should be arranged so a master worksheet can be prepared and reviewed. This should be a detailed function-by-function work list which includes:

- Time and place of all convention functions:
    Meetings
    Food functions
    Exhibits
    Other activities
- Detailed specifications:
    Room set-up
    Type of setting
    Facilities
    Equipment
    Services
    Other

Something Extra

Since the hotel executive knows the property inside and out and has seen what other conventions have achieved there, he or she may maintain a file on outstanding programs that can be passed on to meeting planners if they are stuck for an idea.

FOOD AND BEVERAGE FUNCTIONS _____

Meal functions provide more than food at conventions. As sponsored social events, they are as important as any item on the program. These functions fall into many different categories: banquets, luncheons, breakfasts, cocktail parties, hospitality suites, coffee breaks. But no matter what the function, the convention official is the host.

Type, size, and requirements of functions will determine function room assignment. If the room that is used is oversized, it should be screened off attractively to accommodate the group, if possible. The meeting planner should keep a check on ticket sales to make sure that attendance projections are still on target. Both the hotel executive and meeting planner should be prepared to make necessary adjustments. Guarantees should be checked constantly.

Setting Objectives for Food Service

The convention official or host can be assured of maximum help from the hotel if he or she explains the personality of the group and the convention theme to the catering executive. In addition, he or she should outline the goal of *each function* so that the hotel staff can suggest appropriate set-up and decor.

Once the function planner and hotel executive have this objective clearly in mind, then they can determine *together* the style, location, and menu for the function.

The function planner should let the catering executive and, in some cases, the chef assist in choosing items on each menu. The hotel staff is best able to tell the function planner which foods can be prepared with most success in their facility for large groups. This should include the serving time-table and which substitutions can be made in order to keep the price down.

It is sometimes a good idea to let the hotel serve its specialty. After all, the facility is well known for the dish and may have built a reputation on it. Attendees may be disappointed if the house specialty is Colorado Mountain Trout and you serve them London Broil.

Avoid too many sauces and gravies; many conventioneers are diet conscious. If you want to add some drama to the meal, do it with the dessert. This way, dieting guests can forego the dessert if they desire, while others will enjoy the treat. The meeting planner should consider suggestions of the catering executive who is an expert in arranging group functions.

Determine if the food is to be served French style or by banquet plate service.

For breakfast, one might consider an attractive buffet. This saves serving time and allows for different breakfast habits. In addition, the meal is not delayed by late risers.

Luncheons, on the other hand, may be buffet or table service. However, with a buffet, the convention planner must pay for labor that no one sees. Buffets cost top dollar because of the need of overproduction of food and because most guests will eat more. The hotel executive should provide comparable buffet and sit-down luncheon prices.

Finally, check to avoid meal duplication. With hundreds of meals to prepare for different guests, the catering executive may not notice that a convention group is scheduled for a similar item for two or more functions during a long convention stay.

In determining the objectives for food service, first ask what the group wishes to accomplish as a result of the meal. Is it just a vehicle for getting people together?

Is it a showcase at which an important announcement will be made or a new service revealed? Will the meal be used to relax people after a hard day in the meeting room, or gear them up for a big social evening? Or is it one or more of the following?

1. Provide Nourishment Only

2. Preparation for Following Event

3. Create a Mood
   a. Conviviality
   b. Sophistication
   c. Celebration
   d. Casualness
   e. Seriousness

4. Bridge a Gap
   a. Members/Suppliers
   b. New Members/Established Members
   c. Manufacturers/Retailers

5. Fill Time

6. Entertain

7. Promote Fellowship

8. Eating Ease

9. Vehicle to Get People Together

10. Showcase for Important Announcement

11. Relax People After a Hard Day

12. Gear People Up for a Big Event

13. Keep Attendees from Wandering

14. Assure Attendance at Early Morning Session

15. Develop Spirit of Convention

CONSTRAINTS ON MENU PLANNING

1. Financial Condition of Association

2. Time on Program

3. Budget

4. Room Size

5. Tone Immediately Preceding and Following Events

6. Uncertain Guarantees

7. Customs of the Area

8. Physical Plant

9. Locale and Type of Food Supply

10. Composition of Audience

CONSIDERATIONS IN CHOOSING FACILITY

1. Objective for Food Service
2. Whether Environment Will Enhance Objective
3. Emotional Impact
4. Inspiration
5. Spirit
6. Intimacy
7. Efficiency of Operation
8. Professional Staff
9. Creativity
10. Type of Sites

   A. Hotel
     (1) Show Room
     (2) Ballroom
     (3) Restaurant
     (4) Lobby
     (5) Series of Rooms—Movable Feast
     (6) Exhibit Area
     (7) Pool
     (8) Garden

   B. Public Facilities
     (1) Civic Center
     (2) Amphitheater
     (3) Dinner Theatre
     (4) Park
     (5) Museum
     (6) Historic Buildings
     (7) Malls
     (8) Exposition Centers
     (9) Entertainment Parks
     (10) Government Buildings
     (11) Ball Park
     (12) Armories
     (13) Zoo
     (14) Factory
     (15) Warehouse
     (16) Attractions

   C. Other
     (1) Boats or Ships
     (2) Houses of Local Residents
     (3) Desert
     (4) Beach
     (5) Private Clubs
     (6) Tents

PROVIDING PROPER NUTRITION _____

Diet. A proper diet is important to maintain good physical and mental health and to supply needed energy. Therefore, it must contain adequate amounts of protein, fats, carbohydrates, minerals, salts, vitamins, and water.

Balanced Diet. Carbohydrates (sugars and starches) furnish energy to the body and contribute somewhat to the growth of cells. Fats also provide energy, aid in the conservation of body heat, and constitute food reserves (fried foods, butter, rich pastries, sauces, etc.). Proteins supply an additional source of energy, but are used mainly in the growth and repair of body tissues, which are constantly being broken down. Vitamins, minerals, and salts are not energy producers, but are essential to the proper functioning of the body.

Digestion. Cellulose or bulk in foods such as whole-grain cereals, fruits, and vegetables stimulate the movement of the intestinal muscles and thus aid in the removal of waste matter. Foods that are attractively prepared and carefully seasoned will be more readily digested. The sight and odor of food help to stimulate the flow of digestive juices. Pleasant surroundings and freedom from worry, fatigue, or emotional disturbance are also important to proper digestion.

RULES FOR PROVIDING PROPER NUTRITION AND AIDING DIGESTION DURING GROUP MEALS

1. Include meat or a protein substitute, two vegetables, fresh fruits, and whole-wheat or enriched bread at all lunches or dinners.
2. Do not serve fried foods, especially those dipped in a batter or rolled in flour.
3. Limit crusted pastries or other foods enclosed in crusts.
4. Do not serve meats with a sauce or gravy that includes wine if the meal is followed by a program. Limit all sauces.
5. Check to avoid meal duplication. This is especially important when food events are sponsored.
6. If attendees are required to be attentive for more than six hours, provide quick-energy food (fresh fruit, cookies, candy) at the afternoon break.
7. Make sure hotel dining facilities are open when meals will be required and there are not sponsored events.
8. Inform hotel in advance of room service requirements.

GEAR FOOD PREPARATION AND STYLE TO FACILITY

1. Type Service
   a. French
   b. Plated

c. Buffet
d. Butler or Russian
2. Availability of Food
3. Familiarity with Preparation

HOSPITALITY SUITES

Hospitality suites are best when they are small enough for intimacy. They should be away from the main flow of hotel traffic so that uninvited persons are not tempted to join the convention guests.

Whenever possible, a room separate from the dining area should be arranged for cocktail parties. It is easier to break up a cocktail party when guests must move to some other room for dinner.

Plan to have coffee breaks in a room other than the meeting room whenever possible. Setting up coffee breaks in the meeting room while in session can distract attention. If coffee must be served in the meeting room, make sure it is wheeled in at an appointed coffee time on preset rolling buffets.

The meeting planner should ask for scaled drawings of meal functions when there is assigned seating. Be sure that these drawings contain dimensions of the room and all of its facilities. All obstructions, exits, and restrooms should be clearly marked. If no such drawings are available, the meeting planner should personally make one.

SPACE IS IMPORTANT

Do not try to squeeze too many people at a table. Each person should have about two feet of eating room. Head tables need at least two feet of space per person plus an additional three feet for a podium. Leave room between your tables for comfortable sitting.

Size and shape of tables play an important role in room decoration. Know what size centerpiece can be used without blocking the view or encroaching on the meal.

If it is a reserve-seating function, the meeting planner should provide a diagram listing the number of tables. The diagram should show any changes from the standard number of place settings per table. Both the hotel executive and the meeting planner should check as soon as the set-up is complete to make sure that it is correct. If the function is to be held outside of the hotel, the meeting planner should also give the person responsible for this function a diagram.

When a meal function is set out-of-doors, plan an emergency inside facility in case of inclement weather. Prepare both an indoor and outdoor seating diagram. Try to keep table numbers in the same relative locations.

Facilities of your meal function room can make a big difference in entertainment and speakers. Find out if there is a temporary or permanent stage. Ask about audio-visual facilities, including microphones, projectors, screens, and sound.

SPECIAL ENTERTAINMENT NEEDS ────────────────

Arrange for all staging, lighting, and props required by the entertainers. If the hotel cannot provide all equipment or services that a meeting planner needs for the speakers or entertainers, the meeting planner should ask for a list of reliable outside agencies who can furnish such needs. The meeting planner should check for any problems with use of these outside facilities in the hotel. Generally, the hotel has an outside source that they will recommend for this purpose. Whenever possible, the meeting planner should use the recommended source. On occasion, some staging elements are included in the price of the banquet room, such as microphones, with additional microphones at an additional charge. Be sure to advise the meeting planner about these "extras."

It is best to reserve a room where the meeting planner can meet with head table guests before the meal function. A room should be provided for this purpose near the meal function room. To eliminate confusion, the lineup at the head table, in order of seating, is accomplished in this smaller reception area. Place cards are placed on the chairs which are in the same configuration as that in the larger function room.

For entertainers, you might need to reserve a dressing room with mirrors, hangers, and a restroom. In addition, ask the meeting planner if a rehearsal room with a piano is required.

Let the past be the guide in determining facilities and requirements for the various functions. Be aware of any traffic or parking problems that may arise and be ready with alternative suggestions. Also check on past meal functions of any organization and similar organizations for hints on how to solve problems or make the meal more interesting. Past history plays an important part.

The meeting planner should be advised about hotel and local rules, regulations, licenses, policies, and practices. Local alcoholic beverage laws can affect days and hours during which beverages may be served. Generally, all food and beverages must be provided by the hotel. In some cases, with the approval of management, the hotel may charge a corkage (a tax on liquor brought into the hotel) since liquor is a service of the facility which includes many cost factors to the hotel. Some hotels do not permit liquor to be brought into the hotel under any circumstances.

Various services are taxed locally. Know what these services are and how they add to the convention cost. Unions are contracted for special services. A mistake in union practices can cost you a convention. Know what unions do, their hours, and their pay.

GRATUITIES ────────────────

Gratuities vary from hotel to hotel, but they are always present. The size of the gratuities depends on the type of hotel, the services rendered, and the city of the convention. Generally, gratuities are automatically added to the bill. In addition, many times the meeting planner will provide additional gratuities to individuals who have performed above and beyond the call of duty. Some hotels have tipping guidelines to help the meeting planner decide on who should receive these special and additional gratuities.

It is the duty of the hotel executive to arrange for and determine the cost of all facilities, services, and equipment required for the meal function. If the food program is planned many months in advance, the spiraling costs of food and labor should be considered. Allow a cushion of 6 to 10 percent to cover increased cost.

BASIS FOR PAYMENT

Determine, well in advance, if the meeting planner will be charged for the meal functions by assigned guarantee, by collected tickets, or by the quantity served by the hotel.

If the meal function is included in the price of registration, the meeting planner should be certain that there are enough seats for everyone. The catering executive should be sure to advise the meeting planner what the final cut-off date is for guaranteed number of meals or covers.

If there are meal tickets, the meeting planner and the catering executive should discuss the arrangements for collecting them. After the function the hotel should return the tickets or ticket stubs (after the hotel has used them for its bookkeeping purposes) to the meeting planner. The planner will want the tickets for his or her own control system. The meeting planner should also have a backup procedure for guests without tickets. If table numbers are assigned on tickets, arrange that tickets are honored only at the proper table number. If a registrant wishes to move from his or her assigned table, that person should be referred to the meeting planner or the planner's authorized representative. The situation should not be resolved by the catering executive.

All attendees should be informed how seating reservations will be conducted. The meeting planner should prepare charts and display them if there is assigned seating. If attendees choose their seats, do not have V.I.P. tables listed on the charts. Attendees will be annoyed that the "best tables" are reserved before they can make a choice.

If a reserved-seat function is transferred from one location to another after seats have been reserved, you must take into consideration changes for registrants and room set-up. Registrants should be notified of the change by both verbal announcement and written notice. Directional signs should be posted with notice of the change throughout the hotel.

According to the size and shape of the room(s), head table, stage, orchestra, and dance floor space will need modification. Try to retain relative locations of special registrants for guest tables, tables with more than standard numbers of settings, party groups occupying more than one table, and preferred locations.

Prepare charts that show new locations of table numbers and place them in a noticeable area in the reception area. The hotel should have ushers on hand to direct registrants to assigned tables.

WHAT TYPE BEVERAGE SERVICE?

Beverage services vary from hotel to hotel. It is best to determine the basis of charge for beverage service and what the services include at social functions, hospitality suites, and through room service.

For large functions, such as cocktail parties or hospitality-suite functions, there are three principal beverage services: by the bottle, by the drink, and a flat rate price by the person.

In some hotels, flat bottle rates include waiters and waitresses, bartenders, and service. In others, it covers only the cost of liquor. In either case, you pay extra for hors d'oeuvres and mixers.

When a client buys by the drink, he or she pays only for drinks consumed by the guests. Hotels will have a fixed price for any drink; the convention is billed later. Generally, a per-drink price includes service and mixers, but bartenders are extra. The meeting planner should decide with the catering executive as to the size of each drink and the amount of liquor in each drink.

Drinks "by the person" (or an all-inclusive reception) means that the meeting planner and the hotel agree on a flat price for each guest depending on the length of the function. The rate may or may not include food, gratuities, and taxes.

If the bar is a cash bar, be sure attendees know in advance. Also, the meeting planner should inform the attendees of hotel policy about bringing food and beverage into the hotel.

Relying on previous experience when possible, the meeting planner should provide the hotel executive with the estimated volume of room service. This will help with quick service.

Kosher Catering

KOSHER VERSUS KOSHER-STYLE _____

It is inevitable that everyone engaged in food-service operations will ultimately be confronted with the terms *kosher* and *kosher-style*. The word *kosher* means "fit or proper" and, when applied to foods, identifies those foods that *observant* Jews will eat. To the observant Jews, eating is a discipline of religion and a regulatory principle in their everyday life. Symbolically, the family table becomes an altar—a means of serving God and a medium for bringing God into one's daily life. The nucleus of all these regulations is found in the Old Testament, mostly in Leviticus. These Written Laws, together with the Oral Laws, carried down through the centuries, have developed into a compendium known as the Dietary Laws.

The term, *kosher style,* when applied to foods, is obviously an attempt to mislead and misrepresent. It is only by certain physical identifications, pre-preparation, preparation, and service—and the total fulfillment of each admonishment, regulation, and tradition—that determines whether a food is or could be kosher. The requirements are many and rigid. Many foods must even carry certification by ordained rabbis before they will be considered for use by the observant Jews.

Foods may appear and taste like kosher foods but these similarities do not justify their being called kosher; they could possibly be called "Jewish-type" foods but emphatically *not* kosher foods!

Food processors who advertise or imply that food is kosher when it isn't or who sell nonkosher products as kosher products may, in many states, be subject to court action.

KOSHER: ITS MEANINGS AND RITUALS

Q. What is the meaning of *kosher?*

A. *Kosher* is a term applied to all foods that observant Jews will eat or use that meet the specifications and requirements of the Dietary Laws.

Q. What are the Dietary Laws?

A. These are the laws as set forth in the Bible (Old Testament) and as elaborated upon by the rabbis and scholars (in their commentaries on the Bible).

Q. How can we know which animals, fish, or poultry the Jews are allowed to eat?

A. In animals, Jews may eat only those animals that have split hooves *and chew the cud.* Pigs have split hooves but do not chew their cud, hence Jews are not supposed to eat pork. Specifically, those animals that Jews may eat are cattle, sheep, goats, and deer.

Q. May Jews eat all fish?

A. No. Jews may eat only those fish that swim and that have both scales and fins.

Q. May Jews eat lobster, shrimp, clams, etc.?

A. No. Shellfish and mollusks are forbidden.

Q. May Jews eat all poultry or birds?

A. No. They may eat only domestic birds such as chicken, ducks, geese, turkeys, and Cornish hens. They may not eat birds of prey or scavengers, or birds that are used in the "hunt" (wild birds sought after by the hunters).

Q. If the Jews are permitted to eat only certain fish and certain meats, then may they eat only certain fruits and vegetables?

A. There is no prohibition against anything that grows on the land. All fruits, vegetables, and edible grasses are permitted.

Q. What are the Rituals in Preparation?

A. The Rituals in Preparation relate basically to the slaughter of animals and poultry and how they must be treated after slaughter before being prepared for eating.

Q. Is the method of slaughter different from standard procedures?

A. Yes. This slaughter is according to Ritual. The Torah forbids the infliction of useless pain on any living being. Animals and fowl may be slaughtered only by a highly trained and supervised man called a *shoket,* who must use a razor-keen, blemish-free knife of certain proportions. The jugular vein of the animal must be cut in an area below the larynx. The trachea, esophagus, carotid arteries, and pneumogastric and sympathetic nerves are severed, preventing blood from reaching the brain and cutting off the bodily centers of pain.

Q. Is this the end of the ritual?

A. No. The shoket then carefully examines all the vital organs to make certain that the animal is free of any disease and that the animal shows no sign of wounds or of having any part of it torn from attack of dogs or wild animals. He rejects the entire animal if it does not come up to the specifications. The shoket then attaches stamps and tags to various parts of the forequarters, showing the date and hour of slaughter, the city, and the name of the shoket.

Q. Why is all this information so essential and why only to the forequarters?

Q. Jews may not eat meat or poultry unless it is first "kashered," and this must be done within 72 hours after slaughter. This is the reason the hour and date are stamped on the meat. The forequarters are tagged because it is forbidden to use the hindquarters. (The hindquarters may be used only if all the veins and certain textured fat is first removed. This process is too expensive to make it commercially feasible.)

Q. What is meant by *kashered*?

A. This is the term applied to all acceptably slaughtered meat and poultry. Before the meat can be used it must first be soaked in cold water for one-half hour, in vessels kept specifically for this purpose. The meat is then rinsed with cold water, sprinkled evenly with coarse salt (or so-called kosher salt), and placed upon a grooved board, so as to allow the blood to flow off. The meat must then remain on the board for one hour and then it is washed off. It is then ready for use. (Meat may not be frozen for future use unless it is first kashered.)

Q. Are there any exceptions or exemptions to this rule?

A. Yes. Meat used for broiling does not need to be kashered (if it is used within 72 hours). Livers need not be kashered by the soaking and salting ritual; they may be frozen for future use. When ready to be processed, livers must be completely thawed, sliced, salted, broiled, and then washed off and used for whatever purpose desired.

A. Are there any other regulations for kosher foods?

A. Yes. All meat and meat products may not be cooked with any dairy products or derivatives. (For example, food dishes such as chicken á la king or creamed chipped beef may not be eaten.) Nor may any dairy foods be served at a meal in which meat is used (such as butter with steak, etc.). The pots in which meats have been cooked and the dishes in which they have been served may only be used for meat products, and the same is true of pots and dishes used for dairy food preparation and service. Glassware is interchangeable and may be used for either meat or dairy.

Q. Does fish have to be kashered?

A. No. The fish may be used in its entirety and requires no salting after cleaning. Fish dishes may be combined with dairy foods but must *not* be combined with meat dishes.

Q. Do vegetables require special handling or rituals?

A. Vegetables and fruits may be combined with either dairy or meat dishes. If the vegetables are to be used with meat dishes then they must be cooked in pots used for meat service, and if vegetables are to be served with dairy dishes then they must be cooked in pots used for dairy service. All fruits, vegetables (including vegetable oils), cereals and derivatives, and eggs are called *parve*.

Q. What is meant by *parve*?

A. *Parve* is a term applied to all or any foods that do not contain meat products or derivatives, and to any foods that do not contain any dairy products or derivatives. Parve really means *neutral*—a product that can be used by itself or combined with meat or dairy dishes with complete impunity. Anything that grows or any derivative thereof (e.g., peanut butter, cocoa, applesauce, homogenized or liquid vegetable oils, maple syrup, coffee, tea, etc.) is classified as parve.

Q. There are "imitation" dairy products on the market such as sour cream, coffee whiteners, margarines, imitation bacon, and the like. How may they be classified?

A. Any product that is purely chemical or vegetable in origin, and that does not contain even the slightest amount of either milk or meat products, is considered parve.

Q. Must I check all the ingredients of manufactured products to see if they are kosher or not?

A. Yes. There is also an easy way to determine the classification of the product: check the label. Many products will have a circled *U* imprinted in a conspicuous spot. This means that the product has been investigated by the Union of Orthodox congregations and is certified kosher for use. Alongside this may either be the word *parve* or the letter *P* or the letter *M* which means *milchig* (or dairy foods). If the letter *F* is on the label it means *flaishig* (containing meat or meat products).

Q. Is there any term that is used to denote forbidden foods?

A. Yes. The word *trefe* encompasses all forbidden foods.

Q. Are there any special rules that must be observed when cooking either meat or dairy foods?

A. The important thing to remember is that meat and dairy products must not be cooked in the same oven at the same time. If surface cooking is employed, then pots with meat or dairy dishes may not be so close to each other that the vapors of one may enter the pots of the other.

Q. Do these rules apply all through the year or are there any special times in which they may be relaxed or modified?

A. These rules are never relaxed; they become more rigid or stringent during the one week (eight days) of Passover. (The rules for Passover will be covered later.)

PROMOTING KOSHER CATERING ON YOUR PREMISES

Many hotel managers, particularly in the metropolitan areas of Boston, New York, Miami, Washington, D.C., and Atlanta, find it extremely profitable to make their dining facilities available for kosher functions on occasional or permanent basis. In addition to the basic rental charges, the potential income to be derived from the ensuing additional room rentals, coffee shop and grille room sales, and lobby shop sales add substantially to the dollar-volume income and increased net earnings.

The previous paragraph states that the operators "make their dining facilities available" for kosher functions. Because of the many rigid, complex, and mandated specifications that determine or identify kosher food service, an individual (Jew or Gentile) not thoroughly knowledgeable would not be recognized by local Rabbinic authority. Without this sanction, patronage by certain segments of the Jewish community would be withheld.

If any part of a celebration involves the participation of an Orthodox or Conservative rabbi, then any meal that is to be an integral part of that celebration *must* be kosher. This will be an explicit condition stipulated by the rabbis.

In an ambience where the majority of meals served are not kosher, then the project of converting the premises to make them acceptable—even temporarily—for kosher procedures requires a cleaning that must be so thorough, so inflexible, and so uncompromising that many operators welcome kosher caterers for this basic reason alone. (Of course, the accepted kosher caterer's service and standards must be at least equal to those of the owner/operator.)

All stoves, ranges, and other cooking areas must be meticulously scrubbed and the cleaning must then be finalized by the application of live flame from a propane torch. (This is from the ancient practice and realization that fire is the most effective cleaner. It is continued for its symbolism rather than for its effectiveness as a cleaning tool.) Some rabbis may require coming into direct and immediate contact with the surfaces that have been used for cooking nonkosher foods. This is done when they feel that insufficient time has been allotted for cleaning or that certain areas may have apertures where nonacceptable foods may be trapped.

Any areas that are not cleaned, even if they are not to be used, must be covered with paper, cloths, plastic, or foil. Added to the above are the precautions that must be taken in the actual identification and preparation of foods to qualify them as "fit and proper" in their respective categories so that they conform with the Torah-mandated and/or Rabbinic edicts that make up the Dietary Laws.

To avoid so much responsibility, Gentile operators allow recognized and prestigious kosher caterers to lease or subcontract their prep and dining facilities. Financial arrangements vary with each establishment and involve numerous factors. Convenience of location, ambience, special facilities, size, parking, and an impressive local (and national) reputation are all factors that determine the charges.

The physical area of the dining room, including the reception facility if needed, will include all of the dining room furniture such as tables, chairs, platforms, lecterns, amplification, lighting, and/or display materials. All are exempt from ritualistic preparation. Included with the package, of course, is the kitchen use for the caterer with specially designated prepared areas for freezing, refrigeration, pre-preparation, preparation, and service.

The kosher caterer *must supply all of his or her own* dishes, silverware, glassware, accoutrements, and linens. Once the kitchen has been cleansed according to the prescribed ritual, then, and only then, may the caterer set up his or her own pots, pans, service equipment, and work tools. The intermixing of the on-premises non-kosher equipment is strictly prohibited and could result in the abrogation of the caterer's privileges in the religious Jewish community.

The caterer may use the on-premises sinks and mechanical dishwashing machine if they have been first cleaned to the prescription and satisfaction of the deputized supervisor (called *mashgiach*). This person, who must be Jewish and knowledgeable in all of the requirements, is the representative of the Jewish community or the involved rabbi. He oversees the entire preparation and is responsible for the entire affair being in conformity with the pertaining Dietary Laws. He is also the arbiter of any immediate questions regarding impropriety or breach of religious law. (For want of a better metaphor, he is the "head umpire" and his decisions can only be argued before "the commissioner," who is the involved rabbi.)

Dishwashing machines may be converted for kosher use by the following procedures:

1. Clean the machine thoroughly inside and outside (particularly the feed and exit tables), using water hotter than 125 degrees F.

2. Fill the machine with hot water and detergent and allow to go through one complete cycle (without dishracks).

3. Empty the machine and wash thoroughly again; set up with detergent and hot water and it is ready for use. (Note: Soaps containing animal fats may *never* be used. Soaps with vegetable oils or complete chemical bases are permissible at all times.)

4. Dishracks must be supplied by the kosher caterer and must be used exclusively for kosher dishes. (The caterer must have two separate sets of racks—one for dairy products and one for meat products.)

The bar service remains the dominion of the on-premises licensee and is usually handled in the same manner as it would be for other banquet business—cash bar, limited drinks, bottle or flat rate, corkage, and so on. Many state Alcoholic Beverage Control Boards do not allow a temporary license transfer nor do they have one-day special permits for this type of occasion.

All liquor distilled from grain, fruits, or vegetables are kosher and require no special handling to make them ritually acceptable, except at and for Passover service. At that time all liquor derived from grains and cereals is strictly prohibited. Only those beverages that are specially prepared and specifically labeled "Kosher for Passover" and signed by recognized authority may be used.

The public service of wine, whether still or sparkling, can present some problems. Not all wines, whether home or commercially produced, may be used. From the time the grapes are first gathered and put through the progressive steps necessary to result in the end product of wine, total monitoring by rabbis or mashgiachs must be evidenced. Approved wines will then carry signatures of authenticity. Certain types of wines may not be poured or served tableside by Gentiles or by Jews who are not true Sabbath observers!

This rule is more often invoked by Orthodox rabbis than by their counterparts in the Conservative movement. The dictum of each supervising mashgiach should be sought. Because of the complexity of rules involved in wine handling, it is suggested that the entire wine service should become the responsibility of the subcontracting kosher caterer.

Any byproduct of grapes is subject to Rabbinical scrutiny and decision. Grape juice and grape concentrates used in the flavoring and coloring of candies, soda, and baked goods, and also grape concentrate used as a sweetener in canned fruits instead of sugar (because it is cheaper) could be nonkosher. This is one of the reasons why observant Jews will purchase only manufactured food products that carry a kosher seal of approval.

It should also be noted that kosher public functions are seldom held in rented facilities during the eight days of Passover. The normal preparation of facilities that are required during the rest of the year are negated in favor of a cleaning program that is almost obsessive in its demands. Not all foods are permitted during this period and what is permitted must be prepared to unalterable specs! Certain dishes and serviceware must be used and retained exclusively for Passover use. The extra investment required to purchase such equipment (and to store it for a year) plus the higher cost of Passover foods could make a public meal function outrageously expensive.

Outside Kosher Caterers

All kosher functions handled by outside caterers in your hotel must, of course, be subject to the availability of space *as determined by you*. Since all functions booked in your hotel are your responsibility, your reputation and image in the community are your primary concerns. Therefore, your hotel catering staff should book, contract for, and service all functions. The hotel would bill the customer directly, and the caterer would bill you for his or her food at a predetermined price. This is the only way you would have complete control of all functions taking place in your hotel.

A straight rental arrangement (or a variation of this) is usually negotiated with the caterer, provided the above criteria are met. In any case, since the beverage license is in your name, the hotel should always handle beverage sales and service. In order to protect the facilities of your hotel, your personnel should sell, supervise, and service all functions.

To avoid pilferage and mishandling of equipment you should have a concrete system of control for all equipment and merchandise entering or leaving your hotel. A member of the security department or steward's department should be assigned to check *all* equipment and advance notice should be required for arrival and departure time by the caterer. A checklist should be established as equipment arrives in your hotel. This checklist should be reviewed when the caterer's equipment leaves your hotel and signed by the persons designed to control this.

It is advantageous to make a periodic study of the profitability of your kosher business, taking into consideration the investment by your hotel (dishes, utensils, special kitchen equipment, etc.), the difference in purchase costs for kosher foods (where you do your own kosher catering), the cost of Rabbinical supervision, comparison of selling price of your kosher functions and nonkosher functions, and so on, in order to be certain you are not filling your books with nonprofitable functions. Just as in nonkosher functions, you must be aware of bottom-line profits when all costs have been calculated. Therefore, a profit and loss record should be kept on each kosher function, showing food costs, labor costs (including benefits), beverage costs, controllables, and the like. An annual list of kosher business should be compiled by the director of catering and reviewed with the director of food and beverage.

PASSOVER FOODS AND UTENSILS REGULATIONS

Passover commemorates the deliverance of the Israelites from slavery in Egypt as told in the book of Exodus. It is an eight-day holiday calendared about the same time as Easter. The first two nights are celebrated with the family in an elaborate feast, called the seder, in which the story of the Exodus is read from the Haggadah, with ritual song and food.

The word *seder* in Hebrew means *order* and refers to the traditional order of the Passover ceremony. The following symbolic foods are placed at the head of the table: three whole matzos on a dish covered with a napkin, a roasted egg, a roasted meatbone, charoses, bitter herbs, a dish of salt water, and a vegetable to be dipped in salt water during the service. A glass of wine is placed before each person present and everyone is expected to drink wine during the ceremony.

SEDER SYMBOLS

Bitter Herbs: These herbs, usually horseradish, are a reminder of the bitter lot of the Israelites under bondage in Egypt.

Charoses: This mixture of nuts, apple, and wine symbolizes the mortar used by the Israelite slaves in the erection of the pyramids in ancient Egypt:

> 1 cup chopped apples
> 1/4 cup chopped nuts
> 1 teaspoon sugar or honey
> grated rind of 1/2 lemon
> 1 teaspoon cinnamon
> 2 teaspoons red wine (approx.)

Mix all ingredients. Add enough of the wine to bind the mixture.

Cup of Elijah: This cup of wine is set aside for the prophet Elijah, who was expected to come bearing glad tidings—the word of the coming of the Messiah. With the setting aside of the cup of wine, there are the accompanying customs of opening the door and leaving a vacant chair during the seder to welcome the prophet.

Matzos: Three whole matzos are set aside at the beginning of the seder. These matzos, called Kohen, Levi, and Yisroel, symbolize the three main groups of Israelites: the Priests, the Levites, and the Laymen.

Parsley: This vegetable, as well as other green vegetables, is used as a relish, symbolizing the festive nature of the meal.

Roasted Egg: This is a symbol of a freewill festival offering brought to the Temple, supplementing the Paschal lamb.

Roasted Meatbone: This symbolizes the Paschal lamb, which was sacrificed on Passover eve during the days of the Temple.

Wine: Each person at the seder is expected to drink four cups of wine at specified points in the service. The first follows the Kiddush, as on other festive occasions and on the Sabbath. The second is drunk at the end of the first half of the seder. The third follows the grace at the end of the meal. The fourth is after the praises of God recited toward the end of the Haggadah.

During this time very rigid regulations exist about specific foods that may not be eaten. Also, pots and pans used for food preparation during the rest of the year may not be used during Passover. The same restriction is placed on dishes, silverware, and other utensils. (Certain types of metal pots and certain kinds of dishes may be used again, but the rituals and the time involved are so complicated and time-consuming that most families have separate utensils used only for the holiday of Passover.)

The basic food restrictions concern *all cereals and any derivatives thereof.* Leavening agents of any kind are forbidden. Leavened breads, cakes, biscuits, crackers, cereals, coffee substances derived from cereals, wheat, barley, oats, rice, dry peas, dry beans, corn, and any liquids made from grain alcohol (rye, scotch, vodka, bourbon) are all forbidden. Wines, brandies, cordials—all fruit derivatives—are permissible. Corn oil is prohibited for Passover. All fresh and frozen vegetables (except peas, corn, and beans) are permitted for Passover use and carry a special label signed by competent Rabbinical authority. Foods that do not require labels are sealed packages of natural coffee, sugar, salt, tea, and pepper.

Stoves and ovens used for Passover must be prepared by a thorough scrubbing. This is followed by turning on all jets and heat areas and allowing the oven to heat through for a while. The dishwashing machines may be used after scrubbing with hot water and using new trays.

BASIC KOSHER DIETARY LAWS _____

Kashruth

Jewish dietary laws are based on sound hygienic principles. Certain animals are breeders and carriers of disease germs; consequently the flesh of such animals is harmful to people. Those animals are excluded from the Jewish diet.

According to the laws in the Bible, the flesh of only those animals that have a cleft hoof and chew their cud are permitted. Only the forequarters (not the hindquarters) of permitted animals, which include deer, goats, sheep, and cattle, may be used.

After the animal is killed, the lungs and other vital organs are inspected. If they are found free of all symptoms of disease, the meat is declared *kosher*. To be considered kosher, all meat and poultry must be under the supervision of Jewish authorities.

The hearts of animals must be slit before soaking to free them of any blood. The lungs must be cut to open the large veins before soaking. The liver, which contains a large quantity of blood, cannot be made ready for cooking by the usual process of soaking and salting. It must be seared over a fire in order to draw out the blood and then lightly salted while it is being seared. No meat may be kept after 72 hours unless it is kashered in the interval. Steaks and chops do not have to be kashered if they are to be broiled. No bird or beast of prey is permitted, such as eagles, vultures, owls, or lions.

Rules for Kosher Food

Permitted food and meat must be slaughtered according to Rabbinical specifications and processed for human consumption according to a code of law. Animals or birds must be killed by a man trained to slaughter in accordance with ritual. A knife is specially made and sharpened for the purpose so that little pain is suffered by the animal or fowl when the jugular vein is severed. This method of slaughter causes the maximum effusion of blood in the animal or fowl. The remaining blood is extracted by soaking and salting the meat (kashering).

Glatt kosher is a costly process by which a trained man can remove certain veins and fatty portions of the hindquarters and, in that way, make it kosher. The flesh of an animal or fowl on the permitted list becomes impure if it is not slaughtered in the prescribed manner. Each slaughtered animal must be examined by an expert; if it shows any signs of disease or lesions it must be considered impure and discarded. If the flesh of a permitted animal or fowl has been mutilated in any way, as by being torn by a wild beast, it must be considered impure.

A question that frequently arises concerns the prohibition of pork. There have been a number of theories advanced, particularly that the pig, like certain other animals and seafoods, is a carrier of disease. The prohibition in the Bible is specific and the reason given is similar to the reasons for forbidding the flesh of other animals. Although the pig has cloven hoofs, it does not chew the cud.

Kitchen Regulations

It is necessary to have two sets of dishes, utensils, and tableware because meat and milk products may not be prepared or served in the same pots or dishes. Dairy products may not be served on a dish that contained meat, and vice versa. In fact, most people will not eat at a table where meat and milk products are served simultaneously. Cracked or chipped dishes are considered unclean and should not be used. The utensils used for soaking meat must not be used in the preparation of any other food.

Food known as *parve* is that made without either meat or dairy ingredients and is prepared with separate utensils. Glass dishes are considered parve and may be used for serving either meat or dairy foods. The use of the same towels for wiping meat and dairy dishes and utensils is forbidden. Kosher soap, soap powder, and scouring powders must be used for cleaning dishes and utensils.

An interval of six hours must elapse before one may eat dairy food after a meat meal.

Kashering

Even though meat and poultry are purchased in a kosher market, they must still be kashered to remove thoroughly all blood from the meat before it is cooked. This does not apply to the blood in the flesh of a fish. Meat and poultry must be soaked for a half-hour in cold water in a container used only for that purpose. The meat is then rinsed, placed on a perforated board, and sprinkled with coarse salt. If the board is not perforated, then it should be tilted so as to permit the blood to flow off. The salted meat must remain on the board for one hour and is then washed. Hearts of animals and poultry must be cut open, veins removed, and blood permitted to flow before soaking and salting.

Liver

Liver from permitted animals or poultry must be prepared separately from other meat because it contains so much blood. It does not have to be soaked and salted, however; it may be prepared only by broiling. After it has been broiled, it may be eaten that way or used in other manners.

Broiled Meats

Meats used for broiling need not be salted, since the broiling process permits free flow of blood from the meat.

Poultry

The neck vein of a fowl must be removed by cutting lengthwise along the neck between the tendons. The claws and skin of the feet must be removed and the feet may be used. The clean fowl must be kashered. Eggs found inside poultry require kashering but are kept separate from the meat. Such eggs must not be eaten with dairy foods.

Meat and Milk

Meat may not be cooked in milk or with a milk derivative, or otherwise prepared and served together with milk or a milk derivative. Foods containing milk or milk derivatives may not be served for six hours after meats. Meats may be served after milk dishes.

Fish and Seafood

Only fish that have scales and fins are acceptable. For example, mollusks and eels are prohibited. Permitted fish may be cooked and served together with dairy dishes. Fish may not be cooked together with meat or eaten from the same dishes. Fish may be served before the meat course.

IMPORTANT KOSHER LAW FACTS

A most important fact to know about kosher law, both for the chef and the guests, is that on Saturdays meat cannot be served until three hours after sunset. By starting the dining time at 8:00 P.M. (if sundown is at 5:00 P.M.), the guests will take note and be assured that the dinner is truly kosher and that the hotel is abiding by the dietary laws. During the week, it is permissible to serve kosher meat or fowl at any time.

Most cheeses are nonkosher. Only the soft cheeses, such as cottage cheese, may be served.

Concerning desserts, one must keep in mind that there can be no ice cream with meat meals unless it is kosher ice cream—that is, ice cream made with soybean. Sherbert is also prohibited, except when it is made with ice.

No hard rolls can be served with any dinner. Even margarine is not truly acceptable with meat; marmalade is a better choice. However, if the guests insist on margarine, it should be left in its wrapper when brought to the table.

When sweets are going to be brought into the hotel for an affair, the rabbi must be consulted.

Basically, the cost of the Rabbinical supervision is in the area of $300 to $350. However, the price can be lowered in certain instances. It must be emphasized to the guests that there is a time element and involvement in preparing kosher meals.

The food must be ordered in advance; three or four days is necessary when selecting fowl or meat. Consequently, when the guarantee goes way over, obvious difficulties arise.

For kosher functions, it is customary to set up a "Wash Table" in the room or an adjacent room for all guests, and also one at the headtable for the honored guests. Included on the table should be water, bread (hard rolls), salt, napkins, and yarmulkes.

Another factor to be stressed is that nothing should be written on the event order that is not going to be served. Also, it would be a good practice to state on the event order that the selected menu is "To be prepared in strict accordance with Hebrew Dietary Laws and under the Rabbinical Council."

GLOSSARY OF SPECIAL YIDDISH TERMS ⸺⸺⸺⸺⸺⸺⸺⸺⸺⸺

This glossary of Yiddish names is for information purposes only. When making a menu it is recommended that the American name be substituted whenever possible when referring to food items.

Bar Mitzvah: Literally, a "son of the commandment," a Jewish boy who has reached the age of responsibility, 13 years. The term is also used for the ceremony celebrating this event on the Sabbath nearest his thirteenth birthday. On this occasion, the youth is symbolically acccptcd into thc community of adult Jcws and becomes eligible for a minyan and for participation in the reading of the Torah. Cakes, wines, and liquors are customarily served on this festive occasion, although a complete meal, including a number of holiday dishes, may be served. (This same occasion for a girl is called *Bas Mitzvah.*)

Challah: Twisted loaves of white bread prepared for the Sabbath. They are also made in a variety of forms for the various holidays of the year.

Chanukah: The Feast of Lights, celebrated for eight days, commemorates the historic victory of the Maccabees in the year 165 B.C.E. Today the eight days are commemorated by lighting eight candles, one the first day, two on the second day, and so on. The ninth candle is used to light the others. Among the traditional foods served on Chanukah are potato latkes. Gifts are traditionally given to children.

Chupah: The wedding canopy under which marriages are traditionally solemnized. One theory of its origin is that it is intended as a reminder of the ancient tent life of Israel.

Farfel: Noodle dough chopped into fine grains.

Gefilte Fish: Literally, "stuffed fish." Some variation of this fish is prepared by Jews in every country of Central and Eastern Europe.

Kasher: To soak and salt meats and poultry before cooking, in accordance with the laws of Kashruth.

Kashruth: The Jewish Dietary Laws.

Kiddush: The benediction pronounced over wine on the Sabbath and holidays.

Kishke (Stuffed Derma): A large beef intestine stuffed with various savory fillings and roasted. The most common filling is made of flour and fat and seasoned with onions, salt, and pepper.

Knaidel: A dumpling.

Knish: A baked or fried dumpling or patty, frequently served with soup. Among the most popular knishes are those made of a thinly rolled or stretched dough with fillings of chopped, seasoned meat or mashed potatoes.

Kosher: Literally, "fit." Designates foods that have been selected and prepared in accordance with the Jewish Dietary Laws.

Kosher l'Pesach: Fit for Passover use.

Kreplach: Noodle dough cut into small squares, filled with meat, cheese, or other fillings, and cooked in soups. It is a particular favorite of Eastern European Jews. Traditionally eaten at least three times a year: on Purim, on the day preceding Yom Kippur, and on Hosh'ana Rabba.

Kugel: A pudding, especially one made of potatoes or noodles, and baked.

Latkes: Pancakes, especially pancakes made of grated raw potatoes or matzo meal.

Lox: A variety of smoked salmon.

Mashgiach: An inspector employed by the community to see that kosher meat markets and the like conform to the law of kashruth.

Matzo: Unleavened bread eaten during Passover. The custom of eating unleavened bread grew out of the biblical narrative about the exodus from Egypt. In their haste to depart, the Israelites carried with them dough that was still unleavened. As a yearly reminder of this "bread of affliction," the people were commanded to eat only unleavened bread for one entire week.

Menorah: A candelabrum; specifically the eight-branched candelabrum used during Chanukah.

Parve: Neither a dairy nor meat dish, as fish, fruit, and vegetables.

Rabbi: Literally, "my master." An ordained teacher of the Jewish law, authorized to decide questions of law and ritual and to perform marriages, ceremonies, and so on. Now usually the spiritual head of a congregation.

Rosh Hashana: The festival of the New Year; the first day of the Jewish religious year. Traditional foods associated with the holiday are lekach, carrot tzimmes, and apple slices dipped in honey.

Schmaltz: Rendered chicken fat or goose fat.

Strudel: A pastry of stretched or rolled dough with various fillings.

T'refah: Not kosher; that is, not in accordance with Jewish Dietary Laws.

Tzimmes: A composite dish of meat, sweetening, and vegetables, prepared especially for the Sabbath, Rosh Hashana, or before the Yom Kippur fast. There are many varieties, the most popular of which is carrot tzimmes.

CHAPTER 9

Wedding Planning with Aplomb

In order for the catering executive to assist in planning the perfect wedding, he or she must know all the complications that are involved in arranging a wedding. Therefore, it is vital that you are completely knowledgeable and can exude complete confidence in helping to make the many arrangements of a wedding a reality. You may even choose to write and design a Wedding Planning Guide, such as this, as a give-away to every bride who makes an appointment with you to discuss holding her wedding at your facilities.

SAMPLE GUIDE TO PLANNING THE PERFECT WEDDING

Wedding Etiquette

A message to the bride.   No two couples are alike and every wedding will be different. Incorporate your personal preferences and cultural traditions into the plans for your day to make it uniquely beautiful.

You've imagined your wedding a thousand times in your mind—in your dreams. Now your fantasy is becoming a reality.

The most important thing between now and that day is the planning. You have many decisions to make, but we have a feeling you are going to enjoy every minute of it.

Arranging a wedding of substantial size and formality takes time—at least six months and often longer. Although weddings occur throughout the year, some months are certainly more popular than others. Hence, securing a sought-after reception site, florist, photographer, and musician(s) must be done far in advance for spring, summer, fall, and holiday weddings.

If preparations for this one, albeit very important, day take so much time, is it not perhaps more important to allot at least that much time for marriage preparation? The engagement offers an opportunity for the bride and groom to get to know each other as well as possible before making the marital commitment, to learn in depth about the home and life you each come from, to establish mutual goals and determine how you will best go about accomplishing them, and to learn about who you really are and what kind of expectations you have for yourself and your spouse.

To help you do this, many religions require marriage preparation instruction beginning six months before the wedding. In some faiths, a year's notice must be given so you and your fiancé can take part in group workshops followed by personal meetings with the clergy who will marry you. This is done not to complicate your life, but to help make certain you have thorough awareness of the extent of your commitment to each other and to do everything possible to assure that your beautiful wedding will be your only one. Therefore, once you have decided to marry and have shared the news with your families, you should immediately arrange for the two of you to meet with your clergy. After that takes place and the wedding date is confirmed, you can formulate preferences and establish your time frame with the help of this Wedding Planning Guide.

Once you have met with your clergy, your next step is to visit with the wedding experts of the catering profession. They will assist you in your every move in planning your special day at the caterer's outstanding facilities. To assist you in every possible move, we have designed this wedding planner to provide you with the following indispensable tools for the most efficient completion of your plans and ideas:

- Timely articles providing traditional information sprinkled with contemporary ideas for assistance in your preparation
- Worksheets, checklists, and timetables to keep track of your progress
- A place to jot notes and details when visiting and telephoning the services you want to use

Carry this planner with you throughout your preparation and planning. You will be organized, calm, and have all the necessary information at your finger tips.

We express our sincere wishes for a wedding day laced with your personal touch that fulfills special dreams and creates unforgettable memories. We are honored we can help and we are indeed at your service.

The Wedding Ceremony

Although it may last only a few precious moments, the wedding ceremony is indeed the highlight of this special day. Even the smallest detail should be planned with careful attention and care. Professionals who have been trained to handle details with skill and assurance are required to plan ceremonies, particularly the mid-size to large formal wedding.

The style and ambience of the ceremony can be determined by where you choose to be married. The most popular location has always been the religious site— a church, chapel, or synagogue. Should this be your choice, you should contact your clergy early in your engagement.

You can still enjoy a conventional wedding, however, and can make it memorable by your choice of setting. Outdoor weddings add a touch of whimsy to an otherwise formal affair. If your imagination soars to even greater heights, perhaps a ceremony in a hot air balloon is more to your liking—or on a train, a yacht, or a palm-tree-dotted beach. If you plan to marry in a public location, however, you need to obtain permission from the city or applicable public agency.

However traditional or adventuresome you may want to be, you will want to trust your most memorable day to the professionals who have the talent and experience to assure a wedding with aplomb—and an occasion to remember for a lifetime. In addition to food and beverage, professionals can also assist with arrangements, such as floral designs, music and entertainment, decorations, invitations, photography, and limousine service.

CEREMONY TIMETABLE

- 2–2½ hours before, the bride and her bridesmaids begin to dress.
- 1–1½ hours before, flowers arrive and picture taking begins.
- 45 minutes before, ushers arrive.
- 30 minutes before, organist starts to play as guests are seated.
- 20 minutes before, groom and best man arrive.
- 15 minutes before, the fee is given to officiate.
- 5–10 minutes before, the bride and her wedding party assemble in vestibule or entrance area.
- 5 minutes before, groom's parents are seated. Then the mother of the bride is seated.
- 1 minute before, wedding march and processional begins.

Catering

Perhaps the most important professional you will consult with is the catering executive. His or her expertise will prove invaluable. Remember this is a new experience for you—the professional has the benefit of years of experience and training.

Generally, prices are determined by the lavishness and quality of the menu selections and will include equipment rental and serving costs. There will probably be additional charges for taxes and gratuities. There may also be an extra charge for any special products or service you may desire, such as special crystal, china, silver, white-gloved French Service, or ice carvings.

Many establishments offer a most special wedding package that will insure your day will be everything you wish it to be. However, most caterers will be only too happy to create a menu and arrangements with your special wishes in mind. Price should always be a factor, but your budget should allow for the little extras that will insure a lifetime memory.

Be prepared to leave a nonrefundable deposit at the time you request that a function room reservation be made in your name, for your desired date. A contractual agreement will follow the acceptance of that deposit. If you do not fully understand the terms of the contract, payment due dates, cancellation provisions, and so on, ask questions before you sign the contractual agreement or banquet prospects.

A couple of weeks prior to the wedding, your catering executive will want to know approximately how many guests will be expected. A guaranteed attendance, which will not be subject to reduction, will be required no less than 72 hours prior to the affair.

Although you may have a special menu in mind, keep an open mind to your caterer's suggestions. Reception menus can often be dictated by the time of day, location, and what items will work best for a group of specific size. Take advantage of the creative suggestions, knowledge, and information available to you through your caterer. Remember—this is the part of the day your guests and you will most re-member.

Reception Sites

The reception following the wedding generally corresponds to the ceremony in size and degree of formality. The most popular sites for receptions range from hotel banquet rooms to country clubs. When choosing a locale, keep in mind how much space the facility has and its proximity to the wedding site.

Hotel banquet facilities are by far the most popular location for wedding re-ceptions. Because they offer extensive services and complete reception packages, hotel banquet facilities allow complete freedom to relax and totally enjoy your special day.

Discuss your choice of menu and style of service with your catering executive. You will be able to choose from a buffet of hot and cold hors d'oeuvres to a sit-down dinner complete with cordial cart. The menu should be relatively consistent with the overall formality of your wedding, however.

Your caterer can be of assistance to you also with the ceremony, ceremony rehearsal, rehearsal dinner, and guest room accommodations for your out-of-town wedding guests.

Hotel banquet facilities and the professionals who manage them can provide you with a memorable and cherished event. Rely on them for suggestions and advice, but remember to communicate your own wishes to them.

Receiving Line

Plan A.   The bride's mother is the first in the receiving line, as she is the hostess, then the groom's father, the groom's mother, the bride's father, then the bride and groom. They are followed by any other immediate part of the family, such as brothers and sisters who are in the bridal party, then the grandparents. This is so the bride's mother can introduce the guests from her side to the groom's side and the same thing for the groom's father.

Plan B.   First in the receiving line are the bride's mother and father, the bride and groom, the groom's mother and father, and then the brothers and sisters and grandparents.

Also, if desired, the maid or matron of honor and best man can be included.

Bridal Dance Lineup

Plan A.   In order:

1. Bride and Groom

2. Bride's Mother and Father

3. Groom's Mother and Father

4. Best Man and Matron of Honor

5. Everybody Dances

Plan B.   In order:

1. Bride and Groom

2. Bride's Father and Bride

3. Bride's Mother and Groom

4. Groom's Father and Bride

5. Groom's Mother and Groom

6. Best Man and Bride

7. Matron of Honor and Groom

8. Bride and Groom

9. Everybody Dances

The Jewish Wedding

Orthodox wedding.   Parents of the groom and bride walk up under the canopy. This is the first ruling in the Orthodox Jewish wedding.

As for the procession down the aisle, the grandparents are generally ushered in first. The first grandparents to be ushered in are the grandparents of the groom. The grandparents are not actually part of the procession, but they are the first ones down the aisle before the bridal party, and the processional music does not have to be playing.

Then the procession is started: The best man is the first one down the aisle, and he takes his place under the canopy on the left-hand side.

The groom's mother and father (one on each side of him) start down the aisle. The mother is on the right of the groom going down. They proceed to the canopy area, and the groom takes his place next to the best man under the canopy. The mother and father line up on the side and get under the canopy as much as possible.

The next ones down the aisle are the ushers, according to their height. They can either walk single file or in pairs. They take their places on a 45-degree angle just outside the canopy or on the platform below the canopy. They stand diagonally, facing the audience.

The bridesmaids then come down the aisle and take their places on the right-hand side of the canopy and line up in the same manner as the ushers.

The next person to come down the aisle is the maid of honor and/or the matron of honor. Only one can get under the canopy, and she should be the bride's choice.

It is not always necessary to have the bridal party standing as stated above. This can be varied according to the number of people in attendance.

The bride's mother can be either ushered in after the groom's parents, or, as for the groom, she can enter with the bride and her father. They go down to the base of the platform. At this point, each of them kisses the bride, and the groom comes off the platform and takes the bride under the canopy, followed by the parents, who take their place opposite the groom's parents.

In the recessional, the bride and groom are first, followed by the bride's mother and the maid or matron of honor. (The bride's parents are really the hosts.) The groom's parents, the ushers, and the bridesmaids meet in the center aisle and come back as pairs. Sometimes the groom's father is the best man, and this creates a problem as far as the maid or matron of honor is concerned. In this case, an usher meets the maid or matron of honor at the bottom of the platform and escorts her to the recessional area. The rabbi and cantor are already on the platform before anyone is escorted there.

Conservative wedding.   The procedure is that the rabbi can either be the first one in and take his place, or he can enter from the side with the groom and best man.

The groom and best man stand on the left-hand side of the canopy.

The parents of the groom come down the aisle and take their seats (generally, the first two seats) on the left-hand side of the aisle.

The mother of the bride is ushered in and sits at the right-hand side of the aisle, in the second seat. The usher comes back to go down the aisle again.

The ushers and then the bridesmaids follow—same as before—and take the same positions. The maid or matron of honor takes her place under the canopy opposite the best man.

The bride enters with her father, on his right arm. Again, the same procedure as used in the Orthodox wedding is followed: the groom meets the bride, and so on.

The father of the bride sits in the first seat on the right-hand side.

In a Conservative ceremony, it is permissible for the mother and father of the bride and groom to take their place at the canopy area. It can be done either way.

Reformed ceremony.   A canopy is not required. If there is one, the parents do not go under the canopy. The procedure is the same as the Conservative wedding.

Any minor alterations to these procedures will be conducted at the rehearsal.

Invitations

Invitations and other stationery items should be ordered at least two to three months ahead of time since etiquette requires they be sent to guests one month prior to the wedding date.

More than 50 guests indicates a formal (engraved or printed) invitation. Weddings smaller than 50 guests require a handwritten or telephoned invitation.

If only some guests are invited to the reception, remember to have separate reception cards printed to enclose with the wedding invitation. Otherwise, all pertinent information is included in one invitation.

If necessary, it is acceptable to include a map or directions. Have a map concisely drawn and have your stationer handle the printing.

When ordering invitations, do not forget to order matching note paper and envelopes printed with both your names. (And please respond to gifts within two months of the wedding date.) The following are some guidelines for sending out your invitations as etiquette dictates:

- Use only blue or black ink.
- Abbreviate only Mr., Mrs., Ms., Dr., and Jr.
- Write out titles, such as Senator, the Reverend, etc.
- Write out street, avenue, etc.
- Write out numbered streets (e.g., West Fifteenth Street).
- Do not use "and family" on the outer envelope.
- List the first names of the family members on the outside of the envelopes.
- Single adults within the same family should receive separate invitations.
- Return address should appear on the back flap of the envelope.
- Enclosures should be placed inside the invitation fold.

- When placed in the envelope, the invitation lettering should face the fold.
- Remove the tissue paper the printer has enclosed in the invitation. That was included to prevent ink from smudging when freshly printed.
- Send the invitation by first-class mail one month prior to your wedding date.

Bridal Registry

The bridal registry service allows you to list all items you would like to receive as shower or wedding gifts. This convenience discourages your receiving duplicate gifts while making it easier for your friends and relatives to choose a gift that's sure to please.

Stores that provide a bridal registry service often have a consultant who can assist you in making selections and advise you on workmanship, patterns, colors, and guarantees.

Photography

Other than lasting memories, capturing your wedding on film is the only way to vividly relive your most memorable day. Consequently, trust this most important service only to a professional.

As soon as your wedding date is set, you should begin interviewing photographers since some are booked up to one year in advance.

Photographers usually have wedding packages available that will suit any budget. Ask your photographer for an itemized agreement of the amount of time he or she will spend at your wedding and the number of photos you will ultimately receive.

Videotaping

Videotaping a wedding has become popular in recent years. Such a hectic and exciting time, combined with a possible case of pre-wedding jitters, can mean many details of this special day will be forgotten.

When shopping for a video producer, look for price, experience, and the approach that will be used. Ask to see a demonstration tape before you make a decision.

You can choose a polished, staged production with floodlights and dubbed-in music or a less theatrical approach which will record the event as it happens naturally.

Book your video producer at least three to six months in advance.

Wedding Gowns

Choosing your wedding gown is one of the most pleasurable and exciting decisions you will make for your wedding day. Selecting the perfect gown—one that will flatter you, suit the style and formality of your wedding, fit your budget, and create the once-in-a-lifetime, romantic effect you want—is not an easy task.

Consult bridal magazines and attend bridal fashion shows as soon as you become engaged. Keep abreast of the latest styles; don't be swayed by trends, however, unless your selection is the right look for you.

Wearing antique gowns is currently enjoying popularity. If this idea appeals to you, find a tailor who has had experience in this line to assure satisfactory results.

Accessories should be kept to a minimum and jewelry should be classic, but simple.

Shoes dyed to match the shade of your gown should be purchased after your gown is selected, along with any lingerie you may need.

Order your gown at least six months prior to your wedding to allow ample time for fitting and alterations.

Men's Formal Wear

The formality of the men's attire depends on the overall formality of the wedding, your gown, and the time of day of the ceremony. The color is determined after the bridesmaids' dresses are selected.

Although the ushers can differ somewhat in detail and color, they should be the same style and degree of formality.

The bride's father should dress the same as the ushers, but it is not essential for the groom's father.

Once the selection of formal wear is completed, fittings should be arranged for all men in the bridal party. Out-of-town ushers should send their measurements so their order can be placed at the same time. Each member of the bridal party generally pays for his own rental.

A formal evening wedding usually requires contoured jackets, long or short, matching pants, vest or cummerbund, and white bow tie. Black tie is also acceptable.

Tuxedos can be worn for a semi-formal wedding with a white or colored dress shirt and vest or cummerbund.

Vests and cummerbunds are optional for daytime formal or semi-formal weddings, although contoured jackets, dress shirts, and ascots are appropriate.

Informal weddings require only a solid-colored business suit with a dress shirt and conventional tie. A dark suit is appropriate, although white or off-white can be worn in the summer months.

Tuxedos should be ordered four to five weeks prior to the wedding to assure proper fit.

Music

You should take great care in selecting the music for your wedding since the ambience of the day will be set by the music before and during the ceremony.

The fee will vary depending on the musicians you select. It is a good idea to hear them perform before you make a commitment. Ask about their repertoire—they may offer suggestions for songs you will enjoy hearing, but haven't thought of yourself.

Be sure to get a signed contract at least six to nine months in advance.

Flowers

Flowers will add a traditional, romantic, or elegant touch to your wedding, depending on your selection. Consult florists who specialize in wedding floral arrangements. They can advise you, make suggestions, and show you sample photos of their work.

A good idea is to bring along fabric swatches so the florist can match the color to the attendants' dresses.

Although more expensive, you may want to consider silk flowers for bouquets. They are becoming more popular since you are left with an everlasting remembrance of your very special day.

Attendants' Gifts

The bride should present identical gifts to her attendants, as should the groom. These are usually presented the night of the rehearsal dinner.

The choice of gifts should be a memorable item and is often engraved to add a very special personal touch.

Some suggestions include jewelry, silver picture frames, key rings, money clips, cuff links, or mugs.

Transportation

You may want to consider renting limousines to transport you and your wedding party the day of the wedding. Large weddings often need three limousines to accommodate you, your parents, and a large wedding party.

If you are particularly romantic with a yen for the unique, give some thought to renting a horse-drawn carriage or an antique car.

Investigate at least three or four months in advance and get all details including mileage, minimum rental times, cancellations, and down payments.

Wedding Party

Choose your attendants with great care, since they are an important part of a day you will relive for years to come.

An honor attendant on both sides plus two to four attendants is traditional. The more guests you have, the more attendants you will need. It is customary to have one usher for each bridesmaid; however, additional ushers may be needed for an especially large wedding. One usher per 50 guests is a good guide.

Bride's Trousseau

It is customary for the bride to have a special going-away outfit to wear when leaving for the honeymoon. You will also want several new lingerie items, including negligees and nightgowns.

In packing for your honeymoon, remember to take clothing that is appropriate to climate and planned activities. Clothing should also be easy to pack.

A trousseau can also include the wardrobe you take into your new life. Casual and dressy clothing for two seasons following your wedding is customary. Not everything needs to be new, but supplement your current wardrobe and accessories with new items to add a new look to update an old one.

Honeymoon Packing List

Last-minute packing usually means forgotten items. Pack a day or so before your trip to avoid a hectic scramble and to insure a relaxing bon voyage. The following checklist will help you remember those little items easily left behind.

- Moisture and night creams
- Shaver or depilatory
- Tweezers
- Medicines
- Extra contact lenses or glasses
- Sun cream or tanning lotion
- Soap
- Shower cap
- Sewing kit
- Emery boards, nail polish, polish remover
- Contraceptives
- Travel iron
- Travel hair dryer and hair curlers
- Address book
- Travel/clock radio
- Insect repellant

PACKING TIPS

- Fill shoes with belts, socks, or underwear.
- Pack nonwrinkle items first.

- Fill spaces with small items like travel iron, clock, and hair dryer.
- Next, pack shirts, sweaters, pants, and so on.
- Items that wrinkle easily should go on top.
- Suits and dresses should be hung in a garment bag.
- Pack toiletries and necessities in a small carry-on case.
- Label luggage carefully.

Honeymoon Travel

Although you will begin thinking of your honeymoon as soon as you become engaged, begin planning it four to six months in advance. Discussing your plans with your fiancé in great detail is the key to a memorable honeymoon. Be sure to communicate a few basics such as: How much time and money do you want to spend? What climate and type of activity do you prefer? (Do you like breakfast in bed or camping?) Do you want a honeymoon package or a group tour? Do you want an isolated resort or a bustling inner-city hotel?

Travel agents can provide information on every aspect of your trip, so take advantage of their knowledge and experience. Even small requests should be made in the early planning stages, such as an ocean view or a king-sized bed.

Continue to check with your agent until you have all tickets and confirmations and double check everything!

Beauty

You will want to look more beautiful on your wedding day than you ever have before. You are the star of the production, so you should prepare accordingly.

Consult with your beautician on the best way to wear your hair with your veil or headpiece. Schedule a couple of appointments before your wedding day to experiment with various hair styles.

Have a manicure a day or two before your wedding. Even if you do not currently have regular manicures, this is the time to pamper yourself. It will give you that extra confidence you need to look your very best. If you cannot grow your own nails very long, you may want to try some acrylic nails or the latest nail-wrapping techniques.

Experiment with makeup to achieve a natural look with just the right degree of sophistication. You may even want to visit a salon the day of the wedding for a professional makeup application. Your attendants might be interested in doing the same. Don't forget to coordinate makeup and nails with the colors of attendants' gowns and flowers.

Wedding Consultant

If your career demands a great deal of time or if you do not like to bother with details and you can afford it, you may want to consider hiring a wedding consultant. A

JOE SAGET PHOTO

Bar Mitzvah featuring mylar mirrored tables, mylar dance floor, two-way stretch fabric covering the service door entrances and exits, and a computer-controlled light show over the dance floor.

July 4th centerpieces, real bread baskets, satin table cloths, and individual jelly jars set this tabletop off.

JOE SAGET PHOTO

JOE SAGET PHOTO

Gold Coast Salad: Jumbo Shrimp, Florida Lobster Chunks, sliced Papaya and Avocado, Greek Olives, arranged elegantly on a bed of Colorful Greens, accompanied with Cocktail Sauce.

JOE SAGET PHOTO

Paté displayed on polyure-thaned cypress wood and garnished with tallow American eagles and wildlife.

JOE SAGET PHOTO

Large clam presenting crab claws, displayed on a mir-rored cube with stuffed pink flamingos.

JOE SAGET PHOTO

Mirrored Plexiglas aquarium filled with African Cichlid Fish, on which a mélange of seafood is presented to include: Giant Shrimp, Langostinos and Golden Gulf Crabmeat, garnished with Lemon, Mustard, Remoulade, and Cocktail Sauces.

JOE SAGET PHOTO

Giant lobster display appropriately decorated.

JOE SAGET PHOTO

Paté display on mirrored cube.

JOE SAGET PHOTO

Presented in a mirrored and clear Plexiglas seafood bar, a large fish and coral crystal ice carving, displayed with the following Seafood delicacies: Freshly Shucked Clams and Oysters on the Half Shell, Jumbo Shrimp, Langostinos, Squid a la Marinara, Seaweed, Crabmeat and Lobster Chunks marinated, served in Giant Coconut Shells, garnished with Cocktail Sauce, Sauce Aurora, Remoulade Sauce, Creamy Horseradish and Lemon Crowns.

JOE SAGET PHOTO

Highly polished chafing dishes on 5½-foot mirrored table.

JOE SAGET PHOTO

Fresh fruit display at breakfast.

African art displayed at reception.

JOE SAGET PHOTO

JOE SAGET PHOTO

Fresh seafood display complete with live snapping sea turtle.

JOE SAGET PHOTO

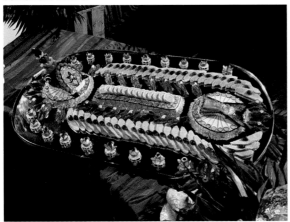

Cold seafood presentation as part of a theme display.

JOE SAGET PHOTO

Table setting with fish-shaped menus in front of entree, which is a Cheese Brioche filled with Marinated Vegetables, laced with Crisp Green Leaves and Fresh Strawberries and topped with Seafood Salad.

JOE SAGET PHOTO

Ballroom setting with lace-covered tables complete with burgundy show-plates trimmed in 18-Karat coin gold.

JOE SAGET PHOTO

West German display to include Smoked Eel, Cold Wurst Variety with Mustards, and Black Forest Cake.

JOE SAGET PHOTO

Display of fresh vegetables.

JOE SAGET PHOTO

Mosaic display of international cheeses.

Fresh vegetable display is highlighted with carved vegetables.

consultant can assume all the responsibilities for your wedding and be an invaluable service during a very hectic time. She or he will also be able to get the best bids for all the services you will need. The larger your wedding, the more important this service will be to you.

Interview for a consultant as soon as possible. Be sure you feel comfortable with your selection and are able to communicate your every desire.

It is advised to secure a written contract to include details, costs, and services. If you are working with the most professional of catering executives, the need for a consultant is diminished.

Budgeting Your Wedding

The diverse range of wedding ceremonies and reception styles create an equally wide range of costs. An integral first step in the overall wedding plan is to determine the type of wedding you will have, keeping in mind the financial resources available to you, and then prepare a budget. Your dream wedding may be an entirely formal affair, including a large church ceremony after which there is a reception with dinner and dancing; or it might be an intimate ceremony at home, in a restaurant, a hotel, or a park setting, surrounded by close friends and relatives only.

Today, the style you choose is open; it can be traditional or contemporary, allowing for your particular tastes.

Here are some general guidelines for ceremonies you might choose:

Formal.   The ceremony usually takes place late in the day, either late afternoon or early evening (formal Roman Catholic ceremonies may follow morning mass). You can choose 6 and even up to 12 or 14 attendants. Most formal weddings are in a church, although they could just as easily be outdoors, in a hotel, or in the home. Usually, the flowers and decorations are abundant, including aisle ribbons and carpet, pew ribbons, and sometimes a canopy from the curb to the church door. Special sections are marked off for reserved seats. You may have a soloist, chamber ensemble, or choir in addition to (or instead of) the traditional organist.

Semi-Formal.   There is little difference between formal and semi-formal ceremonies except in the matter of degree. The time is usually late afternoon or evening. (Roman Catholic semi-formal ceremonies are sometimes held in the morning.) Generally, no more than six attendants are at your side. The decorations are less lavish, omitting the aisle carpet and canopy and cutting down on the flowers. Music is usually simpler, perhaps using only an organist.

Informal.   An informal wedding can take place in the morning or the afternoon. A maid or matron of honor is the only attendant necessary. Whether or not you have music depends largely on the space available for the processional or recessional (if the wedding does not take place in a church). The decorations depend more on a flower's own beauty than on lavish arrangements. No formal seating is required.

Of course, another major cost is the reception. The type of reception and location usually depend on the time of day and the formality of the ceremony. As a rule, the more lavish the reception and the closer to mealtime it is held, the more costly it will be. Remember: Guests attending a wedding will indeed make a meal on the food provided and consume more than the usual amount of alcohol. This must be kept in mind in setting a realistic budget for the occasion.

Bride's Budget Worksheet

ENGAGEMENT PARTY

Invitations...$_____

Food/Catering ....$_____

Beverages...$_____

Gratuities ....$_____

Tax...$_____

Music...$_____

Rental for Place ....$_____

Extra Gratuities ....$_____

Flowers and Decorations...........................$_____

Total ....$_____

STATIONERY

Invitations...$_____

Announcements....................................$_____

Thank-You Notes..................................$_____

Postage ....$_____

Total ....$_____

CLOTHING

Wedding Dress ....$_____

Headpiece and Veil................................$_____

Shoes..$_____

Accessories..$_____

Special Clothes for Showers.......................$_____

Rehearsal Dinner Dress............................$_____

Going-away Outfit.................................$_____

Special Attire for Honeymoon ....$_____

Mother's Dress....................................$_____

Father's Attire. . . . .$_____

Special Attire for Other Family Members. . . . .$_____

Total . . . .$_____

GIFTS

Groom's Wedding Gift. . . . .$_____

Bridesmaids' Gift. . . . .$_____

Gifts for Bride's Parents (optional) . . . .$_____

Groom's Wedding Ring . . . .$_____

Total . . . .$_____

BRIDESMAIDS' LUNCHEON

Food/Catering . . . .$_____

Beverages. . . . .$_____

Gratuities . . . .$_____

Tax. . . . .$_____

Rental for Place . . . .$_____

Extra Gratuities . . . .$_____

Flowers for Tables . . . .$_____

Corsages. . . . .$_____

Invitations and Place Cards. . . . .$_____

Total . . . .$_____

GUESTS

Transportation (in-town) and Lodging for
   Out-of-Town Bridesmaids and Other Guests. . . . . . .$_____

Local Transportation for Out-of-Town Guests . . . .$_____

Total . . . .$_____

PHOTOGRAPHS

Newspaper Engagement Announcement and
   Wedding Story. . . . .$_____

Formal Photos Before and During Wedding
   Ceremony and/or Reception. . . . .$_____

Duplicates to Give to Friends, Relatives, etc. . . . .$_____

Videotaping of Ceremony and/or Reception . . . .$_____

Total . . . .$_____

WEDDING CEREMONY

Music (Organist, Soloist, etc.). . . . .$_____

Flowers in Church (or other location) . . . . $_____

Bridesmaids' Bouquets. . . . . $_____

Flower Girl's Basket of Petals. $_____

Pew Ribbons and Aisle Runner . . . . $_____

Rental of Church (or other location) . . . . $_____

Officiant, Altar Boys, Custodian . . . . $_____

Corsage for Guest Book Attendant . . . . $_____

Candle or Flowers at Guest Book Table. . . . . $_____

Guest Book and Pen. . . . . $_____

Transportation of Bride, Both Families, and
   Bridesmaids to Wedding and Reception. . . . . $_____

Total . . . . $_____

RECEPTION AND/OR MEAL FUNCTION

Flowers on Cake Table . . . . $_____

Floral Centerpieces for Bridal Table, Buffet Table,
   Family Tables, and Guest Tables . . . . $_____

Other Floral Decorations. . . . . $_____

Corsages for Friends and Relatives Who
   Serve (optional) . . . . $_____

Other. . . . . $_____

Rental of Special Equipment. . . . . $_____

Music. . . . . $_____

Reception Hors d'Oeuvres . . . . $_____

Reception Beverages . . . . $_____

Ice Sculpture (optional) . . . . $_____

Challah for Motzi (optional). . . . . $_____

Damask Linen with or without Lace Overlays
   (optional). . . . . $_____

Meal Function . . . . $_____

Meal Beverages . . . . $_____

Wine . . . . $_____

Champagne Toast . . . . $_____

Cordials. . . . . $_____

Wedding Cake. . . . . $_____

Viennese Sweet Table (optional). . . . . $_____

Personalized Matches (optional) . . . . $_____

Table Favors (optional). . . . . $_____

Personalized Napkins (optional) . . . . $_____

Place Cards. . . . . $_____

French Service (optional) . . . . $_____

White Glove (optional) . . . . $_____

Honeymoon Suite. . . . . $_____

Valet Parking . . . . $_____

Rose Petals, Rice, Confetti, or Bird Seed. . . . . $_____

Marriage Cup. . . . . $_____

Bartenders . . . . $_____

Gratuities . . . . $_____

Tax. . . . . $_____

Extra Gratuities . . . . $_____

Total . . . . $_____

FEES

Bridal Consultant (optional) . . . . $_____

Marriage License . . . . $_____

Total . . . . $_____

OTHER

Additional Insurance to Cover Wedding Gifts . . . . $_____

Security Guard to Protect Gifts. . . . . $_____

Sound Recording of Wedding Ceremony. . . . . $_____

Flowers and Gifts Given to Hostesses Who
      Entertain Bride . . . . $_____

Additional Rentals. . . . . $_____

Total . . . . $_____

TOTAL

Engagement Party . . . . $_____

Stationery . . . . $_____

Clothing . . . . $_____

Gifts. . . . . $_____

Bridesmaids' Luncheon . . . . $_____

Guests . . . . $_____

Photographs/Videotapes. . . . . $_____

Wedding Ceremony . . . . $_____

Reception and/or Meal Function . . . . $_____

Fees. . . . . $_____

Other. . . . . $_____

Grand Total . . . . $_____

Bride's Wedding Timetable and Checklist

SIX OR MORE MONTHS BEFORE

- Buy memory album.
- Discuss wedding budget with your parents. If you'll share expenses, include your fiancé and his family.
- Together decide on the wedding style—everything from food to flowers.
- Decide on the ceremony site.
- See your officiant with your fiancé.
- Decide on the reception site, make reservations, and leave deposit.
- Select and book your caterer.
- Plan the color scheme for your wedding and reception.
- Select and order your gown and accessories.
- Select your bridesmaids' gowns.
- Select a formal-wear specialist.
- Decide on the style of the men's attire.
- Select and register silver, china, crystal, and housewares.
- Select the photographer.
- Select the video producer.
- Select the florist and order the flowers.
- Begin the guest list.
- Choose attendants.
- Plan for new home or apartment.
- Send for honeymoon brochures and see a travel agent.
- Order wedding rings.
- Select and book your musicians.

THREE MONTHS BEFORE

- Complete guest list.
- Order invitations and announcements and start addressing them.
- Order all men's formal wear.
- Order gowns for bridesmaids.
- Have a medical checkup.
- Make honeymoon reservations.
- Shop for trousseau.
- Have both mothers choose their gowns.
- Shop for home furnishings.
- Pick up wedding rings and order engraving.
- Get your marriage license. (Check to see how long it is valid.)
- Make an appointment for a makeup consultation for you and your bridesmaids.

- Meet with your caterer and make all final food and beverage arrangements, including rehearsal dinner and wedding reception.
- Plan how you will handle traffic and parking.

ONE MONTH BEFORE

- Buy wedding gifts for each other.
- Mail invitations.
- Have wedding clothes fitted and altered.
- Choose gifts for members of the wedding party.
- Plan bridesmaids' party and bachelor party.
- Write thank-you notes as you receive gifts.
- Arrange for announcements in the newspaper.
- Make lodging arrangements for out-of-town guests.
- Plan how you will record and display your gifts.
- Have your hair styled as you will wear it at the wedding.
- Attend showers and parties given in your honor.
- Have your formal wedding portrait taken.
- Give the approximate attendance figure for the reception to the caterer.

TWO WEEKS BEFORE

- Arrange transportation to the church for the day of the wedding.
- Make necessary hair appointments.
- Confirm honeymoon reservations.
- Continue to record gifts and mail thank-you notes.
- Draw up your reception seating plans; make name cards for the bride's table.
- Go over your personal trousseau for last-minute additions.
- Update the caterer with the latest attendance figure and payment.

SEVENTY-TWO HOURS BEFORE

- Give the caterer the guaranteed attendance for the reception. This figure is not subject to reduction, but generally the caterer will be prepared to serve 3% over and above your guaranteed attendance.
- Prepare formal seating arrangements on the diagram provided by the caterer.
- Through proper planning, you can now relax and enjoy the most spectacular experience in your life.

CHAPTER 10

Beverage Sales

TAKING THE MYSTERY OUT OF SELLING WINE

For centuries, wine has been one of our most accessible civilized pleasures. Artifacts and primitive paintings indicate that wine was a part of our life more than 5,000 years ago, and it has been written about with appreciation and enthusiasm from earliest times. Yet today, despite its ever-growing popularity, the entire area of suggesting wines is still clouded with doubt, mystery, and a snobbishness that goes way back until shortly after the Industrial Revolution when landed aristocrats used wine snobbery to put down the newly rich. The practice dies hard! You do not have to be an expert on wines to enrich the enjoyment of good cookery with a pleasant wine, whether you are a restaurateur, employee, or customer.

The snobbery about wine in the United States surpasses that in France. Why? No one knows for sure, but the connection with the French and others on the European continent somehow infused the drinking of wine with a kind of aura that is associated with diamonds and orchids. That idea, of course, was pure rot, but an inhibition grew out of it that threw people off from drinking what is nothing more than an agricultural product.

Perhaps the worst of the aboriginal ideas of wine drinking stemmed from what was supposed to be a dictate about what one should drink with different foods: white with fish and light-colored meats, red with red meat, and so on. It is easy to find

French people who insist on drinking white wine with *all* foods for the simple reason that they do not like red. It is also easy to find recipes by highly qualified French chefs that call for a red wine for poaching fish.

So, drink the wine you like, and let the soi-disant "experts" look down their bulbous noses. The sooner the public gets over wine snobbism, the better for all of us.

Oenology (the science of wine and wine making) may sound arcane, but it really isn't. Rather, it is personalized by the one who is drinking the wine. So don't be put off by fancy language and labels. Start with the uncomplicated and perhaps inexpensive wines, then graduate to the great ones.

Most Europeans consider wine an everyday beverage, preferable to coffee, soda, beer, or spirits. It is as readily available to the French and Italian person as milk is to us, and often less expensive. Oddly enough, even though Americans drink much less wine than the French or Italians, we have a much greater choice of wine in this country than can be found anywhere else. Someone living in Rome would find it difficult to buy a German wine; similarly, it would be difficult to buy a bottle of French wine in Madrid, and a Frenchman living in Bordeaux might even have trouble buying a bottle of Burgundy. By comparison, not only do we have a great variety of American wines to choose from, but the wines of 15 or 20 countries are available in most cities.

There are four basic types of wine: table wine, sparkling wine, fortified wine, and aromatized wine.

Table wines.   These wines are red, white, or rosé and can be dry or sweet. They contain no more than 14% alcohol, and most of them have somewhat less. Simply stated, it might help to understand that fermentation turns the sugar in grape juice into almost equal parts of alcohol and carbon dioxide gas. Fermentation will usually stop of its own accord when the wine contains 14% alcohol, although occasionally it can continue to 15 or 16%. However, that is unusual and it is also the reason why 14% has been set as the standard or legal upper limit for table wines. Also, "table wine" is properly used to describe all natural (not fortified) and still (not sparkling) wines, at whatever price. Therefore, such popular wines as Beaujolais, Chianti,
Liebfraumilch, and California Burgundy are all table wines, as are such expensive wines as Chateau Lafite-Rothschild and Gevrey Chambertin. Table wines constitute the vast majority of the wines made in the world and come in an enormous range of flavors and quality.

Sparkling wines.   Sparkling wines are usually drunk on festive occasions. Champagne, the most famous one, usually adds gaiety and distinction to any occasion, however, some other sparkling wines are Vouvray, Seyssel, and Burgundy from France, Spumante from Italy, Rosé from Portugal, and Sekt, which is the generic name for the tremendous quantities of German sparkling wines.

Fortified wines.   Fortified wines are those to which spirits have been added at some point, so that they contain between 17 and 21% alcohol. Sherry and Port are the best known. In this country, fortified wines are called "dessert wines," even though they can be dry or sweet, and served before or after a meal.

Aromatized wines. These wines, which are red or white, are fortified and are flavored with herbs, seeds, and/or spices. Vermouth is the best known. Aromatized wines are often combined with spirits to make cocktails or are served alone as before-dinner drinks. Other aperitif wines from France and Italy are Dubonnet (red and white), Campari (red), Byrrh (red), Lillet (white), and Punt e Mes (red). There are also some new flavored wines on the American market—White Satin and Thunderbird are two well-known brands.

WHEN TO SERVE WINES

Wine can be served before, during, and after a meal, or enjoyed alone, just like any other beverage. Before a meal, many people prefer a dry to medium-sweet wine such as Sherry, Vermouth, or any of the aperitif wines known under their brand names (e.g., Campari). All these wines should be served chilled, on the rocks or with soda. Champagne and other not too sweet sparkling wines also make excellent pre-dinner drinks. The reason for not choosing very sweet wines for this purpose is that the pre-dinner drink should lead into the first course of dinner, which is not sweet. For most people a very sweet pre-dinner drink would be like starting the meal with dessert!

Don't forget to suggest a glass of well-chilled white wine before dinner if your guests are not interested in a full or half bottle. A splash of soda added to a glass of wine makes a "spritzer," which is a most refreshing drink. The wine list should be suggested and presented to the guests at the same time as the menu, in order that they can study both and decide which wine to order with what food. Keep in mind that many people have been made to feel uncomfortable about the possibility of not ordering the "appropriate" wine, thus they may shy away from wines altogether. That is when your ability to *suggest* becomes invaluable. Remember—in this day and age the wine that is "appropriate" is the one that the customer enjoys and may want to order again. However, there are some points worth considering to enhance one's appreciation of wine. More people than not will enjoy a full-bodied red wine with a red meat; a delicate wine might be overpowered by a red meat. Conversely, a delicate poultry or seafood dish will be enjoyed by more people if they have a delicate white wine with it. A rosé is a good bet for a couple who order a red meat and a light dish.

In addition, wine does not go well with highly spiced foods like curry, or with vinegary ones like salads and some hors d'oeuvres that have a tart dressing. They make wine taste sour and strange. If you serve cheese with wine, do not suggest a strong cheese because it will overwhelm the wine. If a strong cheese is desired, suggest a heavy red wine to complement it.

BRIEF GUIDELINE OF WINES FOR MENU
ITEMS

Hors d'oeuvres. It is generally understood that salads and antipasto do not lend themselves to wine, but the flavor of a paté or a bite-size quiche and many other hors d'oeuvres are enhanced by a glass of wine. White wine such as Pinot Chardonnay or Pinot Blanc can be served. Patés and shellfish also go very well with a Riesling, as does Quiche Lorraine, since it is a regional dish of Alsace-Lorraine and goes well with an Alsatian wine. The finest wines from Alsace are the Riesling Traminer and Gewurztraminer. Gewurztraminer sometimes is a much sweeter wine and goes well after dinner with dessert and fruit. However, there are many American wines that will do equally well. Use a dry, light, fruity wine such as Pinot Blanc, Riesling, Sylvaner, Chablis, or Rhine. If you are selling to a person who understands wines and you are looking for a wine that complements seafood, especially oysters, you should suggest a Muscadet. You will never be wrong with a French White Loire wine, as this wine has been called "the perfect partner for seafood."

Soup. No wine is needed, particularly for cream soups. At a gourmet dinner, a consommé is often accompanied by an Amontillado Sherry or Madeira. At times, a teaspoon may be added directly into the soup to enhance its flavor.

Fish. Simply prepared fish calls for a light white wine like a Pinot Chardonnay, Alsatian Riesling, Petit Chablis, Moselle, Pouilly Fuissé, or Pouilly Fumé. Full-flavored fish and those made with a rich sauce call for a full-bodied white wine like a Chassagne-Montrachet, a Mersault, or a German Rheingau (but not an Auslese; Auslese are grapes that have been allowed to dry and therefore are sweeter). American wines that can be successfully used, although not a direct counterpart of the German or French wines, are Mountain White Chablis, Chablis, Sauvignon Blanc, Johannisberg Riesling, or Grey Riesling. Dry Sherry is often preferred to a white wine when fish is oily. For shellfish, Chablis is the traditional American choice, especially with oysters, but any refreshing white wine—particularly a Muscadet, Soave, Sylvaner, or Pinot Chardonnay—will also do very well.

Pork and veal. Suggest white wines such as Rieslings (there are many American Rieslings rivaling their German counterparts) or a Graves, which is a class of the white Bordeaux wine. If you wish to serve a light red wine, a Beaujolais, Zinfandel, or a Bardolino is very acceptable. A rich pork dish like those served in Germany calls for a good Riesling, preferably Alsatian, or a good Rheingau, which is a Rhine wine. The best-known Rhine wine name is Liebfraumilch. It is interesting to note that Liebfraumilch is identified by a trade name as well. The best-known examples are: Liebfraumilch "Blue Nun Label," Liebfraumilch "Hanns Christ of Wein," Liebfraumilch "Crown of Crowns," Liebfraumilch "Glockenspiel," and Liebfraumilch "Madonna." Some American-type Rhine wines are Mountain Rhine from Louis Martini, Johannisberg Riesling from Louis Martini or Almaden, Grey Riesling from Wente Bros or Inglenook, Navalle Rhine or Vintage Rhine from Inglenook.

Chicken and other fowl.   Red or white, light or full-bodied wines are all served with poultry. The selection depends somewhat on the preparation of the dish. For example, Coq au Vin, when made with a white wine sauce, should be served with a white wine; when it is made with a red wine sauce, a red wine should be served. Roast chicken or roast duck is complemented very well with a claret (red Bordeaux). Chicken served in a rich sauce calls for a white Burgundy or the American Pinot Blanc or Pinot Chardonnay. Cold chicken can best be served with a Muscadet, a Moselle, or an American equivalent of a dry light white wine. If in doubt, a good chilled rosé or crackling rosé will do very nicely.

Beef and lamb.   Simply broiled or roasted meats are best accompanied by a fine red wine—Bordeaux, Burgundy, or the American types of Burgundy, Pinot Noir, Gamay Beaujolais, Cabernet Sauvignon, or Zinfandel. Stews, especially beef, can be served with a good Beaujolais or a California Cabernet Sauvignon.

Game.   Although we very seldom serve game for dinners, it is interesting to note the two classifications of game and the wine supplied for each. Light-flavored game, like pheasant or quail, is complemented by a light red wine such as Bordeaux Claret or a light Burgundy. Strong game, like venison or wild duck, demands a rich wine—a good Burgundy, although expensive, would be a Pommard, Corton, or Musigny. A less expensive but robust wine is Chateauneuf du Pape from the Rhine. There are several robust full-bodied American Burgundy wines, such as Almaden Burgundy, Napa Burgundy by Louis Martini, Burgundy Wente Brothers, Vintage Burgundy by Inglenook, and Sebastiani Burgundy and Barbera to mention a few.

Ham.   Some people enjoy a light red wine with ham, particularly if it is plainly baked. A chilled rosé is good with ham that is accompanied by something sweet like pineapple, raisin, or cherry sauce.

Cheeses.   There are various flavors of cheeses and many lend themselves very well to almost any wine. If you are using cheese with a white wine, choose lightly flavored cheeses. In most cases, cheese is used to accompany red wines because of their full flavor and their position at the end of a meal. It is well to note that strong pungent cheeses like Roquefort or Liederkranz tend to overwhelm the delicate flavor of good wines; in fact, few people find such strong cheeses compatible with any wine. For some additional guidelines, see the Wine and Cheese Chart.

Dessert.   With cake or fresh fruit (except highly acid citrus fruits), a sweet wine is the most appreciated. In this category are Sauternes, dessert Madeira (Bual or Malmsey, the sweetest classification of Madeira), Cream Sherry, Spatlese, and

Auslese Rhine Wines. Champagne also goes very well with dessert, but choose one that is labeled extra dry rather than the bone-dry brut, as the brut may taste slightly sharp in conjunction with a sweet dessert. The Italian Asti Spumante is oversweet, but it is excellent at the end of a meal. As for Port, reserve it for special occasions; it adds great flavor to fresh melon and complements walnuts and other nuts very well. It also gives Stilton cheese a little extra flavor.

WINE AND CHEESE CHART

Beer Kaese	Cabernet Sauvignon, Meursault, Chianti, Gattinara
Bel Paese	Beaujolais, Orvieto (dry), Moselle, Rhine, Valpolicella, Zinfandel
Bleu (including Wisconsin, Stilton, Roquefort, Danableu)	Barolo, Red Bordeaux, Cabernet Sauvignon, Red Burgundy, Port, Sauternes
Bonbel	Cabernet Sauvignon, Meursault, Red Bordeaux, Traminer, Chablis
Boursault (Boursin)	Rhine, Muscadet, Sauternes, Moselle, Red Graves, Sancerre
Brick, American	Gattinara, Chianti, Barbera, Cotes du Rhone, St. Emilion, Red Burgundy
Brick, German	Any light wine
Brie	Red Burgundy, Dry Sherry, Pinot Noir, Chianti, Rioja
Camembert	Pouilly Fumé, Sancerre, Hermitage, Bergerac, Beaujolais, Rhine, Vouvray, Red Burgundy
Caraway	California Cabernet, Red Bordeaux, Chablis, Pouilly Fuissé, Rhine
Cheddar	Chianti, Rioja, Barbaresco, Red Burgundy, Red Bordeaux
Cheshire	Beaujolais, Macon, Valpolicella, Zinfandel, Cote de Beaune Reds, Bergerac
Edam	Port, Cabernet Sauvignon, Red Burgundy, Claret Sherry
Feta	Pinot Noir, Bardolino, Inferno, Red Burgundy, Cabernet Sauvignon, Rioja
Fontina	Rhine, Corbieres, Orvieto (dry), Beaujolais, Pinot Noir

Gouda	Grignolino, Freisa, Beaujolais, Graves, Cote de Beaune, Macon, Zinfandel
Gourmandise	Moselle, Riesling, Rosé, Sauternes, Vouvray, Soave, Lacrima, Christi
Grape Cheese	Rhine, Sauternes, Asti Spumante, Orvieto (sweet), Riesling, Vouvray, Chiaretto
Gruyere	Chateauneuf du Pape, Barolo, Gattinara, Red Burgundy, Barbaresco
Hand	Chianti, Cotes du Rhone, Pinot Noir, Rioja, St. Emilion, Médoc
Hickory Smoke	Red Bordeaux, Red Burgundy, Cabernet Sauvignon, Barbera, Inferno
Liederkranz	Rheingau, Red Bordeaux, Chablis
Limburger	Barolo, Cote de Nuits, Chateaneuf du Pape, Red Bordeaux, Cabernet Sauvignon
Muenster	Red Burgundy, Beaujolais, Valpolicella, Zinfandel, Red and White Bordeaux
Norbo	Grignolino, Bardolino, Chablis, Riesling, Rhine, Graves, Neuchatel
Port du Salut	Rhine, Red and White Burgundy, Muscadet, Soave, Verdicchio
Provolone	Red Burgundy and Bordeaux, Pinot Noir, Cotes du Rhone, Chianti
Swiss	Cotes du Rhone, Barolo, Red Burgundy, Rioja, Barbaresco

IDEAS TO INCREASE BANQUET WINE SALES

All too often the word *wine* is missing in our conversation between catering managers and meeting and/or banquet planners. The pity of it is that banquet wine sales represent a handsome profit—a profit that is lost if wine is not suggested. Remember: There is *no* additional payroll cost accompanying a wine sale. It is one of the few upsell items with zero addition to labor hours.

Good intentions will not promote wine sales; action will! So perhaps the few promotional steps that follow may be of help. If you commit yourself to these action steps, you will reap that additional profit.

1. Always have a wine display in the catering office with samples on hand at the proper time when promoting sales.

2. Offer a simple banquet Wine List that promotes those wines you wish to sell. Plan for volume sales; *keep prices modest.*

3. Mention wine as often as possible during your conversation. Explain how well it would complement the menu that you are planning. Keep the conversation simple, using the words *white, red, or rosé.* If you find that your prospect has some knowledge of wines you may use more specific terms.

4. Avoid the two major pitfalls in selling wine:
   a. Try not to mention the name of the wine.
   b. Try not to quote wine by the bottle.

   The first is considered a pitfall because the introduction of a foreign name into the conversation may be enough to frighten the planner into saying no. However, if you find your customer knowledgeable or sophisticated enough, proceed accordingly.

   The second is considered a pitfall because it is easier to quote a price by the glass or per person. This is due to the fact that it is much easier to package the price into the overall per-person cost.

5. Know in advance which wines are available in quantity. Major wine merchants will stock some wines for you if they know that they can depend on you selling those in stock consistently. This will help you maintain less inventory while being assured of a good supply.

6. Invite the banquet planner to have a glass of wine during the discussion. It is easier to have him or her taste the wine you are suggesting rather than trying to explain the color, flavor, and bouquet with words. It is also a very hospitable gesture.

The public has accepted wine as a proper part of a meal. Four or five years ago, it was unusual to see a bottle or carafe of wine on most restaurant tables. Today, it is unusual to see a table without a bottle of wine, and that means fewer people are drinking the higher-alcohol content liquors.

FRENCH LAWS PROTECTING CHAMPAGNE

The wine of Champagne is one of the most famous of all French wines. Since it was "invented" by a monk, Dom Perignon, at the end of the seventeenth century, it has been associated worldwide with festivities and celebrations. However, it is also an excellent dinner wine and goes well with almost any dish.

By French law, wines may be called *Champagne* only if they are made from grapes grown in the Champagne region. The process of Champagne making, called *Champagnization,* is widely used elsewhere in France, as well as in other countries, for the making of better sparkling wines. Yet, even the best of the other sparkling wines are not Champagne because only in that region is the combination of soil and climate found which makes for the unique quality of the wine.

Champagne is always a blend. Grapes from different vineyards are pressed separately and blended in the "cuvee." Each great Champagne firm has its own standard in blending and the reputation of the Champagne producer is the best guarantee of quality. Nonvintage wines from a reputable firm often equal or even surpass a vintage wine from an obscure house.

According to the degree of dryness of the wine, Champagne may be labeled as follows:

Brut—The driest

Extra-Dry—Sweet

Sec—Medium dry, which is very sweet. (Champagne is the only region in which the word *sec* (dry) has such meaning.)

The wines of Champagne are fruity, light, and sparkling. They are generally of a pale yellow color, although some pink Champagne is also made.

COOKING WITH WINE

Any chef worth a small grating of sea salt would be repelled at the idea of using anything called "cooking sherry" or any other kind of wine that is supposed to be used only in cooking. The rule is simple: A wine to be used in cooking must be drinkable; if it isn't, the addition of such a liquid to a dish will only be deleterious.

That is not to say that if a red wine is called for in a recipe one uses Chateau Lafite or Romanée-Conti. Nor does the home cook pick a Pouilly-Fuisse if a white is in order for whatever he or she may be cooking. Modest wines are acceptable for cooking, and they turn out very well. A quick tour through some of any city's most prestigious restaurants shows gallon jugs of domestic wines used for cooking that results in meals of distinction.

DEVELOP A GREATER WINE KNOWLEDGE

Perhaps wine has not been an important factor in your establishment because your customers or your catering staff are not familiar with the hundreds of names tossed about casually. Learn to be an expert. Start small, then graduate to a variety. Learn two red wines, two white wines, and two rosés as a starter, and if you feel awkward about foreign names, start with the United States, but list and use their names properly. The following list of terms and the guide to pronunciation will assist you to that end. You will also find that Appendix B will aid you greatly.

List of Terms

AGING Maturation of the wine. The aging of the wine is at first very active in casks in the producer's cellars. It continues at a much slower pace in the bottle. Properly controlled aging makes the wine mellow and supple. Excessive aging results in the "passing out" of the wine. Only greater wines may gain by aging for decades. Most other wines are at their best when young—from one to five years, depending on the region of origin and the conditions of the vintage.

AROMA The scent of a wine. The aroma of red wines improves when it comes into contact with the air. To get the full aroma of a red wine, the bottle is opened one hour before serving and the wine is swirled in the glass before tasting.

BODY The density, consistency, or "weight" of a wine. Light-bodied wines go best with delicately flavored foods; full-bodied wines go best with foods of stronger flavor or that are highly spiced. When more than one wine is served during the same meal, the light-bodied ones are served first and the fuller-bodied ones last.

BOUQUET Same as Aroma.

BRUT Maximum of dryness.

CHILL To cool the wine prior to serving it. This is done by letting the bottle stand for one hour in the refrigerator or for about 25 minutes in an ice bucket. Too low a temperature is not advisable because it would freeze the aroma and flavor of the wine.

CLARET A dry, red table wine; true claret is red Bordeaux wine.

DRY Opposite of sweet. The dry wines are served before the sweet ones.

FRUITY Quality of a wine in which the aroma and flavor of the grape are recognizable.

LABEL The "credentials" of a wine. By French law, the label gives the following information:

1. The name of the wine, which is usually the place of origin or sometimes a proprietary name

2. The exact place (or at least the country) of origin

3. The mention of "Appellation d'Origine" or "Appellation Controllée" or "V.D.Q.S." (if the wine is entitled to any one of them)

4. A statement that mentions if bottling was done by the owner of the vineyard

5. Name of the shipper

6. Name of the importer

7. Alcoholic content of the wine

8. Volume content of the bottle

9. Vintage, if any

Bottles of Bordeaux may also bear a seal bearing "Qualité Approuvée par ADEB," meaning that the wine has passed the special test of quality established by the Association pour le Developpement de l'Exportation du Vin de Bordeaux (ADEB). Estate or chateau bottled wines represent only a minute portion of all the wine produced in France. Parish and regional wines entitled to an "Appellation Controlée" or a "V.D.Q.S." are very high-quality wines. They represent no more than 10% of the total crop of France, the first wine-producing country in the world.

MEDIUM DRY   Slightly sweet.

MISE EN BOUTEILLE   Bottling. When these words appear on a label, they are followed by an indication of who did the bottling. Any one of the following expressions means that the wine has been produced, aged, and bottled in the same estate:

"Mise en bouteille au Chateau"

"Mise en la Propriété"

"Mise en bouteille par le Propriétaire"

"Mise du Domaine"

"Mise en bouteille au Domaine"

NONVINTAGE WINES   Wines blended from several vintages in order to obtain high quality. Only nonvintage wines can be the same in quality from year to year.

ROOM TEMPERATURE   The temperature at which red wines are usually served (between 60 and 65 degrees F). Older and greater red wines are better at room temperature. Other red wines, particularly young ones, are often preferred when slightly cool. Wine is never brought to room temperature by abrupt "warming," which would spoil it, but it is left to stand for a few hours before serving.

ROSÉ   Pink wine served chilled.

SEDIMENT   Deposit that results from aging in the bottle. Sediment does not harm the wine in any way. It is very often an indication that the wine is of an older and better quality.

Guide to Pronunciation

ANJOU (ahn-joo)   French wine district along the Loire

AUSLESE (aw-slay-zuh)   Sweet German wine

BARBERA (bar-bear-ah)   Red wine grape from Piedmont region of Italy

BARDOLINO (bar-doe-lee-no)   Light Italian red wine

BARSAC (bar-sack)   Wine village in the Sauterne district of Bordeaux

BEAUJOLAIS (bo-jo-lay)   Red wine from southern Burgundy

BERNKASTEL (bearn-castle)   German wine village along the Moselle

BORDEAUX (bore-doe)   City and important wine region in France

BRUT (brute)   The driest Champagne

CABERNET SAUVIGNON (ca-bear-nay saw-vee-n'yon)   Red wine grape, Bordeaux

CHABLIS (sha-blee)   Famous white wine village of Burgundy

CHATEAUNEUF-DU-PAPE (sha-toe-nuff-doo-pop)   Red wine from Rhone region

CRU CLASSE (crew clah-say)   Classified growth or vineyard of Bordeaux

CUVEE (coo-vay)   A blend of wines

FINO (fee-no)   A particular style of dry Sherry

FRASCATI (frahss-ca-tee)   Wine village near Rome

GAMAY (gam-may)   Red wine grape used to make Beaujolais

GEVREY-CHAMBERTIN (jev-ray shahm-bear-tan)   Wine village in Burgundy

GRAVES (grahv)   Red and white wine district of Bordeaux

GRENACHE (greh-nahsh)   Grape used to make red and rosé wines

HAUT (oh)   Literally, high; not necessarily of higher quality

MACON (mah-kon)   Extensive red and white region in Burgundy

MARGAUX (mahr-go)   Wine village in the Medoc district of Bordeaux

MEDOC (meh-dock)   Important red wine district in Bordeaux

MONTRACHET (mon-trah-shay)   Famous white wine vineyard in Burgundy

NIERSTEIN (neer-shtine)   Important German wine village on Rhine

ORVIETO (or-vee-ay-toe)   White wine village in central Italy

PINOT CHARDONNAY (pee-no shar-doe-nay)   Classic white wine grape, Burgundy

PINOT NOIR (pee-noe nwahr)   Classic red wine grape of Burgundy

POMMARD (poh-mar)   Village in Burgundy

POUILLY-FUISSE (poo-yee fwee-say)   Dry white wine of southern Burgundy

POUILLY-FUME (poo-yee foo-may)   Dry white wine from the Loire

PULIGNY-MONTRACHET (poo-lee-nyee mon-trah-shay)   White wine of Burgundy

RIESLING (reece-ling)   Classic white wine grape of Germany

RIOJA (ree-oh-ha)   Finest wine district of Spain

ROSÉ (roh-zay)   Any pink wine

SAUTERNES (saw-tairn)   Sweet wine district of Bordeaux

SAUVIGNON BLANC (saw-vee-n'yohn blahn)   Classic white grape of Bordeaux

SEMILLON (seh-mee-yohn)   Fine white wine grape of Bordeaux

SOAVE (so-ah-vay)   Italian village producing light dry white wine

SPUMANTE (spoo-mahn-tay)   Italian sparkling wine

TAVEL (tah-vell)   Wine village in the Rhone, produces a rosé (dry)

VALPOLICELLA (val-poh-lee-t'chel-ah)   Light dry red wine of Verona

VERDICCHIO (vehr-dee-kee-oh)   Dry white Italian wine

CHAPTER 11

Think Success to Gain Success

Everyday, all over this nation, young people start working in new jobs. Many hope they will someday enjoy the success that goes with reaching the top. However, the majority of these young people simply do not have the faith it takes to reach the top rungs—and so they don't. Believing it is impossible to climb high, they do not discover the steps that lead to great heights.

A small number of these young people truly do believe in success. They approach their work with the "I'm-going-to-the-top" attitude. Believing they will succeed—and that it is not impossible—these budding individuals study and observe the behavior of senior executives. They observe the attitudes of successful people and learn how to approach problems and make decisions.

Believe in yourself! Have faith in your abilities! Without a humble but reasonable confidence in your own powers, you cannot be successful. A sense of inferiority and inadequacy interferes with the attainment of your goals, but self-confidence leads to self-realization and achievement. Because of the importance of this mental attitude, this book has tried to help you believe in yourself by providing you with the knowledge you need in order to be successful in your chosen industry.

It pays in every way to think big. Remember:

1. Don't sell yourself short. Concentrate on your assets.

2. Use the big thinker's vocabulary. Use bright, cheerful words. Use words that promise victory, hope, happiness, and pleasure; avoid words that create unpleasant images of failure, defeat, and grief.

3. Stretch your vision. See what can *be,* not just what *is.* Practice adding value to things, to people, and to yourself.

4. Get the big view of your job. Believe your present job is important. That next promotion depends a great deal on how you feel toward your present job.

5. Think above trivial things. Focus your attention on big objectives. Before getting involved in petty matters, ask yourself, "Is it really important?"

Success depends on the support of other people. The only hurdle between you and what you want to be is the support of others. You are not pulled to high levels of success; rather, you are lifted there by those working beside and below you. Gaining the support and cooperation of others requires leadership ability. Success and the ability to lead others—getting them to do things they would not do otherwise—go hand-in-hand. Live by these four simple leadership principles:

1. Trade minds with the people you want to influence.

2. Ask yourself, "What is the *human way* to handle this?"

3. Think progress, believe in progress, and push for progress.

4. Take time out to confer with yourself.

Practicing these rules will produce results. Putting them to use in everyday situations takes the mystery out of that gold-plated word, *leadership.*

Check the example you set. Use this old (source unknown) but ever-accurate quatrain as a guide:

> What kind of world
> would this world be,
> If everyone in it
> were just like me?

To add meaning to this self-imposed test, substitute the word *company* for *world* so it reads:

> What kind of company
> would this company be,
> If everyone in it
> were just like me?

Think, talk, act, and live the way you want your subordinates to think, talk, act, and live. Over a period of time, subordinates tend to become carbon copies of their chief. The simplest way to get high-level performance is to be sure the master-copy is worth duplicating.

Leaders in every field agree that there is a shortage of top-flight, expertly qualified persons to fill key positions. As the saying goes, there really is plenty of room at the top. As one executive explained, there are many *almost*-qualified people, but there is one success ingredient often missing—the ability to get things done, to get results.

In the words of Publilius Syrus: "A wise man will be/ Master of his mind/ A fool will be its slave."

Glossary of Hotel Terms

A common problem in the hotel business is the difference in terminology used by hotel people within the organization and between them and the prospective client. This Glossary is standard in the industry, and when these terms are referred to in dealing with customers, an explanation should be given.

ROOM ACCOMMODATIONS

ADJOINING ROOMS Two or more rooms side by side without a connecting door between them. (Rooms can be adjoining without being connecting.)

CABANA A room adjacent to the pool area, with or without sleeping facilities, usually separate from the hotel's main building.

CONNECTING ROOMS Two or more rooms with private connecting doors permitting access between rooms without going into the corridor.

DOUBLE Room occupied by two people.

DOUBLE/DOUBLE* Two double-size beds (54″ × 80″). *Twin double* is now more commonly used over *double double*.

*Refers only to accommodations, *not* to the number of people in the room. Rate is not based on accommodations (i.e., a Twin, King, Queen, or Dbl/Dbl can be sold to a single at the same rate).

DUPLEX   A two-story suite (parlor and bedroom(s) connected by a stairway).

EFFICIENCY   An accommodation containing some type of kitchen facility.

EXTRA PERSON   Occupancy of more than two.

HOSPITALITY   A room used for entertaining (cocktail parties, etc.); usually a function room or a parlor.

HOSPITALITY SUITE   A parlor with connecting bedroom(s).

JOINER   Person joining another person in the same room.

JUNIOR SUITE   A large room with a partition separating the bedroom from the sitting area.

KING*   One king-size bed (size of two singles put together) (72″ × 84″).

LANAI   A room overlooking the water or a garden with a balcony or patio (resort hotels mainly).

PARLOR   One or two rooms comprising a suite, with a pullout sofa—sold as part of the suite or sold separately (called *salon* in some parts of Europe).

PENTHOUSE SUITES   Suites located on the top floor(s) of the hotel. These will be handled by management. Front office inquiries should be referred to the supervisor or front office manager.

QUEEN*   One queen-size bed (60″ × 80″).

QUADRUPLE   Room occupied by four people.

ROLL-A-WAY BEDS   Beds that can be installed in bedrooms or parlors for extra persons occupying the room; available in most hotels at a nominal price.

SAMPLE   A display room for showing merchandise; with or without sleeping facilities.

SHARE   Room occupied by two people under both names and usually separate accounts.

SINGLE   Room occupied by one person.

STUDIO   A one-room parlor set-up having one or two couches that convert to a bed (sometimes called an *executive room*).

SUITE   Two connecting rooms: one is a sleeping room and the second is a parlor. Both are more luxuriously decorated than regular rooms. A suite could have more than one bedroom. Note: When requesting a suite, always designate the number of bedrooms needed.

TRIPLE   Room occupied by three people.

TWIN*   Two single beds (38″ × 80″).

*Refers only to accommodations, *not* to the number of people in the room. Rate is not based on accommodations (i.e., a Twin, King, Queen, or Dbl/Dbl can be sold to a single at the same rate).

ROOM RESERVATIONS _____

ADVANCE DEPOSIT   Partial payment sent in prior to guest arrival.

COMMERCIAL RATE   The rate agreed upon by a company and the hotel for all individual room reservations.

CONFIRMED RESERVATION   An oral or written confirmation by the hotel that a reservation has been accepted (written confirmations are preferred). There is usually a 6:00 p.m. (local time) check-in deadline. If the guest arrives after 6:00 p.m. and the hotel is filled, the assistant manager will make every effort to secure accommodations in another hotel. (This does not apply to guests with confirmed reservations where a specific time "late arrival" has been specified.)

DAY-RATE   Usually one-half the regular rate of a room for use by the guest during a given day until 5:00 p.m. Sometimes called a *Use Rate*.

DEPOSIT RESERVATION   A reservation for which the hotel has received cash payment for at least the first night's lodging in advance and is obligated to hold the room regardless of the guest's time of arrival. The hotel should preregister this type of guest. This type of reservation should be cancelled as early as possible but a minimum of 48 hours prior to scheduled date of arrival is required in a commercial-type hotel. For the resort hotels the customer should verify cancellation policy at the time of making the reservation.

FLAT RATE   The specific room rate for a group agreed upon by the hotel and group in advance. Sometimes called *Convention Rate*.

GUARANTEED PAYMENT RESERVATION   A room is set aside by the hotel at the request of the customer in advance of the guest's arrival. Payment for the room is guaranteed and will be paid by the company or organization even though the guest may not arrive (unless the cancellation procedure in effect at the hotel is followed). The company or organization should receive a cancellation code or the name of the person accepting the cancellation.

GROUP BOOKING ORDER   Reference material for a number of reservations made under one company or group.

HOUSING BUREAU   The local convention bureau (for certain convention groups), acting as a "housing bureau," assigns rooms in various participating hotels in the city or area. In some parts of the world, a "hotel clearing house" is a semi-official organization that assigns rooms in hotels for individuals and/ or groups seeking accommodations.

MULTIPLE RESERVATION   A number of reservations usually made under a group name (may be made as individual reservations).

NO SHOW   A confirmed reservation that has not been fulfilled or cancelled by the customer.

PAYMENT ON ACCOUNT   Partial or full payment of guest's account made during his or her stay.

PREPAID (PAID IN ADVANCE)   Full amount of room and tax paid by guest before checking in or during his or her stay.

PREREGISTRATION   The guest is preassigned a room by the hotel to be available upon the guest's arrival. This procedure is also used for some types of group business. Some hotels have a special "preregistration" desk or rack near the front desk.

RACK RATE   The current rate charge for each accommodation as established by the hotel's management.

RUN OF THE HOUSE RATE   An agreed upon rate generally priced at an average figure between minimum and maximum for group accommodations for all available rooms except suites. Room assignments are usually made on a "best available" basis.

TUBS   This term designates the receptacles in which all guest registrations in the house are kept.

ROOM OCCUPANCY

CHECK-IN   When this term is used in context with the Room Revenue Report, it will designate a room that will check in the same day. The hotel day starts at 6:00 a.m.; however, occupancy of rooms by arriving guests may not be possible until after the established check-out time (usually 1:00 p.m.). Guests are required to sign the hotel's registration card.

CHECK-OUT   When this term is used in context with the Room Revenue Report, it will designate a room that will check out by noon on the next day.

HOUSEKEEPER'S REPORT   Report made out by housekeeper that shows the status of rooms (whether they are occupied or vacant and ready). The housekeeper will also inform the desk if the rooms were used that should not have been used, or if rooms were not used that should have been used according to the Room Revenue Report. The housekeeper will also inform the desk of people staying over that should have checked out and of check-outs that should have stayed over.

PICK-UP   When this term is used in context with the Housekeeper's Report, it will designate a room that had to have a light cleaning before it could be sold to another guest. The room was reported vacant according to the Room Revenue Report. Usually this situation occurs on a late check-out.

ROOM REVENUE REPORT   Report made out by night auditor showing revenue received for each room, the number of occupants in the room, and if the guest will be checking out.

SET-UP   This term designates a room that is set up for a meeting. When this term is used in the Housekeeper's Report it will refer to a room that has been cleaned and readied but tables, chairs, and so on are still in the room. The Banquet Department has to be notified to remove these items so the room can be sold as a sleeping room.

SLEEP OUT   When this term is used in context with the Housekeeper's Report, it will designate a room in which there is luggage or clothing but the room did not have to be made up by the maid because it was not slept in.

SLEEPER   This term designates a room on which revenue was added by the night auditor but the room was reported vacant and ready on the Housekeeper's Report. The folio should have been pulled by the desk clerk upon verifying the Housekeeper's Report, but was not, thus revenue on the room was lost.

STAY-OVER   When this term is used in context with the Room Revenue Report, it will designate a room that will stay at least one more night.

EUROPEAN HOTEL DESIGNATIONS

DELUXE   Finest type hotel (private bath and full service).

FIRST CLASS   Medium range (usually has private or semi-private bath).

HOTEL GARNI   A hotel without dining facilities (except breakfast).

TOURIST OR ECONOMY   Commercial-type hotel (usually without private bath).

FOOD PLANS

AP—FULL AMERICAN PLAN   Rate includes three full meals and room. Full board and full pension.

CONTINENTAL BREAKFAST   Consists of juice, Danish pastry (sweet roll, hard roll, or toast), and coffee, tea, or milk. (In some countries only coffee and roll are offered.)

CONTINENTAL PLAN   Rate includes breakfast and room. Commonly called *Bed and Breakfast*.

DEMI-PENSION   Rate includes breakfast, dinner, and room.

EP—EUROPEAN PLAN   No meals included in room rate.

MAP—MODIFIED AMERICAN PLAN   Rate includes two selected meals and room.

BANQUET FUNCTIONS

A LA CARTE A meal where each item on the menu is priced separately.

CASH BAR A private room bar set-up where guests pay for drinks. Sometimes known as a *COD Bar* or *a la Carte Bar*. This type of bar is usually set up by the hotel for groups of 100 guests or more.

CONSUMPTION BAR A private room bar set-up where drinks are served and charges are made on an "as consumed" basis. If it is a "by the drink" basis, the charges reflect the actual number of drinks consumed on an individual $1\frac{1}{4}$ oz. drink basis. If the guest selects "by the bottle" basis, the charges are made to reflect all bottles opened, and charged accordingly, at the conclusion of the affair. In some cases, mix charges are included; in others, it is an additional charge.

COVERS The number of persons served at a food function.

FLAT RATE BAR A private room bar set-up where drinks are served on an unlimited basis at a predetermined flat rate price, regardless of consumption, for a specific time period. Generally, bartender charges are included and the number charged is based on food function guarantee or the number in attendance, whichever is greater. (For groups of 100 or more.)

FRENCH SERVICE Each food item individually served on a plate at the table by a waiter, as opposed to serving a completely set-up plate.

GUARANTEE For all private functions, the hotel must have a definite specified attendance. The Catering Office must be notified no later than 12 noon, two days prior to scheduled function, of the exact attendance expected. For functions scheduled on Monday or Tuesday, the exact expected attendance must be given to the Catering Office no later than 12 noon of the preceding Friday, due to the weekend. This number shall constitute a guarantee, not subject to reduction, and charges will be made accordingly. The hotel cannot be responsible for service to more than 3% over and above the guarantee. If no guarantee is given at the appropriate time, the hotel will assume the indicated anticipated attendance previously discussed to be correct, and charges will be made accordingly.

HOST BAR A private room bar set-up where drinks are prepaid by the sponsor. Sometimes known as a *Sponsored Bar*.

OPEN BAR A private room bar set-up where guests do not pay for drinks. A host bar is a form of open bar.

PAID BAR A private room bar set-up where all drinks are prepaid. Tickets for drinks are sometimes used.

SET-UP CHARGE On all seated meal functions, if 15 or fewer guests are guaranteed, an additional $50.00 (or higher) set-up charge is added to the account.

TABLE D'HOTE A full-course meal with limited choice.

NEGOTIATIONS AND ARRANGEMENTS _____

CUT-OFF DATE   The designated day when the buyer (upon request) must release or add to function room or sleeping room commitment. On certain types of groups, rooming lists should be sent to the hotel at least three weeks prior to arrival.

COMMITMENT   The detailed arrangements that have been agreed upon by the hotel and/or buyer. Same as proposal or agreement, but not used in the legal sense.

LETTER OF AGREEMENT   Letter from the buyer accepting the proposal. This may be the hotel's proposal initialed by the buyer. No legal agreement exists unless both sides have exchanged letters or duplicates of letters have been okayed.

OPTION DATE   The date agreed upon when a tentative agreement is to become a definite commitment by the buyer and seller.

PROPOSAL   First letter sent by the hotel outlining the understanding between the buyer and the hotel.

PROSPECTUS   The contractual agreement that conveys the information and menu of each particular function to responsible departments in the hotel. Copies of the prospectus are also sent to the customer for verification of all outlined arrangements and charges. The customer must sign one copy of the prospectus and return it to the hotel, prior to the planned affair. The information included on the prospectus should possess clarity and should be printed in terms that are understandable to the respective hotel departments. More often than not, the prospectus is the last communication between the catering salesperson and the responsible departments. Sometimes the prospectus is called a *Catering Event Order*.

ROOMING LIST   A list of names submitted by the buyer (in advance) of guests to occupy the previously reserved accommodations.

TYPES OF MEETINGS _____

CLINIC   Usually face-to-face small groups, but may have general sessions where staff provides most of the training resources to train in one particular subject.

COLLOQUIUM   A program in which the participants determine the matter to be discussed. The leaders would then construct the program around the most frequent problems. Usually attended by 35 persons or less with equal emphasis on instruction and discussion.

CONFERENCE   Usually general sessions and face-to-face groups with high partic-ipation to plan, get facts, or solve organization and member problems.

CONGRESS   More commonly used European designation for convention (mainly international in scope).

CONVENTION   Usually general sessions and committee meetings; mostly information giving and generally accepted traditional form of annual meeting.

FORUM   A panel discussion taking opposite sides of an issue by experts in a given field with liberal opportunity for audience participation.

INSTITUTE   General sessions and face-to-face groups discussing several facets of a subject. Primarily a substitute for formal education where staff provides most of the training resources.

LECTURE   A formal presentation by an expert sometimes followed by a question-and-answer period.

PANEL   Two or more speakers each stating a viewpoint with discussion between speakers. Discussion is guided by a moderator.

SEMINAR   Usually one face-to-face group sharing experiences in a particular field under the guidance of an expert discussion leader. Attendance is generally 30 persons or less.

SYMPOSIUM   A panel discussion by experts in a given field before a large audience. There is some audience participation, but appreciably less than a forum.

WORKSHOP   Usually a general session and face-to-face group of participants training each other to gain new knowledge, skills, or insights into problems. Attendance is generally no more than 30 to 35 participants.

MEETING ROOMS

AUDITORIUM OR THEATER STYLE   A series of chairs set up in rows (with aisles) facing the head table, stage, or speaker. Sometimes called *Classroom Style*.

BOARD OF DIRECTORS   A series of tables set up in rectangular fashion with chairs on both sides and ends. Can also be set up with ends in oval shape.

DAIS   A raised platform on which the head table is placed.

E-SHAPE   A series of tables set up in the shape of the block letter *E*, with chairs usually on the outside of the closed end and on both sides of each leg.

FLOOR LECTERN   A podium placed on the floor or on a platform. Part of the equipment permanently attached to these podiums is a light with an extension cord to reach a wall outlet. Sometimes called a *Standing or Floor Podium*.

HOLLOW CIRCULAR   Same set-up as *Horseshoe*, except both ends are closed and chairs are set up only on the outside. Sometimes called *Hollow Horseshoe*.

HOLLOW SQUARE   A series of tables set up in a square with middle hollow. Chairs on each of four sides (outside of square).

HORSESHOE   A series of tables set in the shape of a horseshoe, with chairs set up usually around the outside. Chairs may be placed inside as well.

SCHOOLROOM   A series of 6-foot × 18-inch tables lined up in rows (one behind the other) on each side of a good-sized center aisle. Usually six chairs to two tables. All tables and chairs face the head table.

SCHOOLROOM PERPENDICULAR   Same as *Schoolroom* set-up, except that tables are perpendicular to the head table and chairs are placed on both sides of the tables. Sometimes called *Union Style*.

SCHOOLROOM V-SHAPED   Same as *Schoolroom* set-up, except that tables (and chairs) are tilted like the letter *V*, with the base of the *V* at the center aisle. Also called *Schoolroom—Herringbone Style*.

SENATE STYLE   Same as *Auditorium*, except chairs are set up in a semicircular fashion facing the head table. Sometimes referred to as *Auditorium, Semicircular*.

SET-UP AND BREAK-DOWN TIME   The time needed before and after a function to arrange and rearrange the facility.

T-SHAPE   A series of tables set up in the shape of the block letter *T*, with chairs usually on the outside of the top of the *T* and on both sides of the leg.

TABLE LECTERN   A raised reading desk that holds the speaker's papers. It rests on a table and is sometimes called a *Table Podium*.

TABLET ARM-CHAIR SET-UP   A series of armchairs with attachable writing tablets, set up in auditorium or theater style.

U-SHAPE   A series of tables set up in the shape of the block letter *U*, with chairs usually on the outside of the closed end and on both sides of each leg.

V-SHAPE   Same as *Auditorium*, except chairs are set up in the shape of a *V*, with the base of the *V* at the center aisle. Also called *Auditorium—Herringbone Style*.

MEETING ROOM EQUIPMENT

CORDLESS MIKE   A small portable microphone without an electrical connection.

EASEL   A three-legged stand used to hold blackboards, cork boards, magnetic boards, posters, signs, and the like.

FLIP-CHART STANDS   A large pad, usually 20 × 24 inches or larger, on a three-legged stand. Used by a speaker for illustration purposes.

LAVALIERE MIKE   A small portable microphone that hooks around neck by ribbon or cord; commonly known as a *Necklace, Lapel, Neck* or *Pendant Mike*.

OPAQUE PROJECTOR Equipment that projects an image of an actual object.

OVERHEAD PROJECTOR Equipment that projects an image from a transparency.

PA SYSTEM The sound system, portable or built-in, available for amplification in one or more rooms.

ROVING MIKE A hand microphone on a long electrical cord for speaker who roams around stage or in audience.

STANDING MIKE A microphone attached to a metal stand from the floor. Adjustable to the height of the speaker.

TABLE MIKE A microphone on a short stand that is placed on a table for seated speakers.

EXHIBITS

ACCESS PANEL Removable panel or section of exhibit to permit access to lamps, projectors, mechanisms, and so on.

BOOTH Space alloted to exhibit or on contract (usually 6 × 8 feet or 8 × 10 feet).

BOX FRAMING Technique for reinforcing a frame, using nonstructural panel material around all sides.

DRAYAGE Transportation of material from point of arrival to exhibit area.

FLOOR LOAD Weight per square foot that the exhibit floor can safely accommodate.

LOADING DOCK Entrance to the area where exhibit shipments are received.

NET SQUARE FEET Actual saleable exhibit space.

TRAVEL INDUSTRY

ADVERTISED TOUR Any travel program for which a brochure has been prepared. Specifically, a tour that meets airline requirements for an IT number.

AFFINITY GROUP An organization formed for virtually any purpose other than travel that subsequently elects to sponsor group travel programs on scheduled or charter aircraft for and at the pro rata expense of individual members. Clubs, schools, companies, trade associations, religious organizations, and so on are affinity groups if they fall within certain limits established by the CAB.

AGENCY   Apart from its broader meanings, the business place of a retail travel agent or the administrative arm of a government (e.g., the Federal Aviation Administration).

AGENT   In the travel industry, one who acts for or as the representative of another, such as (1) a retail travel agent; (2) a carrier employee who sells tickets, a counter agent, or a ticket agent; (3) one with broad powers to act for a principal, a general agent; (4) more usually outside the United States and Canada, anyone in the travel business other than a principal—a retail travel agent, a receiving agent or local operator, a wholesaler.

ALL-EXPENSE TOUR   A tour offering all or most services (transportation, lodging, meals, porterage, sightseeing, etc.) for a preestablished price. The terms *all-expense* and *all-inclusive* are much misused. Virtually no tour rate covers everything. The terms and conditions of a tour contract should specify exactly what is covered.

AMERICAN HOTEL AND MOTEL ASSOCIATION (AHMA)   A federation of state and regional lodging industry trade associations covering the United States, Canada, Mexico, and Central and South America.

AMERICAN PLAN (AP)   A hotel rate that includes a bed and three meals a day.

AMERICAN SOCIETY OF TRAVEL AGENTS (ASTA)   The leading trade association of U.S. and Canadian travel agents and tour operators.

BERMUDA PLAN   Hotel accommodation with full American breakfast included in the rate.

BLOCKED SPACE   Reservations, often subject to deposit forfeiture, made with suppliers by wholesalers or travel agents in anticipation of resale.

CARRIAGE   The act or process of transporting or carrying; the charge for transporting, as in passenger carriage or freight carriage.

CARRIER   Any organization that deals in transporting passengers or goods.

CHARTER FLIGHT   A flight booked exclusively for a specific group or groups of people who generally belong to the same organization, who are guests of a single host, or who are traveling on an inclusive tour charter program. Charters are much cheaper than scheduled air services but are available only under rigidly specified conditions. They may be carried out by scheduled or supplemental airlines.

CIVIL AERONAUTICS BOARD (CAB)   The federal agency that regulates U.S. domestic air commerce and international air commerce to and from the United States. The CAB has authority to license air carriers and exercise control over their routes, schedules and rates, and their dealings with one another, other travel industry segments, and the public.

COMMERCIAL RATE   A special rate agreed upon by a company (or other multipurchaser) and a hotel. Usually the hotel agrees to supply rooms of a specified quality (or better) at a flat rate.

CONDUCTED TOUR A prearranged travel program, usually for a group, escorted by a courier; in a fully conducted tour, escort and/or guide service are provided throughout. Also refers to a sightseeing program conducted by a guide.

CONTINENTAL PLAN A hotel rate that includes bed and continental breakfast.

COUPON, TOUR See *Vouchers*.

DEMI-PENSION A hotel rate including bed, breakfast, and either lunch or dinner.

DOUBLE OCCUPANCY RATE The full price per person for a room to be shared with another person. The rate most frequently quoted in tour brochures.

DOUBLE ROOM RATE The full price of a room for two people. Be careful: Some people say *double* when they mean "double occupancy."

ECONOMY HOTEL Budget hotel. Few or no private baths; limited services.

EUROPEAN PLAN (EP) A hotel rate that includes bed only; meals are extra.

EXCHANGE ORDER A document issued by a carrier or its agent requesting issue of a ticket or provision of other specified services to the person named in the document.

FAMILIARIZATION TOUR A complimentary or reduced rate travel program for travel agents and/or airline employees that is designed to acquaint them with a specific destination(s) to stimulate the sale of travel. Also known as *FAM Tour*.

FREE SALE The practice of permitting the confirmation of a specified number of reservations (within specified dates) without reference to the principal for confirmation.

FULL PENSION Particularly in Europe, a hotel rate that includes three meals daily (an American plan rate).

HOTEL CLASSIFICATION The following designations are generally understood throughout Europe and, to an extent, the world. But it is sometimes difficult to know whether a hotel is being described by a reliable source or at the whim of a promoter. There is neither an official nor generally accepted rating system for U.S. hotels.

> **DELUXE** A top-grade hotel. All rooms have a private bath. All the usual public rooms and services are provided. A high standard of decor and service is maintained.

> **FIRST CLASS** A medium-range hotel. At least some rooms have a private bath. Most of the usual public rooms and service provided.

> **TOURIST (ECONOMY OR SECOND CLASS)** Budget operations. Few or no private baths. Services may be very limited.

HOTEL PACKAGE A typical offering might include transportation and transfers plus room, board, and the use of sports facilities at a resort hotel.

HOUSING BUREAU Usually a government-sponsored organization that acts as a clearing house for accommodations, particularly for conventions and other large meetings. Often established on an *ad hoc* basis during major touristic events to maintain a list of private accommodations to supplement regular lodging.

INCLUSIVE TOUR A tour where specific elements (airfare, hotels, transfers, etc.) are offered at a flat rate. Inclusive tours do not necessarily cover all costs.

IT NUMBER The code designation on an inclusive tour folder indicating that the tour has been approved by ATC or IATA. Agents who sell such tours qualify for override commissions on air tickets sold in connection with them.

ITINERARY The travel schedule provided by a travel agent for the client. A proposed or preliminary itinerary may be vague or specific; a final itinerary spells out all details (flight numbers, departure items, etc.), as well as describes planned activities. It should be delivered shortly before departure.

LOW SEASON That time of the year at any given destination when tourist traffic (and often rates) is at its lowest.

MISCELLANEOUS CHARGE ORDER (MCO) A document issued by an airline or its agent requesting the issue of a ticket or provision of services to the person named in the order.

MODIFIED AMERICAN PLAN (MAP) A hotel room rate including breakfast and either lunch or dinner.

NET RATE A wholesale rate to be marked up for eventual resale to the consumer.

OVERRIDE An extra commission. Sometimes called an *Overriding Commission*. Airlines pay overrides on ticket sales made in conjunction with tour sales. Wholesalers pay them as bonuses for volume business. Suppliers pay them to provide a profit margin for wholesalers (who must themselves pay commissions). Hotel groups or governments pay them as a volume incentive to wholesalers.

PENSION In Europe, a guest or boarding house.

POST-CONVENTION TOUR An extension designed to supplement the basic travel home from a convention.

PRE-CONVENTION TOUR An extension designed to supplement the basic travel to a convention.

RACK RATE The official tariff as established and posted by a principal.

RETAIL AGENCY The business establishment of a retailer; a subdivision of a wholesale and retail travel organization.

RUN-OF-THE-HOUSE RATE A flat price at which a hotel agrees to offer any of its rooms to a group.

SINGLE   Any facility or reservation to be used by one person.

SUPPLIER   The actual producer of a unit of travel merchandise (a carrier, hotel, sightseeing operator, etc.).

TARIFF   (1) Any individual fare or rate quoted by any supplier; (2) any class of fares or rates (e.g., a youth tariff); (3) any published list of fares or rates established by any supplier; (4) a published compendium of listed fares or rates for any category of supplier; (5) an official publication containing all fares or rates, conditions of service, and so on.

TICKET   The written or printed evidence that an individual or group of individuals is entitled to transportation, entry, and the like. For airlines, the passenger ticket and baggage checks, including all flight, passenger, and other coupons therein issued by the carrier, which provides for the carriage of the passenger and his or her baggage.

TICKET STOCK   Ticket blanks held by carrier employees and travel agents to be filled out and validated, at which point they become tickets. Standard ticket stock may be used on any U.S. airline that is a member of ATA and on many foreign IATA carriers. Some carriers print their own ticket stock.

TOUR OPERATOR   A company that creates and/or markets inclusive tours, performs tour services, or subcontracts their performance. Most tour operators sell through travel agents and directly to clients.

TOUR ORGANIZER   An individual, sometimes a travel agent, who organizes a group of passengers to participate in a special, prepaid tour. An organizer does not necessarily have conference appointments or pay commissions.

UNITED STATES TRAVEL SERVICES (USTS)   The official U.S. agency for the promotion of tourism.

VALIDATION   Imprinting a piece of airline ticket stock with the special stamp that makes it a legal ticket.

VOUCHERS, TOUR   Documents issued by tour operators to be exchanged for accommodations, meals, sightseeing, and other services. Sometimes called *Coupons*.

WAITLIST   A list established by a supplier, particularly an airline, of customers who seek space for a date or a time that is sold out.

FOODS

Classic Culinary Terms

AMANDINE (ah-mahn-deen)   Prepared or served with almonds.

AU GRATIN (oh-grah-tan)   With a browned topping of bread or grated cheese, or both. Also *Gratine* (grah-te-nay).

AUX CHAMPIGNONS (oh-shahm-pee-nyohn)   With mushrooms.

BONNE FEMME (bun-fahm)   Prepared with sliced mushrooms and white wine sauce.

BOUQUETIERE (boo-kuh-tyehr)   Garnished with "bouquets" of vegetables.

BOURGUIGNONNE (boorg-ee-nyun)   Refers to Burgundian cookery and usually features a red wine sauce, mushrooms, and onions.

BRAISE (breh-zay)   Braised. Vegetables or fish or meats are subjected to long, slow cooking in a covered pot in fat and a little moisture, usually a seasoned stock.

CACCIATORE (ka-cha-toh'-reh)   Italian for "hunter's style." A stew commonly made with chicken, simmered with herbs and other seasonings. French equivalent is *Chasseur* (shah-sir).

CREOLE   Prepared with rice, okra, tomatoes, and peppers; highly seasoned. Also denotes Louisiana French.

EN BROCHETTE (ahn-broh-shet)   On a skewer.

EN CROUTE (ahn kroot)   In a pastry shell.

ESCALOPES DE VEAU, SCALOPPINE, SCHNITZEL (eh-skah-loph duh voh, ska-lohp-pee-neh, shnit-z'l)   French, Italian, and German terms for thin veal steaks.

FINES HERBES (feen zairb)   Mixture of chopped herbs used as seasonings, or whole herbs used as garnish.

FLORENTINE   Prepared with spinach.

FORESTIERE (foh-reh-styehr)   Garnished with mushrooms, bacon, and diced potatoes fried in butter.

GALANTINE (gal-ahn-teen)   A dish made of boned poultry, seafood, or meat, stuffed, pressed, cooked, covered with aspic, and served cold.

LYONNAISE (lee-ohn-nehz)   Prepared with onions and usually sprinkled with chopped parsley.

MACEDOINE (ma-say-dwahn)   A mixture of raw or cooked fruits or vegetables cut in pieces and served hot or cold as a salad, cocktail, or dessert.

A LA MAISON (meh-zohn)   French term indicating a dish that has been prepared according to a recipe developed by the restaurateur or the staff. The Italian equivalent is *Della Case* (de-la-kah-zah).

MARINIERE (ma-ree-nyehr)   Refers to seafood cooked in white wine, and often garnished with mussels.

NICOISE (nee-swahz)   Prepared with tomatoes, and usually flavored with garlic.

PERIGOURDINE (pay-ree-gour-deen)   With truffles. Foie gras sometimes is included.

PROVENCALE (pro-vahn-sahl)   Containing garlic and usually tomato, with olive oil used instead of butter.

ROUX (roo)   Butter and flour cooked together to serve as a thickening agent for sauces.

SAUTÉ (soh-tay)   Pan fried.

TEMPURA (tem-poo-ra)   Refers to seafood or vegetables deep fried in fat, as fritters.

Hors d'Oeuvres

BLINI A LA RUSSE (blee-nee ah la roos)   Small pancakes spread with sour cream and topped with caviar.

CAVIAR   Salted roe of sturgeon and other large fish. The finest caviar is lightly salted (Malassol) roe from the Beluga, largest of the sturgeon family.

ESCARGOTS BOURGUIGNONNE (eh-skar-go boorg-ee-nyun)   Snails served hot in shells or earthenware cups, butter flavored, with shallots, garlic, and parsley.

FOIS GRAS (fwah grah)   Literally, "fat liver," especially of a goose, usually in the form of a paté, puree, or terrine.

OEUF EN GELEE (oof-ahn-zhuh-lay)   Poached or soft boiled egg in aspic.

PROSCIUTTO (proh-shoo'-toh)   Dry-cured Italian ham that is salted, spiced, and pressed, but not smoked or sugar-cured. Served in paper-thin slices, often with melon.

Soups

BISQUE (beesk)   Thick cream soup made of pureed seafood, poultry, meat, or vegetables.

BORSCH   Russian beet soup. Most common phonetic spelling of Russian word, but others are used, such as *Borscht.*

BOUILLABAISSE (boo-ya-bess)   French stew made with a variety of fish and shellfish, oil and tomatoes, flavored and colored with saffron.

BOULA (boo-la)   Green pea puree added to green turtle soup, served hot and topped with lightly browned whipped cream. Sometimes called *Boula-Boula.*

CIOPPINO (chop-pee′-no)   Italian fish stew.

GAZPACHO (gahs-pah′-cho)   A soup-salad made of uncooked tomatoes, cucumbers, sweet peppers, onion, oil, vinegar, and condiments, thickened with bread crumbs or slices of bread, and served cold.

MADRILENE (ma-dree-lenn)   A clear consomme flavored with tomato and usually served cold.

MINESTRONE (mee-neh-strohn′-eh)   Thick Italian vegetable soup.

PETITE MARMITE (p′teet mar-meet)   A consomme with pieces of beef, chicken, and vegetables, served in the small earthenware pot (petite marmite) in which it was cooked.

POTAGE SAINT GERMAIN (po-tahzh san zhair-man)   Green pea puree made with dried peas, fresh peas, greens, onion, salt pork, herbs, and sometimes cream.

POT-AU-FEU (paw-toh-fuh)   Literally, "pot on the fire." A thick French soup of meat and vegetables.

SENEGALESE   Creamed and curried chicken stock, served cold and thick. This is the English word. The French name is *Senegalaise* (say-nay-gah-lez).

SOUPE A L'OIGNON (soup ah lo-nyohn)   Onion soup.

VICHYSSOISE (vee-shee-swahz)   Soup made of pureed leeks or onions, potatoes, cream, chicken stock, and seasonings; usually served cold.

Seafood

COQUILLE SAINT JACQUES (ko-kee san zhahk)   Celebrated variety of French scallops, prepared in various ways, such as fried, creamed, sauced, and au gratin.

GRENOUILLES PROVENCALE (gruh-noo-ee pro-vahn-sahl)   Frog legs sauteed in olive oil with garlic and parsley.

HOMARD A L'AMERICAINE (oh-mar da la may-ree-ken)   Lobster sauteed in olive oil, then cooked in a sauce of tomatoes, garlic, onion, shallots, white wine, brandy, tarragon, and parsley. Despite its name, Homard a l'Americaine is not an American dish. It is believed to have originated in France's Brittany region, and the original designation, Homard a l'Americaine, was corrupted to its present form.

LOBSTER NEWBURG   Cooked lobster meat heated, usually in a chafing dish, in a sauce of cream, egg yolks, and Sherry or Madeira.

LOBSTER THERMIDOR   Diced cooked lobster meat and cream sauce spooned into halved lobster shells, topped with grated Parmesan cheese and oven-browned.

OYSTERS ROCKEFELLER   Oysters served hot on the half shell with a topping of chopped spinach, bread crumbs, and condiments.

POMPANO EN PAPILLOTE (pahm'-pa-no ahn pa-pee-yoht)   Cooked filet of pompano, a sole-like fish, baked with a sauce in a papilotte, which is an oiled, greased, or buttered paper wrapper. The fish is served in its papillote. Many meats and fishes are cooked en papillote.

QUENELLES DE BROCHET (kuh-nell duh bro-shay)   Dumplings made of pike forcemeat, served as hors d'oeuvres or main course. Many other types of quenelles are made with forcemeat (mixture of finely chopped ground or sieved ingredients and seasonings) prepared from meat, poultry, or seafood.

SCAMPI FRITTI (skahm'-pee free'-tee)   Fried shrimps, or prawns, of Italy, usually sauteed in olive oil and usually served with a sauce of olive oil, garlic, and parsley.

SOLE MARGUERY (mar-geh-ree)   French dish named for the Restaurant Marguery, where it was originated. Basically, filets of sole are poached in white wine and fish stock, then put in an ovenproof dish together with mussels, shrimps, and a white sauce, and glazed in the oven. This preparation is used for other fish such as trout.

SOLE VERONIQUE (vay-roh-neek)   Baked filets of sole with cream sauce and seedless white grapes heated under a broiler until the sauce browns.

SOLE WALEWSKA   Poached sole filets garnished with lobster and truffles, coated with Mornay sauce and oven-browned. Known also as *Sole Waleska*.

TRUITE AU BLEU (troo-ee toh bluh)   Literally, "blue trout." Trout must be alive until cleaning time, then should be cooked in court-bouillon immediately. Usually served with Hollandaise sauce or melted butter and garnished with parsley.

Meat

BEEF STROGANOFF   Beef filet sliced in thin strips, sauteed in butter with onion, and simmered in a sour cream sauce.

BLANQUETTE DE VEAU (blahn-kett duh voh)   Ragout of veal with onion, carrot, seasonings, and a white sauce.

CARRÉ D'AGNEAU (kar-ray dahn-yo)   Rack of lamb.

CHATEAUBRIAND (sha-toh-bree-ahn)   A thick slice of beef filet, grilled and traditionally served with chateau potatoes or soufflé potatoes. A wide variety of garnishes are used, so there are Chateaubriand Bouquetiere, Chateaubriand Forestiere, and so on. Most common sauce used is Bearnaise, but any of the dozens that are suitable for steak are frequent companions for this filet cut.

FILET DE BOEUF WELLINGTON (fee-lay duh buhf)   Roasted filet of beef coated with foie gras, wrapped in pastry and baked until crust is a golden brown.

GRENADINS DE BOEUF (gruh-nah-dan)   Slices of beef larded with fat pork, braised with vegetables and seasonings. There are also grenadins of chicken (volaille) and veal (veau).

LONDON BROIL   Flank steak broiled and carved diagonally across the grain.

OSSO BUCCO (oh'-so book'-ko)   Braised shin or knuckle of veal.

RIS DE VEAU (ree duh voh)   Sweetbreads of veal.

ROGNONS DE VEAU FLAMBES (rohn-yohn duh voh flahm-bay)   Veal kidneys flamed in brandy. Usually prepared at table.

SALTIMBOCCA (salt-eem-bohk'-ka)   Veal scallops topped with thin slices of prosciutto ham, sauteed and served with a sauce.

SAUERBRATEN (zow-'er-brah'-t'n)   Beef roast marinated with vinegar and seasonings, then oven-roasted and pot-roasted.

SELLE D'AGNEAU (sell dhan-yo)   Saddle of lamb.

SHISH KEBAB   Pieces of marinated meat, most often lamb, broiled on a skewer. Also known as *Shashlik*.

STEAK DIANE   Beefsteak sauteed in butter with chopped shallots, and sometimes flamed.

STEAK AU POIVRE (oh pwahv)   Steak cooked with a covering of coarsely ground black pepper.

STEAK TARTARE (tar-tar)   A patty of ground or chopped beefsteak served uncooked with a raw egg yolk on top and garnished with chopped onion, capers, and parsley.

SUKIYAKI (skee-yah-kee)   Japanese dish made with sliced beef or chicken cooked with soy sauce, bamboo shoots, soybean curd, onions, and other vegetables. Usually prepared at the table.

TERIYAKI   Cubes of pork marinated with soy sauce and broiled on skewers. Other meats prepared in the same way.

TOURNEDOS ROSSINI (toor-nuh-doh)   Small slices from the heart of the filet of beef, sauteed in butter, placed in croutons, garnished with foie gras and truffles, and served with Madeira-flavored brown sauce. Tournedos is both singular and plural, spelled and pronounced the same. It is probably the most mispronounced menu word in this country, often incorrectly pronounced "tornado."

VEAL SCALLOPPINE ALLA MARSALA   Veal scallops sauteed and served with a Marsala wine sauce.

WIENER SCHNITZEL   Veal scallops breaded, sauteed and served with slices of lemon.

Poultry

ARROZ CON POLLO (ar-rohs′ kon po′-yo)   Rice with chicken. Usually chicken is sauteed in oil, then simmered with tomatoes, stock, saffron, Sherry, and seasonings. Rice is cooked in the mixture.

CANARD A LA PRESSE (ka-nahr da la press)   Pressed duck. Roasted duck served with a sauce made with the mashed liver, juices extracted from the carcass in the duck press, Cognac, and wine. The legs are grilled and served as a second course. Also known as *Canard Pressé* (ka-nahr pray-say′).

CANETON A L'ORANGE (ka-nuh-tohn ah lo-rahnzh)   Oven-roasted or pan-fried duckling served with an orange-flavored sauce and often garnished with orange wedges or slices. Also known as *Caneton a la Bigarate* (bee-gah-rahd).

CHICKEN CACCIATORE (ka-cha-tor′-eh)   Italy's chicken hunter's style. A stew simmered with herbs and other seasonings.

CHICKEN KIEV   Filets of chicken breast pounded and rolled with seasoned butter inside, dipped in beaten egg and bread crumbs, then deep fried in fat. Sometimes the filets are rolled around drumstick bones.

CHICKEN MARENGO   Chicken sauteed in oil and cooked with garlic and tomatoes, traditionally served with a garnish of cooked crayfish, and often with fried eggs and mushrooms. Named for the Battle of Marengo, following which Napoleon's chef created the dish with ingredients at hand.

CHICKEN TETRAZZINI   Strips of cooked chicken combined with cooked spaghetti and a cream sauce, topped with grated Parmesan cheese and oven-browned.

COQ AU VIN (kohk oh van)   Chicken cooked in wine and served with a sauce rich with mushrooms, onions, and bits of bacon. Red wine is traditional for the Burgundy version, but white wine often is used. Thus, we have *Coq au Riesling*.

PEKING DUCK   Duck stuffed with mixture of soy sauce, garlic, leeks, brown sugar, and condiments, then roasted and basted with a mixture of soy sauce and honey until browned and crisp.

SUPREME DE VOLAILLE (soo-prem duh vo-lye)   Breast of chicken, served in a variety of ways, but most often with a rich cream sauce.

Sauces

MARCHAND DE VINS (mar-shahn duh van)   This is a butter commonly used with broiled steaks. Cooked-down and cooled red wine and shallots are blended with butter which has been creamed with a little parsley. The Marchand de Vins butter is often used to enrich a basic brown sauce to serve with roasted meats. This sauce is then virtually a Bordelaise, but without the marrow.

SAUCE BEARNAISE (bay-ar-nez)   A creamy egg yolk and butter sauce whose flavoring comes from cooked-down white wine, vinegar, shallots, and tarragon.

SAUCE BECHAMEL (bay-shah-mehl)   A basic white sauce made with milk and using a roux of flour and butter as thickening agent. This sauce has many enrichments and variations.

SAUCE BORDELAISE (bor-duh-lez)   A basic brown sauce (made from brown meat stock) enriched with cooked-down red wine, shallots, and herbs. Cooked diced marrow is added before serving.

SAUCE HOLLANDAISE (ohl-lahn-dez)   A creamy basic egg yolk and butter sauce, flavored with lemon juice.

SAUCE MORNAY (mor-nay)   Grated cheese (Parmesan, Gruyere, Emmenthal, or any combination of these) melted in a basic white sauce.

SAUCE VINAIGRETTE (vee-nay-gret)   Basic "French" dressing used for salads and simple marinades. Consists of wine vinegar, oil, sometimes mustard, and sometimes fresh herbs.

Pasta and Cereals

CANNELLONI (kahn-nuh-lo'-nee)   Largish rolls of noodle-like dough stuffed with a savory meat/cheese filling.

FETTUCCINI (fet-too-chee'-neh)   Narrow strips of thin pasta.

GNOCCHI (nyawk'-kee)   Italian dumplings, often made with mashed potatoes mixed into the dough.

LASAGNE (la-zahn'-yeh)   Very wide noodles often based in casserole dishes with ground beef.

PILAFF (pee-lahf)   Cereal, usually rice, sauteed with onion and other aromatics, then steamed, usually in a savory stock, until tender. Sometimes combined with meat, seafood, or vegetables. Also known as *Pilaf* or *Pilau*.

RISOTTO (ree-zawt'-toh)   Rice cooked in meat stock, sauced and seasoned in a variety of ways, with meat, seafood, or cheese often added. The famed Risotto alla Milanese is flavored and colored with saffron.

Vegetables

CHATEAU POTATOES   Raw potato, cut into thick strips or into the shape of large olives, sauteed slowly in butter and served with sprinkled chopped parsley.

FIDDLEHEADS The young unfurling fronds of certain ferns (e.g., the cinnamon fern and ostrich fern) that are served as a green vegetable.

FRITTO MISTO (free'-toh mee'-stoh) Italian mixed fry. Vegetables alone, or vegetables and meats, cut in chunks, coated with batter or crumbs, and deep-fried.

POMMES DE TERRE (pum duh tehr) French for potatoes. Literally apples of the earth. Often shortened to *Pommes* on menus, even though pommes is the generic word for apples.

POMMES DE TERRE DUCHESSE (doo-shess) Potato mashed and mixed with raw eggs, used as a garnish or made into patties and oven-browned.

POMMES DE TERRE LYONNAISE (lee-oh-nez) Sliced boiled potatoes browned in butter with a little minced onion. Served sprinkled with chopped parsley.

POMMES SOUFFLEES Souffléed potatoes are thin slices of raw potato puffed into little balloons by a double-frying process.

Salads

ASPICS Meat, fish, or vegetables molded with clear jelly made from stock thickened with gelatin.

BELGIAN ENDIVE The developing crown of an endive plant (which has been bleached by depriving it of sunlight while growing). It is a tight, elongated, green-tipped bundle of succulent leaves, looking like a smallish unshucked ear of corn. It is often cut in half and dressed for salad, but it is also cooked in many ways, primarily in a simple butter braise.

CAESAR SALAD Romaine lettuce with a dressing that includes coddled egg. Grated Parmesan cheese, fried croutons, crisp bacon bits, and finely chopped anchovy filets are standard ingredients.

HEARTS OF PALM Terminal buds of palm dressed as a salad.

MOUSSES (moose) Purees of meat, fish, or vegetables combined with jellied stock and softened butter or whipped cream.

SALADE NICOISE (sa-lahd nee-swahz) Sliced cooked potatoes and string beans dressed with oil and vinegar and garnished with capers, olives, and anchovy filets. Other ingredients often used are tomatoes, cucumbers, tuna, and hard-boiled eggs.

Cheeses

BEL PAESE (bell-pah-ayz'-eh) Italian cheese that is mild, soft, creamy, and ivory in color. The edible rind is white and rather firm.

BRIE (bree)   One of the great monarchs of French cheeses. A creamy-textured, pale-gold cheese with a soft, leathery white rind. It has a delicate, somewhat nutty taste.

CAMEMBERT (ka-mahm-behr)   Probably the most popular cheese in France. It is creamy in color and texture, with a white-flecked gold crust. It can be unpleasantly strong when overripe.

GORGONZOLA   The great Italian blue; robust both in odor and flavor. Very rich. Rather soft when quite ripe.

LIEDERKRANZ (lee'-der-krahnts)   Deep-gold, almost runny; American counterpart of Limburger. Robust flavor and aroma.

PORT SALUT (pohr sa-loo)   A fresh, fairly firm, buttery cheese originally made by French Trappist monks. It can become robust with age. Also called *Port du Salut*.

PROVOLONE (pro-vo-lohn'-eh)   A quite firm, rather dry Italian cheese, usually having a pleasant sharpness. It is often smoked.

ROQUEFORT (rohk-for)   The great French blue; made from sheep's milk. A rich, creamy, crumbly cheese with blue-green veining.

STILTON   The great English blue. A little more delicate than Roquefort. It is very rich, but never becomes soft. Even at warm room temperature it retains the pebbly texture of aged Cheddar, and has a mellowness with its pungency.

Desserts

BABA AU RHUM (bah-bah oh rum)   A rich, yeast-leavened cake, containing raisins and currants, which is often baked in a large ring mold. After it cools, it is thoroughly soaked with a rum-flavored sugar syrup. Sometimes a rum-fruit syrup is used, or a spice is added to the syrup. The cake is served plain or with the ring filled with pastry cream or ice cream.

BAKLAVA (bahk-luh-vah')   Many thin layers of pastry put together with honey and nuts. Often flavored with rose water. Turkish in origin.

BAVARIAN CREAM   A gelatin-custard cream of any flavor (vanilla, chocolate, strawberry, etc.).

CHARLOTTE RUSSE   A round mold covered on sides and bottom with sponge fingers (ladyfingers) and filled with Bavarian Cream of any flavor, or ice cream. The French fruit charlottes are baked, and are quite a different dessert.

CHERRIES JUBILEE   Cooked cherries in their own slightly thickened syrup, flamed with Kirsch at the moment of serving. Served alone or over ice cream.

COUPE JACQUES (koop-zhahk)   The classic French sundae, and a prototype of all other coupes. Placed in a sherbet glass are one scoop of lemon and one of strawberry ice or ice cream. Placed between the scoops is a heaping tablespoon of fresh fruit steeped in Kirsch. The garnish is halved almonds and glazed cherries. A few drops of Kirsch are sprinkled on top.

CREME BRULEE (krem broo-lay)   A Creole dish that is a rich custard cream topped by a crisp glaze of brown sugar that has been caramelized under a broiler.

CREME AU CARAMEL (krem oh ka-ra-mel)   A custard cream cooked in a mold that first has been coated with caramelized sugar that was allowed to harden. During the cooking, the caramel becomes a liquid sauce for the set custard.

CREPES SUZETTE (krep soo-zett)   Thin French pancakes served in an orange-flavored sauce. May or may not be flamed.

MERINGUES GLACEES (muh-rang glah-say)   Two baked meringues placed on edge of either side of a scoop of ice cream and decorated with whipped cream.

PECHE MELBA (pesh)   Peach Melba. Half a peach filled with cream, set on a bed of vanilla ice cream and covered with raspberry sauce.

PETITS FOURS (p'tee foor)   Bite-size cakes iced with fondant and decorated imaginatively. Also little fancy cookies (macaroons, shortbreads, etc.). Even, by extension, confections such as Marrons Glaces (glazed chestnuts) or marzipan fruits.

PROFITEROLE AU CHOCOLAT (pro-fee-teh-roll oh shoh-koh-lah)   Small cream puffs filled with ice cream, pastry cream, or sweetened whipped cream, served with a thin chocolate sauce. A Profiterole is any miniature cream puff filled with whipped cream or pastry cream (soft custard) and frosted with fondant icing. Savory fillings are also often used (e.g., for hors d'oeuvres service).

SOUFFLE AU GRAND MARNIER (oh grahn-mar-nyay)   Dessert souffle flavored with the famed French orange liqueur. Many other flavoring agents are used for dessert souffles.

TORTE (tohr-tuh)   An Austrian (or German) cake or pastry made with many eggs, sugar, and often grated nuts or dry bread crumbs in place of flour. Baked in large flat layers, served plain, or often sliced into still thinner layers after baking. Put together with jam or cream fillings, and usually covered with rich frostings or meringues. Famous varieties of torten are Sacher, Linzer, and Dobos (also written "Dobosch").

ZABAGLIONE (dzah-bah-yoh-neh)   A mixture of eggs, sugar, and wine, usually Marsala or Sherry, beaten over simmering water until thick and light, and served warm or cold in a glass. Also Zabaione and Zabajone. The French is *Sabayon* (sah-ba-yohn).

Glossary of Wines

AMERICAN

Cocktail and Dessert Wines

PALE DRY SHERRY   Extra dry and light with a pleasing smoothness and bouquet

MEDIUM DRY SHERRY   A rich, medium Sherry with a mellow, nutty flavor

GOLDEN CREAM SHERRY   Deliciously rich and smooth; sweet, but not too sweet

COCKTAIL SHERRY   Dry, smooth, and mellow—the perfect aperitif

TAWNY PORT   Medium-sweet, rich, and russet-colored with a mellow bouquet; a masterpiece

RICH RUBY PORT   An elegant, full bodied, rich, sweet, robust Port with an enticing fragrance; exquisite!

MUSCATEL   A brilliant golden-amber wine with a delicate, spicy aroma; a superbly smooth dessert wine; very fruity and rich

MADEIRA   A mellow, medium-dry nectar with an enticing nutty flavor

RARE FLOR SHERRY   The driest and most delicate of all Sherries—the perfect aperitif

RARE DRY SHERRY   A magnificent cocktail wine; extra aging gives this unsurpassed Dry Sherry a wonderful bouquet and nutty flavor

RARE CREAM SHERRY   A sweet, golden, luxury wine of exquisite flavor and aroma—delightful after dinner

SOLERA COCKTAIL SHERRY   Very dry, delicate, and truly appetizing

SOLERA GOLDEN SHERRY   Mellow with considerable flavor

Champagne and Sparkling Wines

BLANC DE PINOT   A fine Champagne made entirely from delicate Pinot grapes; for great occasions

EXTRA DRY CHAMPAGNE   Medium dry, delightfully mellow—a celebration favorite

PINK CHAMPAGNE   Delicate, light-bodied, full of zest and sparkle

SPARKLING BURGUNDY   Combines the rich flavor of Burgundy with the effervescence of Champagne; fruity, full-bodied, brilliant ruby red

CRACKLING ROSÉ   A gay, zestful, sparkling pink wine; naturally bubbles like fine Champagne

BLANC DE BLANCS   The choice American Blanc de Blancs; elegant, pale dry

BRUT CHAMPAGNE   Classic, distinguished, very dry, wonderful flavor and bouquet; the connaisseur's choice

ROSÉ CHAMPAGNE   A delicate sparkling Grenache rosé

BRUT CHAMPAGNE   Somewhat dry but full of zest

SELECT COLD DUCK   A unique blend of Sparkling Burgundy and Champagne, with a touch of Concord

Red Dinner Wines

GAMAY BEAUJOLAIS   A winelover's favorite—dry, flavorful, with a fine bouquet

CABERNET SAUVIGNON   An elegant wine with a rich taste, full bouquet, and deep color; smooth and fruity; an extraordinary Claret

PINOT NOIR   A wine of unabashed gusto with a bountiful flavor yet a polished taste; an especially superb Burgundy

CHIANTI   Fresh and delightful

BURGUNDY   Full-bodied, dry, smooth, and mellow—great aroma and bouquet

RUBION   A dry, velvety soft member of the Claret family that goes with everything

BAROQUE   A wine in the taste tradition of a dry, opulent Burgundy

ZINFANDEL   A fresh and zestful red varietal with youthful fruitiness and a lovely, subtle bouquet

Rosé Wines

GRENACHE ROSÉ   Fresh and fragrant

VIN ROSÉ   Like fresh ripe fruit; trace of pleasing sweetness

PINK   Medium dry vin Rose; the "anytime" wine

VIN ROSÉ SEC   A varietal with a distinctively dry character and a light fresh taste and bouquet

White Dinner Wines

EMERALD DRY   Emerald-gold; sprightly, delectably dry

RHINE CASTLE   A light white wine of delicate natural sweetness

RIESLING   Pleasurably dry, pale greenish-gold in color, and piquant in taste

RHINE   Light and delicate with a soft, pleasing taste and fragrance

DRY SAUTERNE   Light-bodied with a distinctive bouquet and softness

CHABLIS   A wine with zest, personality, crisp clarity, and fresh bouquet

PINOT CHARDONNAY   A wine of great dignity with exquisite flavor and rich bouquet; the "champagne" of still white Burgundy

PINOT BLANC   A light golden varietal wine—agreeably dry with a delicious flavor; dry and fruity

JOHANNISBERG RIESLING   Exquisitely dry with a taste of elegant freshness

CHENIN BLANC   A wine with a dancing pale gold color and a savory bouquet; a trace of sweetness

SEMILLON   Very dry and subtle

SAUVIGNON BLANC (FUMÉ BLANC)   A classic; fresh and dry

GREY RIESLING   Dry, light, and altogether charming

SYLVANER   Rare and delicately aromatic; a Rhine type

GEWURZTRAMINER   Unique spicy flavor; extraordinary bouquet

FRENCH

Red Bordeaux Wines

MEDOC   Well-balanced, medium-bodied Claret; fairly dry

ST. JULIEN   Charming and delicately dry

MARGAUX   Excellent bouquet, full of character, and pleasantly dry

ST. ESTEPHE   Fruity, rich, and dry with velvety soft aftertaste

CHATEAU ST. EMILION   A superior St. Emilion; generous and full-bodied with a fine bouquet combined with great delicacy; classified a Grand Cru

White Bordeaux Wines

GRAVES   Medium dry, clean, fresh, with a fruity bouquet

BARSAC   Gracious and sweet; slightly dryer than Sauternes

SAUTERNES   Luscious, soft, sweet, and full-bodied

BLANC DE BLANCS   A light, dry Bordeaux wine that combines a clear taste with fine character

Red Burgundy Wines

POMMARD   Fruity bouquet, full-bodied, yet soft and gracious

GEVREY-CHAMBERTIN   Generous and full-flavored; strong character with a mellow finish

NUITS ST. GEORGES   Generous, soft, well-balanced; an exemplary Burgundy

VOSNE-ROMANEE   Breeding, elegance, exceptional balance, fine bouquet

CHASSAGNE-MONTRACHET   An earthy red wine from the Cote d'Or; excellent value

COTE DE BEAUNE   A high-quality, well-balanced, graceful red wine from the principal center of the Burgundy area

ALOXE-CORTON   A light-bodied red wine; delicate, attractive, and early maturing

CHAMBOLLE-MUSIGNY   An outstanding delicate red wine with the charm and fragrance of the best Burgundies

BEAUJOLAIS   Most popular Burgundy, lively and fruity, with a refreshing flavor

White Burgundy Wines

POUILLY FUISSE   A fine white Burgundy, delicate with a balance in dryness; pleasant bouquet

CHABLIS   Crisp and dry with delicate bouquet

PULIGNY MONTRACHET   An excellent Burgundy; dry, soft, and rich in flavor

Red Rhone Wines

CHATEAUNEUF DU PAPE   Soft, agreeably fresh, rich, and round with character

White Loire Wines

POUILLY FUME   Full-bodied with an earthy taste and perfumy bouquet (Loire Valley)

MUSCADET   Fresh, delicate, dry, with a hint of gunflint (Loire Valley)

SANCERRE   Dry with a lingering fragrance

VOUVRAY   Smooth and soft, medium dry, excellent bouquet

Sparkling Wines

SPARKLING BURGUNDY   Medium dry, fragrant, and full-bodied; serve with all foods

CANARD FROID, FROID (COLD, COLD DUCK)   A delightful and very popular combination of red and white sparkling wines; serve chilled

Rose Wines

TAVEL ROSÉ (Rhone)   A rosé wine with certain delicate lightness that will suit all foods and occasions

ROSE D'ANJOU   From Anjou, a medium dry rosé, fragrant, soft, and smooth; excellent with all foods.

Sparkling Wines

CRACKLING NECTAROSE   A festive, exuberantly sparkling rosé from the Loire Valley

FRENCH CHAMPAGNE REGION

Champagnes

EXTRA DRY   Superior Champagne with a light body; medium dry

BRUT   The red stripe on the label is recognized worldwide; gay, light, and dry

BRUT (Vintage)   Only the finest harvest can result in this elegant light Champagne

ROSE   A special note of elegance; superb pink Champagne

GERMAN

Rhine Wines

NIERSTEINER   A delicious white wine with a distinctive fragrance and softness

LIEBFRAUMILCH   A clean-tasting, flavorful white wine; everyone's favorite

Moselle Wines

MOSELLE BLUEMCHEN   A light, tingly tasting and fragrant white wine

PIESPORTER RIESLING   A superb, light, fresh, dry, and tingly Moselle white wine

BERNKASTELER RIESLING   A light, fruity, full, flowery white wine

ZELLER SCHWARZE KATZ   Light-bodied, crisp, and fruity; an excellent Moselle

Franconian Wines

STEINWEIN   A fine, dry Franconian wine of outstanding quality

Sparkling Wines

MOSELLE SPARKEL   Kaysersekt—a fresh, sparkling wine with a heady bouquet

ITALIAN

Red Dinner Wines

GRIGNOLINO D'ASTI   Crisp, nicely dry, and delicious with a beautiful ruby color

DOLCETTO AMARO D'ALBA   Delightfully dry and rich; perfect complement to main course

BARBERA D'ASTI   Rich, full-bodied, and fragrant

BARBARESCO   A robust, ruby red wine sometimes referred to as the master of Piedmontese wines

BAROLO   A rich, red giant of a wine with an unmatched softness and fragrance

BARBERA   A full-bodied, dry Barbera with a robust taste and full fragrance

NEBBIOLO SECCO   Beautiful dark ruby color; crisp, delicate flavor

CHIANTI   Dry, smooth, and well-balanced

VALPOLICELLA   Light, velvety, fragrant, and fruity

BARDOLINO   A delightful, light, fruity red wine

RISERVA   The finest of all Chiantis; full-bodied, dry with superior bouquet

CHIANTI CLASSICO   The fine Chianti; dry, full-bodied, smooth with a pleasant bouquet

CHIANTIGIANA   Dry, full-bodied, and smooth

White Dinner Wines

SOAVE   Dry, light, clean; fresh to the palate

BIANCO   Light-bodied, crisp, dry, and agreeably fresh tasting

Rosé Dinner Wines

ROSÉ   An exceptionally distinguished Italian rosé; medium dry and delicious

ROSOLINO DELLA CREMOSINA   A subtle and delicate rosé wine

BELPAIS   A delightfully robust Piedmontese rosé

Sparkling Wines

ASTI SPUMANTE   Bubbly, fresh white wine with a delightfully soft sweet quality

Glossary of Alcoholic Beverages

ABISANTE A distinctive liqueur produced by subtle blending of aniseed and aromatic herbs. Clear green in color; becomes milky in water. Enjoyed especially in the Absinthe Drip and Suissesse Cocktails.

ABRICOTINE Apricot liqueur.

ABSINTHE Light yellow-green high-proof liqueur with a pronounced aromatic aroma in which licorice dominates. The primary aromatic is Artemisia, or wormwood. Absinthe with wormwood has been prohibited in the United States and a number of other countries. Absinthe substitutes are marketed; they are without wormwood and are sweeter and not as strong.

ADVOKAAT Creamy, thick egg liqueur, similar in taste to prepared egg nog, but still delightfully different. Made by addition of fresh yolks of eggs to basic liqueur.

ALLASCH KUMMEL Traditional Kuemmel. Not as dry as Berliner or Doeppel Kuemmel.

ANESONE White liqueur with licorice-like flavor. Higher in proof and drier than Anisette. Produced by distillation of aniseed.

ANISETTE Sweet, mild, delicate, aromatic, white or red liqueur with pleasant flavor reminiscent of licorice; sweeter and lower in proof than Anesone. Produced as a flavor-blend of aniseed and aromatic herbs.

APPLEJACK (Apple Brandy)   Brandy distilled from apples; mild, pleasant apple flavor.

APRICOT-FLAVORED BRANDY   Pure grape brandy, with the true flavor and aroma of fresh, ripe apricots; generally drier, lighter bodied, and more potent than Apricot Liqueur. Classified as a cordial. Amber in color.

APRICOT LIQUEUR   Sweet, rich liqueur with the flavor and aroma of fresh, ripe apricots; sweeter, fuller-bodied, and lighter proof than Apricot-Flavored Brandy. Amber in color.

APRY   Apricot Liqueur.

AQUAVIT (Akvavit)   Smooth, light, dry, white liquor with the flavor of caraway; like Kummel, but much drier. National beverage of the Scandinavian countries. Produced as highly refined spirit flavored with caraway seeds and other aromatics.

ARMAGNAC   A great grape brandy of France, probably second only to Cognac. Produced in a legally delimited region in the Gers Department of southwest France. It is dry, less delicate, and less ethereal than Cognac, but compensates with fuller body.

BANANA LIQUEUR   Sweet, yellow liqueur with the full flavor of fresh, ripe bananas.

BARBADOS RUM   Medium-bodied rum; dry, heavier, and more pungent than Puerto Rican Rum, but lighter and not as pungent as Jamaican Rum. Produced in pot stills. Amber in color.

BARENFANG LIQUEUR   Honey-flavored German liqueur.

BATAVIA ARRAC   Dry, highly aromatic, colorless, brandy-like rum of great pungency and rumminess; distilled in Indonesia in the East Indies.

BENAI   Herb-flavored cordial, produced as a flavor in old brandy. Amber in color.

BERLINER KUEMMEL   Traditional Kuemmel. Drier than Allasch Kuemmel.

BITTERS   An infusion of roots, barks, herbs, and other botanicals, produced by private formulas. There are three primary varieties: aromatic, flavoring, and laxative. One should never be substituted for the others. Aromatic Bitters are aromatic and pungent with distinctive aroma and bouquet. They whet the appetite, stimulate the digestive processes, and are frequently used in cocktails that are primarily appetizers. Flavoring Bitters (e.g., Orange Bitters) are important as flavorings in a number of drinks, particularly when a fragrant aroma is sought.

BLACKBERRY-FLAVORED BRANDY   Pure grape brandy with the true flavor and aroma of fresh, ripe blackberries. Generally drier, lighter-bodied, and more potent than Blackberry Liqueur. Classified as a cordial. Blue-black in color.

BLACKBERRY LIQUEUR   Sweet, rich liqueur with the flavor and aroma of fresh, ripe blackberries. Sweeter, fuller-bodied, and lighter proof than Blackberry-Flavored Brandy. Blue-black in color.

BOURBON   Type name for one of the two great American whiskies. Named for Bourbon County, Kentucky, where Bourbon was first produced soon after the Revolutionary War.

BOURBON WHISKEY   Like Straight Bourbon Whiskey except for age. When the label says only "Bourbon Whiskey" (without the word "Straight"), the whiskey may have any age up to two years. Straight Bourbon Whiskey must be a minimum of two years old.

BRANDY   A family of liquors distilled from the wines of grapes or other fruits. Brandy is a soft, smooth, velvety liquor, amber in color, distinguished by its great bouquet and the subtle fragrance of grapes. Unless otherwise identified on the label, Brandy is always a distillation of the wines of pure grapes. When Brandy is distilled from other fruits, the fruit must be stated (e.g., Apple Brandy or Apricot Brandy). Brandy is famed as an after-dinner drink, straight or half and half with many cordials. Brandy and Soda Brandy are basic ingredients in favorite cocktails, making a perfect blend in drinks that call for fruit juices and wines. Over fruit salad and compote, Brandy brings out the natural flavors of the fruit.

CALVADOS   Apple Brandy produced in a legally delimited region of Normandy, France.

CANADIAN WHISKEY   Distinctive whiskey of Canada. Characteristically light, mild, and delicate. Most Canadian Whiskies are blended whiskies, combining heavy- and light-bodied whiskies. They are distilled from mashes of corn, rye, and malted barley, much like those used by U.S. distillers, and are aged in new white oak barrels or in reused barrels. Most are blended during the aging process, although a final blending usually precedes the bottling of the brand. Canadian regulations require that all whiskies be aged a minimum of two years. Most brands sold in the United States are aged a much greater period.

CHERRY LIQUEUR   Sweet, rich liqueur with the flavor and aroma of fresh, ripe cherries. Sweeter, fuller-bodied, and lighter proof than Cherry-Flavored Brandy. Cherry-red in color.

COFFEE LIQUEUR   Delicious piquant liqueur with distinctive coffee flavor.

COGNAC   Superb brandy of France; probably one of the most delicate and ethereal of all alcoholic beverages, with great aroma and the bouquet of grapes. Cognac is produced in a legally delimited 150,000-acre area surrounding the ancient city of Cognac in the departments of Charente and Charente-Maritime in the southwest of France. For the classification of Cognacs, the district is subdivided into seven sections, which, in order of quality, are: Grande Champagne, Petite Champagne, Borderies, Fins Bois, Bons Bois, Bois Ordinaires, and Bois Communs. This division is based primarily on the composition of the soil, which by nature is limy. The more lime, the finer the wines produced for the Cognac.

The Grande Champagne has the most lime—the other sections contain a successively lower lime content. Under French law, only brandy distilled from wine made from grapes grown within this district may be called Cognac. Various qualities of Cognac are sometimes indicated by stars in ascending quality and by letters: *E* ("Especial"), *F* ("Fine"), *V* ("Very"), *O* ("Old"), *S* ("Superior"), *P* ("Pale"), *X* ("Extra"), and *C* ("Cognac"). Thus, *V.S.O.P.* on a Cognac label means "Very Superior Old Pale."

CORN WHISKEY Like Straight Corn Whiskey, except for age. When the label says only "Corn Whiskey" (without the word, "Straight"), the whiskey may have any age up to two years. Straight Corn Whiskey will be a minimum of two years old.

CREME DE ALMOND Rich, nutty cordial; brilliant clear red. Made by a distillation of the almonds of apricot kernels.

CREME DE CACAO (Creme de Cocoa) Rich, creamy cordial blending cocoa-chocolate and vanilla flavors. Made from selected cacao and vanilla beans. Brown (regular) or white in color.

CREME DE CASSIS Sweet, reddish-brown cordial, fairly heavy with the flavor of currants. Made by macerating black currants in spirit.

CREME DE COFFEE Coffee-flavored cordial made by the percolation of coffee and vanilla beans.

CREME DE MENTHE Refreshing, tangy, natural mint-flavored cordial; cool, clean, and very pleasant to the taste. Made as a spirit, flavored with slips of fresh peppermint plant. Green or white in color.

CREME DE MENTHE (Gold) Same mint flavor as other Creme de Menthes (above) but with a gold color.

CREME DE NOYA (Creme de Noyaux) Exquisite, rich liqueur with delicious nutty flavor. Flavoring derived primarily from oil of bitter almonds or the oil of apricot kernels.

CREME DE ROSES Cordial; flavor obtained from essential oils of rose petals and vanilla.

CREME DE VANILLE (Vanilla) Velvety brown liqueur with the pleasant flavor of vanilla.

CREME DE VIOLET Cordial; flavor obtained from the essential oils of violets and vanilla.

CREME DE YVETTE Cordial of violet color; flavor drawn from the petals of fresh violets.

CUBAN RUM Dry, light rum, brandy-like to the taste, with slight molasses flavor. Produced in two labels: White Label (more delicate in flavor and aroma) and Gold Label (a little sweeter and with more pronounced rum flavor). Cuban

Gold Label tends to be slightly bolder than Puerto Rican Gold. Distilled at high proof in column stills.

CURACAO   Light, delicate, orange-flavored cordial, produced as a flavor blending of the peels of tangy Curacao and sweet oranges. Amber Curacao has a subtle orange character, contains slightly less total flavor than Triple Sec, has more sweet orange peel taste, contains more sugar, and is lower in proof.

DELECTA LIQUEUR   Light herb-flavored cordial produced as a flavor blending of spices and many varieties of honey. Amber in color.

DEMERARA RUM   Full-bodied dark rum made from molasses of sugar cane grown along the Demerara River in British Guiana; distilled in pot stills.

DOEPPEL KUEMMEL   Traditional Kuemmel. Drier than Allasch Kuemmel.

DRY GIN   The version of gin (also called London Dry Gin) that dominates the U.S. Market. Dry Gin is the gin product of the United States and England. It is a crisp, clean, delicate, white liquor, aromatic of juniper, with the flavor toned down, but with enough of the bouquet to give it independent character. There is no grain taste. Like Dry Gin, the Dutch Gin types (Hollands and Geneva Gins) draw their primary flavor from juniper, but otherwise differ completely from the U.S. and English gins. Dry Gin may be enjoyed straight (chilled), but is geared most to combine with other flavors—Vermouth, fruit juices, peels, quinine water, cordials, and other liquors. Taste-tempting mixed drinks have earned Dry Gin its following. Dry Gin is produced by distillation or redistillation of Neutral Spirits in the presence of juniper and other roots, herbs, and berries such as angelica root, coriander, cardamom, and cassia.

DUTCH GIN   Gin pungent of juniper and with pronounced grain flavor.

FLAVORED GIN   Traditional Dry Gin with fruit or other flavors added, together with sweetening. Flavored Gin is classified as a Cordial by U.S. Government regulations. Sugar, or dextrose, or both must be added in an amount not less than 2½% by weight of the finished product.

FRUIT-FLAVORED BRANDY   A fruit flavoring of a previously prepared brandy spirit base—unlike Fruit Brandy which is made by distilling the fruit. Generally, the Fruit-Flavored Brandy is produced by soaking the fruit in the spirit until it takes on the color and pronounced flavor of the fruit. Fruit-Flavored Brandy is classified as a cordial. Sweetening (sugar, or dextrose, or both) must be added in an amount not less than 2½% by weight of the finished product.

GENEVA GIN (also Genever Gin; Hollands Gin)   A Dutch Gin; the national drink of Holland. Unlike mildly flavored Dry Gin, Geneva Gin is heavy in body and pungent of juniper, with pronounced grain character. Geneva Gin is distilled at low proof from a fermented mash of barley, malt, rye, and corn. After this distillation, juniper berries, which give the Gin its typical flavor, are added to the malt-wine and it is then redistilled. Geneva Gin should always be served ice cold, never at room temperature. It is served straight and, except for the possible addition of a dash of bitters, is never used in mixed drinks.

GERMAN BRANDY   A blend of especially selected distillates of European wines, matured in oak wood; characteristic mellow brandy taste.

GIN   A family of liquors flavored with juniper and other aromatics. Except for Blended Whiskey and Straight Whiskey, gin outsells every type of distilled spirit in the U.S. market. Two distinctive types of gin are produced: the Dry Gin (or London Dry Gin type) that dominates the U.S. market and the Dutch Geneva or Hollands Gin.

GINGER-FLAVORED BRANDY   Pure grape brandy with the true flavor and aroma of ginger roots and other aromatics. Light brown in color.

GOLDWASSER (Liqueur d'Or; Gold Liqueur)   Literally, gold water. Sweet white cordial with a citrus fruit peel and spice flavor. Contains tiny flakes of gold leaf so slight they cannot be felt on the tongue.

GRAPPA   Brandy distilled from the pulpy residue—the grape pomace—of the wine press. In France, this brandy is called *Marc* (Eau de Vie de Marc).

GREEK BRANDY   Soft, mellow liquor, comparatively sweet, as Cognac used to be. Distilled from grapes, with the gum part of native Greek pine added to impart much of its unique flavor.

GRENADINE   Bright red flavoring syrup blending the tastes of pomegranate, strawberry, and raspberry fruits.

HOLLANDS GIN   A Dutch Gin type, also called *Geneva Gin*.

IRISH WHISKEY   Distinctive whiskey of Ireland. This whiskey is produced in two types: The traditional Irish (a blend of straight pot still whiskies; hearty and full-bodied) and the new style (a blend of the heavy pot still and lighter column still grain whiskies; light, soft, and mellow in taste). Irish Whiskey is made from barley, both malted and unmalted, principally together with oats, wheat, and sometimes a small proportion of rye. Unlike Scotch, Irish Whiskey does not have a smokey taste—the malted barley is dried in kilns constructed so that the smoke from the fuel does not come in contact with the malt.

IRISH WHISKEY—A BLEND   Label designated; also authorized by U.S. regulation for Irish Whiskey produced as a mixture of distilled spirits.

JACOBINER   Rich, German monastery-type liqueur prepared by ancient formula of selected fruits, herbs, and flowers; aged in grape brandy.

JAMAICA RUM   Full-bodied rum, heavy in rum flavor and pungent of bouquet and body; rich golden hue and dark color; distilled in pot stills.

KIRSCHWASSER (Kirsch)   Fruit Brandy distilled from cherries; smooth, mellow, with the subtle fragrance of cherries. Colorless.

KUMMEL (Kuemmel)   White liqueur with the pleasing, piquant flavor of the caraway seed. Neither too sweet nor too dry, and thus an appealing flavor-blend of caraway and other seeds, herbs, and spices.

LIQUEUR   Sweetened, flavored family of liquors; also termed *Cordial*.

LIQUEUR D'OR   Also called *Goldwasser*.

LIQUEUR MONASTIQUE   Herb-like liqueur of monastic tradition; produced from ancient formula using over 30 herbs, seeds, roots, and flowers.

LONDON DRY GIN   Crisp, clean, white liquor, aromatic of juniper to the taste.

MALT WHISKEY   Like Straight Malt Whiskey except for age. When the label says only "Malt Whiskey" (without the word "Straight"), the whiskey may have any age up to two years. Straight Malt Whiskey will be a minimum of two years old.

MARASCHINO   White aromatic liqueur with the clean, rich taste of maraschino cherries.

MARTINIQUE RUM   Rum distilled in Martinique and shipped to Bordeaux, France, where it is blended and reshipped to world markets. Pronounced rum flavor. Amber in color.

MASTIC   Sweet, white Greek liqueur, licorice-like in flavor, slightly drier than Ouzo; much drier and more potent than Anisette. Flavor derived from aniseed and sap of tree of Cashew family.

MOCHA   Coffee liqueur type. Aromatic coffee flavor drawn from mocha and vanilla beans.

NEUTRAL SPIRITS   An alcoholic spirit purified in the still to a minimum of 95% of the absolute alcoholic purity. At that degree of proof (190 degrees) the spirit is considered to have no important taste and little body or flavor. By U.S. law, Neutral Spirits may be distilled from "any material." Almost always, they are distilled from grain. Neutral Spirits are used to make Blended Whiskey. In original distillation, or redistillation, over juniper berries and other aromatics, Neutral Spirits become Dry Gin; filtered through charcoal, Neutral Spirits become Vodka. Neutral Spirits are also the base for many cordials and liqueurs.

NEW ENGLAND RUM   Full-bodied rum produced in the United States from molasses shipped from West Indies; distilled at less than 160 degrees proof and also a straight rum.

OCHA   Japanese cordial. Produced with flavor drawn from green tea. Rich, sweet tea taste. Green in color.

OLD TOM GIN   Traditional Dry Gin sweetened by the addition of sugar syrup.

OUZO   Sweet, white Greek liqueur, licorice-like in flavor. Slightly sweeter than Mastic; much drier and more potent than Anisette. Flavor derived from aniseed.

PEACH-FLAVORED BRANDY   Pure grape brandy with the true flavor and aroma of fresh, ripe peaches; generally dryer, lighter-bodied, and more potent than Apricot Liqueur. Classified as a cordial. Amber in color.

PEPPERMINT SCHNAPPS Dry, white peppermint-flavored liqueur; lighter bodied and not as sweet as Creme de Menthe. Has pleasant aftertaste in which the odor of alcohol is not discernible.

PERONETTE Light green cordial with anise taste.

PFLUMIWASSER German plum brandy.

PUERTO RICAN RUM Dry, light rum, brandy-like to the taste, with slight molasses flavor. White Label is more delicate in aroma and flavor. Gold Label is a little bit sweeter with a more pronounced rum flavor. Distilled at high proof in column stills, aged one to three years and blended by traditional methods.

QUETSCH Fruit Brandy distilled from plums.

ROCK & RYE Sweet, hearty, rye whiskey-flavored cordial. Made as a blending of rye whiskey with rock candy and fruits (lemons, oranges, and cherries). Amber in color.

RUM A family of liquors distilled from the fermented juice of sugar cane or molasses. Rum is produced in virtually all of the various sugar countries and in New England (from West Indies molasses). There are many differences in these rums; thus, the rum's geography is important. The differences result from the methods of distilling, aging, and blending, and the water, climates, and soil in which the sugar cane grows. Rum is attractive straight, but earns its major following in the United States with fruits and other liquors, making an ideal base for a great many cocktails pleasing to most people.

RYE Popular eastern name for Blended Whiskey. *Rye* is widely applied to this whiskey type, although by federal definition, it is a misnomer. Actually, the typical Blended Whiskey brand is likely to contain both Straight Bourbon and possibly other grain flavors, balanced with Neutral Spirits.

SCOTCH WHISKEY Distinctive whiskey of Scotland. Scotch is renowned as a blending of hearty barley malt whiskies produced in traditional pot stills and the light grain whiskies made in column stills. Scotch is soft, light-bodied, mellow to the taste with the subtle, gentle aroma of peat (heather evergreen and fern compressed by nature over the ages)—the smokey flavor for which Scotch is famed. Scotch draws its special character from two primary factors: the drying of the malted barley over peat fires (the smoke impregnates the barley and gives Scotch its smokey taste) and the use of the original mash of the native soft waters that flow down from the highlands.

SCOTCH-TYPE WHISKEY No longer authorized by the U.S. government. Classification of whiskies labeled "Scotch-Type" was discontinued on April 3, 1961. Scotch-Type Whiskey was whiskey produced outside Great Britain in the pattern of the distinctive Scotch Whiskies of Scotland.

SLIVOVITZ Fruity brandy distilled from plums; soft, pleasant, with mellow plum fragrance. Gold in color or colorless.

SLOE GIN   Rich, red cordial with delicate bouquet and tangy fruity flavor resembling wild cherries. Made generally as blend of sloe cherries, from which it derives its primary flavor, and other fruits in a pure spirit.

SOUR MASH   Term often used in connection with Straight Whiskey. Identifies a production process, distinguished from the "Sweet Mash" technique of distillation. The name has nothing to do with the taste of the whiskey. Sour Mash whiskies are rich and mellow. It is inherited from the early distillers and refers to the natural fermentation of the yeast and the grain. In the Sour Mash process, strained fermentation is mixed with the mash of grain. This is done because certain properties in the spent "beer" are said to aid in developing the individuality of the whiskey.

SPANISH BRANDY   Brandy distilled from sherry wine; soft, mellow, and not quite as dry as traditional brandy. Used straight as an after-dinner drink, with soda or tonic in a highball, in coffee, as an ingredient in many cocktails, in cooking recipes, and as flavoring for desserts.

SPIRIT WHISKEY   A whiskey type, unimportant in today's market, containing less than 20% Whiskey or Straight Whiskey in combination with Neutral Spirits. By legal definition, it may consist of Neutral Spirits and not less than 5% by volume of Straight Whiskey or Neutral Spirits and less than 20% by volume of Straight Whiskey, but not less than 5% by volume of Straight Whiskey or Straight Whiskey and Whiskey.

STEINHAGER   German Westphalian Gin, white and dry like the London Dry types. Steinhager has the faint taste of herbs like all Dry Gins, but with slightly more pronounced juniper character.

STRAIGHT BOURBON WHISKEY   Mellow, full-bodied whiskey with characteristic bourbon flavor and taste; light and yet well-defined in aroma and bouquet. This distinctive whiskey type is produced from fermented mash of corn, rye, and barley malt and is aged a minimum of two years in new charred oak barrels. The grain formula for Straight Bourbon must, by law, contain not less than 51% corn (usually the proportion is higher—about 65 to 75%). A larger proportion of corn tends to produce a lighter-bodied whiskey; more of the rye and barley grains produce heavier-bodied bourbon. Straight Bourbon is the most important of the Straight Whiskey types identified by a grain tag.

STRAIGHT WHISKEY   An alcoholic distillate of a fermented mash of grain. Identified by characteristic taste, body, and aroma, and bottled exactly as it comes from the barrel in which it has matured, except for the addition of pure water to reduce the proof to bottle proof. By law, Straight Whiskey is aged a minimum of two years in new charred oak barrels. Distillation may not exceed 160 degrees proof; it must be withdrawn from the cistern room for barreling at not more than 110 degrees, or less than 80 degrees proof. The distiller may call this product Straight Whiskey without a grain tag whether one grain predominates in the mash from which it is made or not. The grain tag may be used (as Straight Bourbon Whiskey or Straight Rye Whiskey) when 51% or more of the grain from which it is fermented consists of that grain. Straight Corn Whiskey, an exception, is made from a mash containing at least 80% corn. Two or more Straight Whiskies may also be combined as Blends of Straight Whiskies or Blends of Straight Bourbon (or Rye) Whiskies. Bottled-in-Bond Whiskies are blood brothers of the Straight Whiskies. Among the Straight Whiskies identified by a grain tag, primarily Straight Bourbon and Straight Rye are the only whiskies important in the market. Federal law also identifies Straight Corn Whiskey, Straight Wheat Whiskey, Straight Malt Whiskey, and Straight Rye Malt Whiskey. Each is distilled from a mash in which the grain specified constitutes 51% of the formula.

TAFEI AQUAVIT   See *Aquavit*.

TEQUILA   Mexican spirits distilled from the fermented juice of the Mescal plant. The Mescal plant takes years to grow; when picked, it resembles a huge pineapple. The plant is baked in ovens, crushed, and the juice extracted. Juice is fermented and distilled in pot stills. Spirit comes from still white. Tequila Gold is the result of aging in oak barrels. Distinctive dry character. White or gold in color.

TRIPLE SEC   White orange-flavored liqueur. Made from the same ingredients as Curacao—a flavor blend of the peels of oranges, but different from Curacao in that Triple Sec has more tangy orange character, has more total flavor, is higher in proof, is drier and is water clear.

VIRGIN ISLAND RUM   Light and dry rum; also produced as more intermediate type. White Label is pale and light; Gold Label has more pronounced rum flavor.

VODKA   Light, crisp, dry distilled spirit—colorless and flavorless—leaves little if any aromatic odor on the breath. Vodka is made by passing highly refined Neutral Spirits through charcoal by redistillation or other government-approved process. Total apparent consumption of vodka in that year reached 19.4 million gallons.

WHISKEY   America's national alcoholic beverage. Whiskey is distilled from a fermented mash of grain, identified by aroma, and distilled in conformity with the laws of the federal government. Federal Standards of Identity list more than 30 different types of whiskey. In this family of whiskies are Straight Whiskies (whiskies as they come from the barrel, aged two or more years, and including also the Blends of Straight Whiskies), Blended Whiskies (whiskies containing Straight Whiskies and Neutral Spirits), Whiskies (whiskies without age or brief age), and the imported whiskies (Scotch, Canadian, Irish).

PROPRIETARY BRANDS ───────────────────────────────────

AMER PICON   French aperitif produced by redistilling brandy in the presence of Spanish orange peel and infusing it with a formula of barks, roots, and herbs.

B & B Prepared blend of Benedictine D.O.M. and Cognac.

BENEDICTINE D.O.M. Liqueur produced with formula of barks, roots, and herbs dried and macerated in brandy, distilled twice, then blended with Cognac and aged in oak casks.

BOLSBERRY A liqueur, also popular in Holland as an aperitif; a blend of black currants and other fruits, notably raspberry.

BYRRH Aperitif wine made in France, rather sweet, contains aromatics.

CAMPARI Dry, brisk-flavored Italian aperitif; also an ingredient in a number of cocktails.

CARLSBAD LIQUEUR White Czechoslovakian liqueur with the taste of bitters, blended from 86 different herbs.

CHARTREUSE Aromatic French liqueur of great delicacy, made from private formula of plants, herbs, and spices. Yellow is 86 proof; green is 110 proof. Green is drier, more aromatic.

CHERRY BESTLE Danish cherry liqueur.

CHERRY HERRING Danish cherry liqueur produced by private formula since 1818.

CHERRY KARISE Cherry-flavored liqueur produced as a spirit flavored with juice of fresh cherries.

CHERRY MARNIER French after-dinner liqueur, cherry flavored, has slight taste of the cherry pit.

CHOCOLATE SUISSE Chocolate-flavored Swiss liqueur produced with miniature squares of chocolate floating in bottle.

CHOKALU Mexican dessert liqueur; mint-flavored chocolate.

COINTREAU & BRANDY Balanced blend of Cointreau liqueur and French brandy; dry orange taste.

COINTREAU LIQUEUR Rich orange-flavored white liqueur; private formula.

CORDIAL MEDOC A cocktail of liqueurs; a blend of Orange, Curacao, Creme de Cacao, and Brandy.

DRAMBUIE Old Scotch Whiskey delicately honeyed and spiced.

EXPRESSO Italian coffee liqueur, dry: distinctive aroma of coffee.

GRAND MARNIER Golden French liqueur with orange flavor and Cognac base; private formula.

GRAND MOUQUIN LIQUEUR Sweet, rich cordial with characteristics of the monastery cordials.

IRISH MIST   Irish liqueur; a blend of Irish Whiskey, heather honey, and herbal flavoring.

KAHLUA   Mexican coffee liqueur, drawn from the beans.

LIQUORE GALLIANO   Golden Italian liqueur; private formula.

PERNOD   A tonic beverage, opaline in color; subtle blend of aniseed and other aromatic seeds and plants. Use in ice water, or as a cocktail ingredient.

PIMM'S CUPS   Tall coolers prepared by private formula dating back a century to the proprietor of Pimm's Restaurant, London, who compounded a beverage he called "Gin Sling" for his favorite customers. The drink later became known as "Pimm's Cup No. 1" and was bottled and shipped throughout the empire for Londoners on duty at military outposts. Today, four Pimm's Cups are marketed: No. 1, Gin Sling; No. 2, Whiskey Sling; No. 3, Brandy Sling; and No. 4, Rum and Brandy Sling.

SOUTHERN COMFORT   100-proof American liqueur. Amber colored, rich tasting; a combination of fruit flavors; private formula.

STREGA   Italian plant liqueur, century-old formula utilizing more than 70 herbs; delicate orange flavor.

TIA MARIA   Jamaican coffee liqueur, ancient recipe known over 200 years ago.

VAN DER HUM   Spicy, aromatic South African liqueur, made with fruits, plants, seeds, and barks. Principal flavor drawn from the mandarine.

VIEILLE CURE LIQUEUR   Straw-yellow cordial made from 52 aromatic herbs, blended with Cognac and Armagnac Brandy.

Diagrams for Meetings, Food Functions, and Buffets

Auditorium or Theater

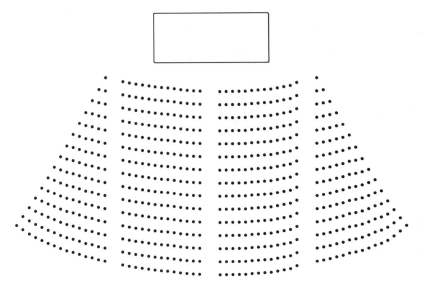

Auditorium or Theater—Semicircular with Center Aisle

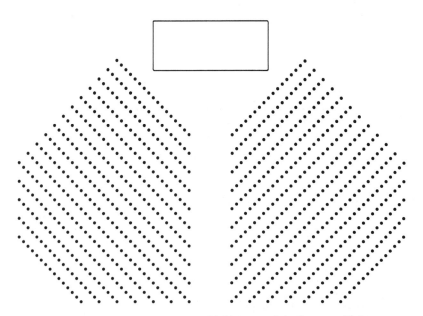

Auditorium or Theater—*V*-Shape with Center Aisle

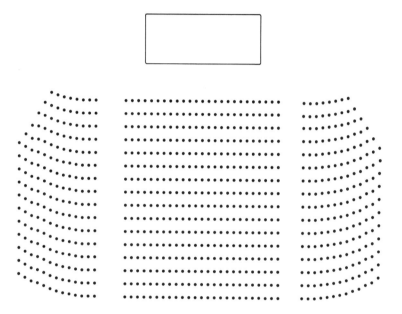

Auditorium or Theater—Semicircular with Center Block and Curved Wings

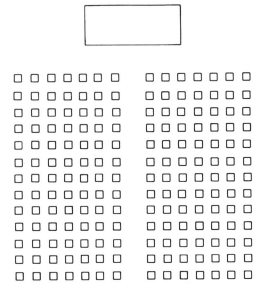

Tablet Chairs

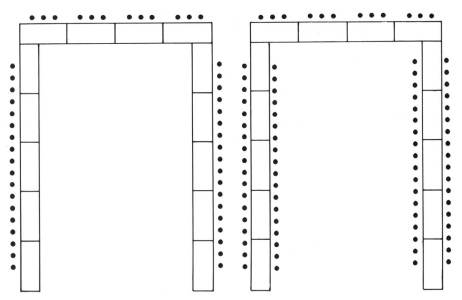

U-Shape—Outside Seating Only   *U*-Shape—Inside and Outside Seating

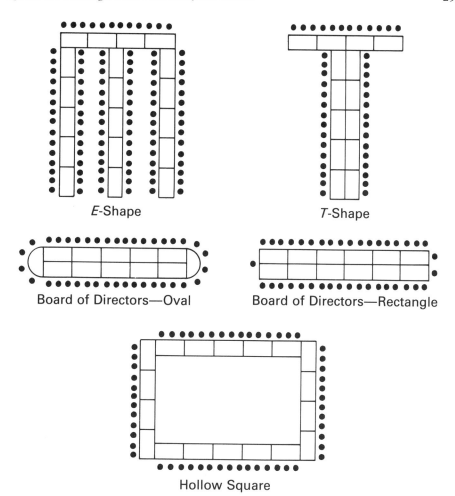

E-Shape

T-Shape

Board of Directors—Oval

Board of Directors—Rectangle

Hollow Square

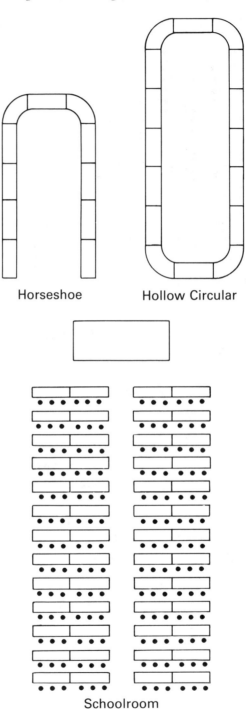

Horseshoe　　Hollow Circular

Schoolroom

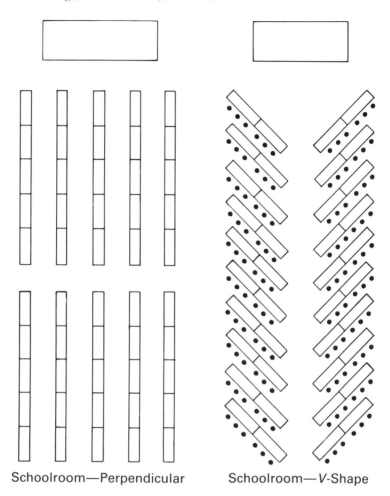

Schoolroom—Perpendicular   Schoolroom—V-Shape

Round Tables—Even Rows

Round Tables—Staggered Rows

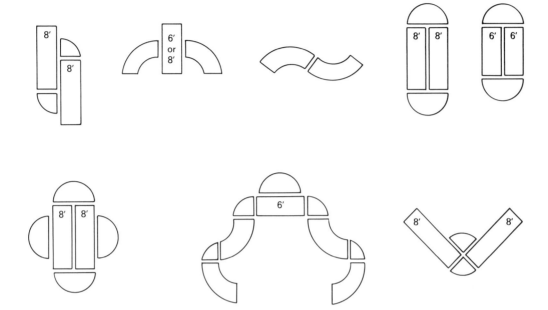

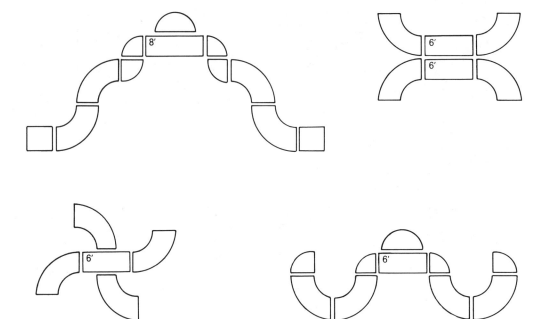

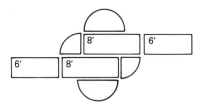

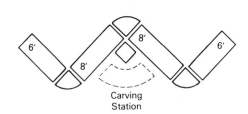

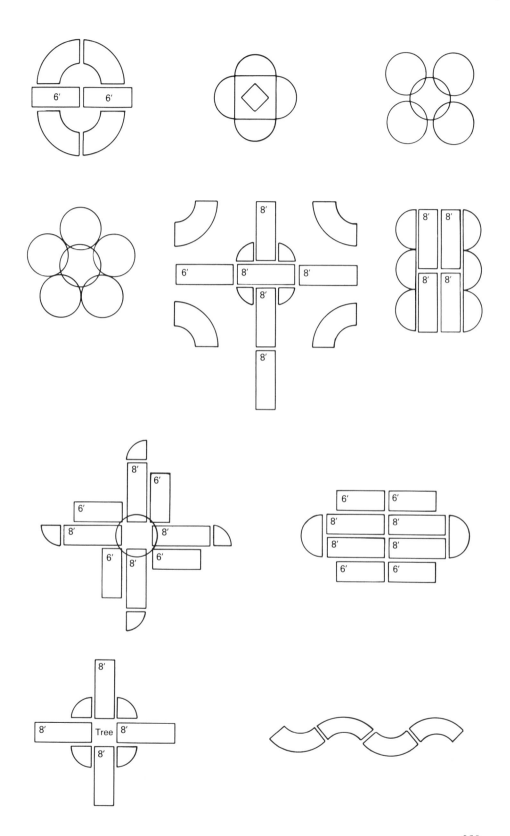

Carving
Station

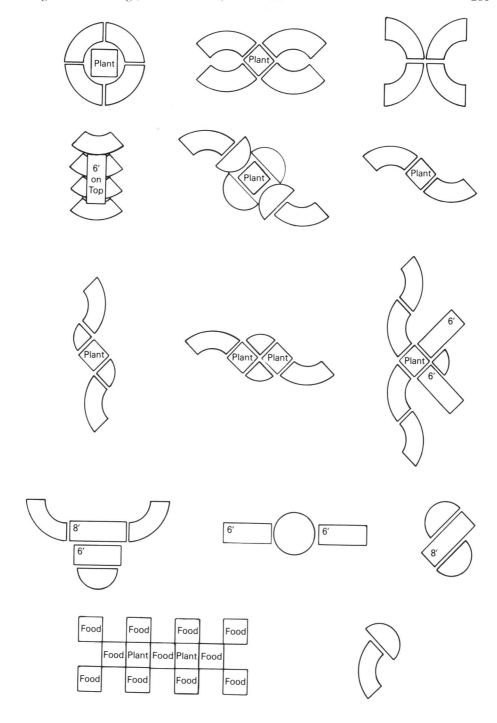

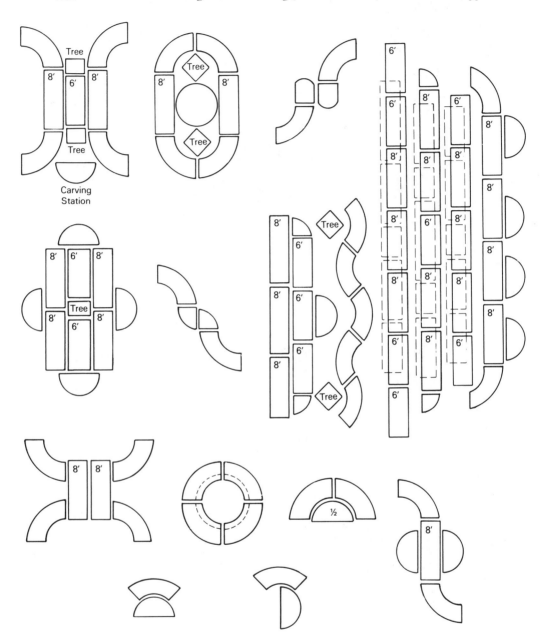

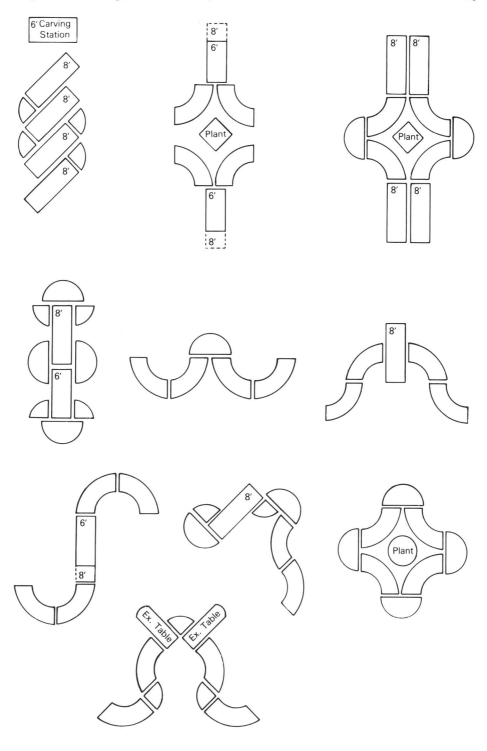

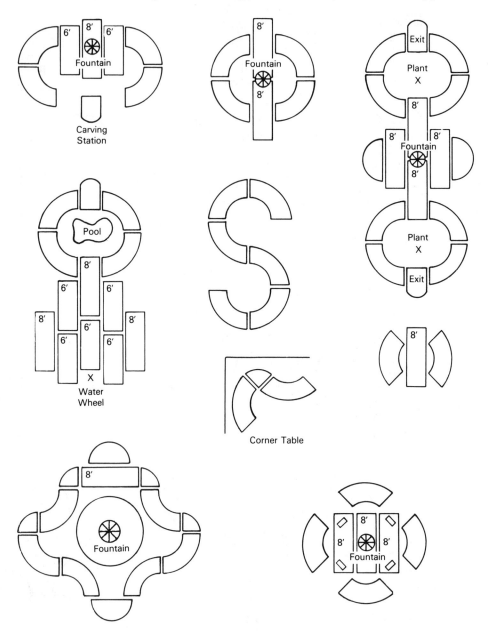

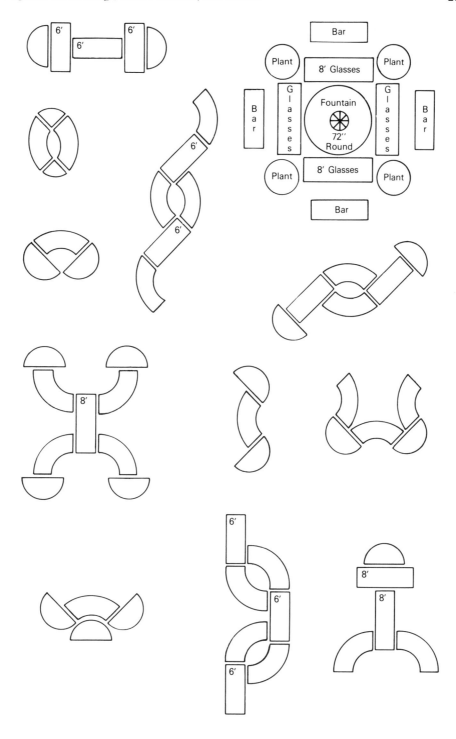

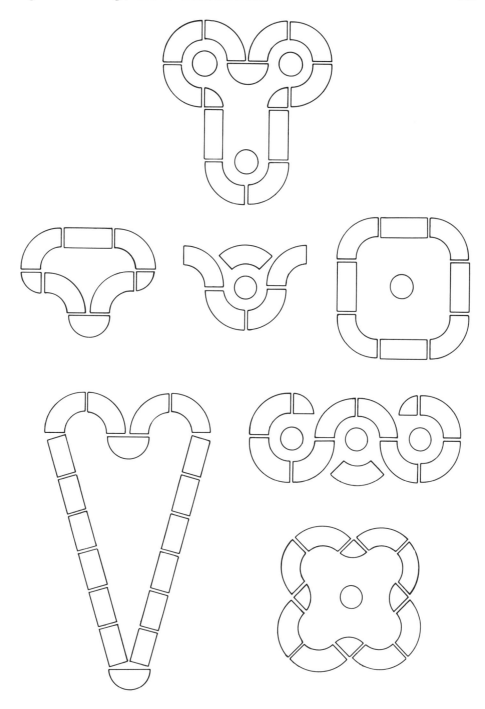

Inedible Centerpiece

Center
Piece
(extra high)

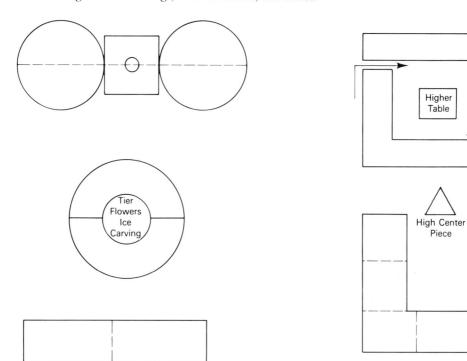

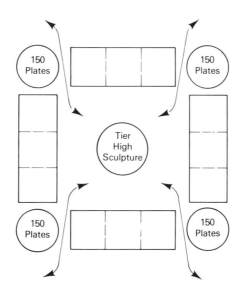

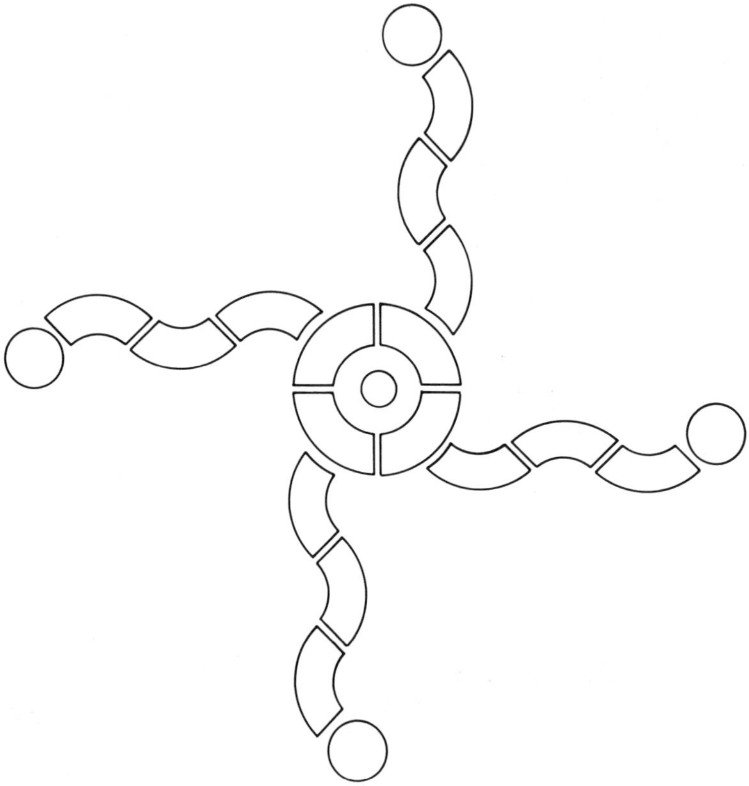

Index

St. Scholastica Library
Duluth, Minnesota 55811